# ENTREPRENEURSHIP DEVELOPMENT FOR WOMEN THROUGH COOPERATIVE SECTOR

# ENTREPRENEURSHIP DEVELOPMENT FOR WOMEN THROUGH COOPERATIVE SECTOR

**Muzamil Jan**

SERIALS PUBLICATIONS
NEW DELHI

First Published–2009

ISBN: 978-81-8387-247-8



*Published by*
**SERIALS PUBLICATIONS**
4830/24, Prahlad Street, Ansari Road
Darya Ganj, New Delhi-110002 (India)
Phone : 23245225 Fax : 91-11-23272135
E-mail: serials@satyam.net.in

## DEDICATION

**To My Neice and Nephew**

**SAHREEN**

*&*

**SAALIM**

# CONTENTS

# PREFACE

Women make substantial contribution to the family income through home-based activities. However, this is treated as supplemental as it is unrecognised. This is in contrast to many research findings that highlight the crucial role played by women in their family's economy and well-being. The implications of this on women's status are far reaching. Women are willing to take up any job to support the family. Without women's wages, many families would live below the substance level. The majority of women contribute up to 50 per cent of their family income. Yet, familial attitudes and social norms have relegated women to the status of supplementary earners.

The status of women would improve if the existing gap between their access to resources and cooperative sector is narrowed, by establishing their cooperatives and thereby exploring their entrepreneurship skills. In the organised sector of cooperatives, women are entering new avenues and improving their skills or acquire new skills. Recognition of women under cooperative sector may help to eliminate the many socio-economic ills that she is subjected to. Such recognition through cooperatives may provide women's access to resources and technology, which can elevate their status in society. In this context, this book highlights the opportunities for women to earn enough through cooperatives and is a platform for entrepreneurship development of women.

During the study of the subject and the field experience of more than six years, where from the present book has taken shape, I have sought help from various persons including Dr. Neeru Sharma, Reader in Post Graduate Department of Human Development, University of Jammu; Dr. A. A. Khan,

Associate Professor of Department of Agriculture-Economics, SKAUST-K, Srinagar; Dr. A. R. Rather, Head and Dean Faculty of Education, University of Kashmir; and Dr. Yasmeen Ashai, Cordinator of Post Graduate Department of Human Development, Government College for Women, Srinagar. I am fully aware that I have benefited largely from them but I cannot resolve how much is due to each. I owe much to them and I gladly take this opportunity of acknowledge my indebtedness to them.

The Department of Cooperative in Kashmir province is extended my thanks for many helpful criticisms, most of which I have used. I shall be failing in my duty if I do not express my sense of gratitude to *Mr. Shahnawaz Taing,* Deputy Registrar, who encouraged me at every step in writing this book. Other Officers in the Department are also expressed my deepest sense of gratitude, namely, *Dr. G.M. Dar,* Ex-Registrar; *Mr. Mohd Syed Shah,* Administrator Planning; *Mr. Farooq Ahmad Khan,* Joint Registrar; and Deputy Registrars/District Audit Officers namely *Mr. Hafiz-Ullah Shah; Mr. Muzzafar Ahmad Pir, Mr. Gul Mohd Jalali; Mr. Mehmood Shah; Mrs. Shahida Khanam; Ms. Tahira Mir* and *Mrs. Poornima Mittal. Mr. Munshi Abdul Majid,* Principal and *Mrs. Hajira,* Law Instructor; of Cooperative Training School, Kashmir; are also acknowledged for their suggestions. Beyond words, is my sincere gratitude to *Mr. Muzaffar Mirza* and *Mr. Shameem Anderabi,* Senior Supervisors, Kashmir, who kept cheering me whenever I felt disheartened. I hope this book will inspire the Cooperative Department to acquire up-to-date and innovative knowledge in the arena of Cooperative Movement.

I have also to thank my brothers Mr. M. Idrees Zaroo and Dr. M. Younus Zaroo; and my sister whom I call Meena, for timely moral support, which helped me long in writing this book. I also acknowledge my colleague Mrs. Shaista Mir, who helped me at various stages in the writing of this book. Finally, I am grateful to the publisher of this book Mr. S. K. Jha, Director, Serials Publications, New Delhi, who took serious efforts in present the book in current form.

**Muzamil Jan**

# 1

# INTRODUCTION TO COOPERATIVES

India like any other developing country has a large unorganised sector where the majority of women work. This sector has been largely neglected in so far as provision of social services and social security benefits are concerned. Things are changing for Indian women, slowly but surely. Over five decades, in the areas of women's programmes, there has been a shift from the purely welfare and consumption oriented approach to a more pragmatic and development oriented one, which recognises the women as a productive worker and the contributor to the country's economy. In this connection, Cooperatives serve as the main organisation providing the self-employment opportunities even with small means, thereby improving the socio-economic conditions of the area, ensuring the upliftment of women and strengthening the sustainable development. Cooperatives are autonomous bodies. Their main aim is raising the socio-economic status of members (Kapoor, 1998).

Cooperation is derived from a Latin word 'corporate' meaning 'working together'. In its special sense, it means the system of people voluntarily associated, working together in terms of equality to eliminate their economic exploitation by middlemen in respect of any economic need common to them (Weeramaman,1990). Sociologists, Economists and Lawyers view Cooperatives differently. To a Sociologist; it is a social order in which man is free from class struggle. Economists believe that the Cooperative is a business organization in which there is no scope of exploitation by intermediaries. Lawyers view it as a legal entity in which members enjoy special privileges and concessions conferred by law (Sehgal, 1990).

## Definitions

The definitions of Cooperatives given by various authors, organizations and others are as:

**V. L. Mehta** 'Cooperation is only one aspect of a vast movement, which promotes voluntary association of individuals having common need, who combine for the achievement of the common economic ends they have in view and who bring into this combination moral effort and a progressively developing realization of moral obligation'.

**Saligam** 'Cooperation in legal sense means abandonment of competition in production and distribution and elimination of middlemen at all stages'.

**Swiss Definition** 'A Cooperative Society is one constituted by varying number of members organized cooperatively, which aims at contributing towards the economic prosperity of the members by joint action and mutual support' (Agha and *et al.* 1960).

**C. R. Fay** regards a Cooperative Organization as, 'an association for the purpose of joint trading, originating among the weak and conducted always in a cooperative spirit, on such terms that all who are prepared to assume the duties of membership share in its rewards in proportion to the degree in which they make use of their association'.

**Calvert** 'Cooperation is a form of organization wherein people voluntarily associate together as human beings on a basis of equality for the promotion of economic interests of themselves'.

**Herrick** 'Cooperation is the act of poor persons voluntarily united for utilizing reciprocally their own forces, resources or both, under their mutual management to the common profit or loss'.

**Holyeake** has defined Cooperation as 'a voluntary concert with equitable participation and control among all concerned in any enterprise'.

**Lambert** defines a Cooperative Society as, 'an enterprise formed and directed by an association of users, applying within it the rules of democracy and directly intended to serve both its own members, and the community as a whole'.

**Watkins** 'Cooperative Society is a system of social organization based on the principles of unity, economy, democracy, equality and liberty'.

**E. M. Hough** says that 'Cooperation may be defined simply as voluntary association in a joint undertaking for mutual benefit' (Chatt, 1996).

**Cooperative Planning Committee of India** in 1946 defined Cooperative as 'a form of organization in which persons voluntarily associate together on a basis of equality for the promotion of their economic interests' (Saeed and Ansari, 1990).

**Cooperative Societies Act 1912** 'Cooperative Organization is a society which has as its objectives the promotion of the interests of its members in accordance with the principles of cooperation'.

**International Labour Organization (ILO)** 'It is an association of persons, usually of limited means, who have voluntarily joined together to achieve a common economic end, through the formation of a democratically controlled business organization, making equitable contributions to the capital required and accepting a full share of risks and benefits of the undertaking' (Gupta, 1993).

**Income-Tax Act 1961** Under section 2(19) of this Act 'Cooperative Society means society registered under the Cooperative Societies Act, 1912 or under any other law for the time-being in force in any state' (Gaur and Narang, 1992).

**International Cooperative Alliance (ICA)** 'A Cooperative is an autonomous association of persons united voluntarily to meet their common economic, social and cultural needs and aspirations through a jointly-owned and democratically controlled enterprise' (Cooperative Initiative Panel, 1999).

Thus, it is clear from above definitions that a Cooperative Organization or a Cooperative Society is an association of persons who join together on a voluntary basis for the furtherance of their common interests (Dhingra, 1992).

## Characteristic Features of Cooperatives

Cooperation is a social revolution of a fundamental nature. By Cooperating people cease to exploit one another's needs and instead join hands to solve their common economic problems for their own social and economic betterment (Weeraman, 1990). Cooperatives have some special features, which tend to make them distinctly different. Most of Cooperatives are state sponsored units, which have to function in close collaboration with the state administrative apparatus, without being a formal part of it (Taimni, 1979). Cooperative is an association of persons as human beings and not as capitalists. It is a form of business organization adopting all business principles and practices. It has a democratic management. One-person one-vote is the rule. Democracy is the heart of cooperation. It is not a mere tool of profit maximization. Service is primary and profit motive is incidental. Equity in distribution of surplus is honoured. The surplus is distributed in proportion to the business contributed by each member to the enterprise and not according to share-holding. Cooperatives are socio-economic institutions having their own environment and are expected to adjust with changing economic and social aspirations or demands of the community (Sherlekar, 1985). For communication purposes in Cooperative Institutions, a number of communication media is available such as Cooperative Societies Act and Rules, By-Laws, meetings, resolutions, circulars, order or instructions, annual reports, statements and communication with employees, beneficiaries and external world (Shah, 1984). A Cooperative Society inherently denies exploitation of its members and consumers. Basically, the society takes care of the mutual economic benefits of its own members. In this way, the Cooperative Society rejects any exploitation, which was the basis of the intermediaries (Doshi and Jain, 1999).

## Types of Cooperatives

Different types of Cooperatives offer distinct benefits to their members. ***Primary Agricultural Cooperative Societies*** (PACS) are the most important instrument for breaking the monopoly of moneylenders exploiting the rural poor masses. The primary function of Primary Agricultural Cooperative Societies is to raise resources and lend to members for agricultural production and investment in allied activities. ***Consumer Cooperatives*** or retail stores owned and organized by people with small means to make available to themselves their daily requirements of goods at cheaper prices. Such stores buy goods of daily use from manufacturers and wholesalers and sell them to members and non-members at concession rates. ***Cooperative Marketing Societies*** are established to form a process of marketing through a cooperative association. Farmers for selling their produce at remunerative prices form such Cooperatives. It provides the benefits of collective purchases and sales. ***Sale and Service Cooperatives*** are also known as 'Farmers Service Cooperative Societies'. These also act as Marketing Societies at the block level for the development of small farm economy. ***Credit Cooperatives*** are Societies set up to pool the savings of members and to make them available as loans to those members who need credit on favourable terms. Such Societies encourage the habit of thrift and savings among the members. ***Women Cooperatives*** can be classified into three categories i.e. Industrial Cooperatives, Credit Cooperatives, and other types of Cooperatives or multipurpose welfare Cooperatives etc. ***Other Cooperatives*** comprise Fishery Cooperatives, Transport Cooperatives, Housing Cooperatives, Dairy Cooperatives, Labour Co-operatives, etc. All these Cooperatives provide specific services to members in order to improve their standard of living.

In addition to the District and State level Cooperatives Societies, Central Apex Cooperative Institutions or Federations of Cooperatives have been established in India. National Cooperative Union of India, National Agricultural Cooperative Marketing Federation of India, National Federation of Industrial Cooperatives, National Cooperative Dairy Federation, National Consumer's Cooperative Federation, and Indian Farmers Fertilizer Cooperatives are some examples of such apex bodies of Cooperatives at national level.

## Advantages of Cooperatives

Cooperatives have an advantage over other forms of ownership in that the loyalty of their members and group support to the principles of the cooperative movement frequently transcend the profit motive present in capitalistic enterprises. Individual bargaining power of relatively weak consumer or producer groups is strengthened, and some of the bad effects of competition are removed. Furthermore, Government support and encouragement of Cooperatives have led to the amendment of tax laws so as to exempt Cooperatives and their subsidiary corporations from tax burdens normally applicable to profit-seeking enterprises. Government assistance has also been obtained in the direction of low-cost credit facilities.

## Disadvantages of Cooperatives

Although many new Cooperatives are formed each year, hundreds of other falls short of their goals. Some associations go out of business because they were poorly planned or because of lack of capital. Others are discontinued because of an inadequate volume of business, because of competition that they cannot meet, or because of lack of intelligent educational work among members, and a few because of dishonest officers or employees. However, many associations have ceased to function because of inefficient or corrupt management or lack of cooperation among the members. Most Agricultural Cooperatives have the weaknesses of large organizations, which depend upon the loyalty of thousands of members whose allegiance cannot, in the nature of the case, be secured through ironclad agreements (Dhingra, 1992).

## Principles of Cooperatives

The International Cooperative Alliance (ICA) in its centennial congress, Manchester, United Kingdom on 23rd September 1995, put down the following principles of Cooperatives:

**First Principle: Voluntary and Open Membership:** Cooperatives are voluntary organization, open to all persons able to use their services and willing to accept the responsibilities of membership, without gender, social, racial, political, or religious discrimination.

**Second Principle: Democratic Member Control:** Cooperatives are democratic organizations controlled by their members, who actively, participate in their policies and making decisions; men and women serving as elected representatives are accountable to the membership. In Primary Cooperatives, members have equal voting rights (one member one vote), and Cooperatives at other levels are also organized in a democratic manner.

**Third Principle: Members' Economic Participation:** Members contribute equitably to, and democratically control, the capital of their Cooperatives. At least part of that capital is usually the common property of the Cooperative. Members usually receive limited compensation, if any, on capital subscribed as a condition of membership. Members allocate surpluses for developing their Cooperatives, possibly by setting up reserves, part of which at least would be indivisible, benefiting members in proportion to their transactions with the Cooperative, and supporting other activities approved by the membership.

**Fourth Principle: Autonomy and Independence:** Cooperatives are autonomous, self-help organizations controlled by their members. If they enter into agreements with other organizations, including Governments or raise capital from external sources, they do so on terms that ensure democratic control by their members and maintain their Cooperative autonomy.

**Fifth Principle: Education, Training and Information:** Cooperatives provide education and training for their members, elected representatives, managers, and employees so that they can contribute effectively to the development of their Cooperatives. They inform the general public—particularly young people and opinion leaders—about the nature and benefits of cooperation.

**Sixth Principle: Cooperation Among Cooperatives:** Cooperatives serve their members most effectively and strengthen the Cooperative movement by working together through local, regional, national and international structures.

**Seventh Principle: Concern for Community:** Cooperatives work for the sustainable development of their communities through policies approved by their members.

## Philosophy and Values of Cooperatives

Service not profit; cooperation not competition; self-help not dependence on the profit-hungry businessmen and moral solidarity not unscrupulous undercutting; forms the philosophy of Cooperatives. Cooperation is a way of life, a philosophy, and an approach to human problems. All human beings are equal in their right to live and to develop and can be free, only if they are not exploited by others but are independently productive and create members of society (SEWA Academy, 2000).

According to International Cooperative Alliance (ICA), Cooperatives are based on the values of self-help, self-responsibility, democracy, equality and solidarity. In the tradition of their founders, Cooperative members believe in the ethical values of honesty, openness, social responsibility and caring for others (Cooperative Initiative Panel, 1999).

## Cooperatives Abroad

***Britain*** is the home-land of Cooperative movement. It was the outcome of radical changes that took place in the latter half of the 18th century in the economic and social systems of Britain under the impact of the Industrial Revolution. In 1844, the 'Rochdale Pioneers' established a first Industrial society in England with the working capital of 28 pounds only. It was registered under the "English Friendly Societies Act, 1793" (Hajela, 1982). Vague complaints in the Cooperatives press and a decline in consumer movement rates suggest that wheel-like changes may have occurred in the British Cooperative Movement (Britt and Boyd, 1968).

***Germany*** is the birthplace of Cooperative Credit movement. 'Raiffasan' and 'Herrfranz Schulze' were the pioneers of *Credit Cooperative Society* which they established in 1850. The first *Cooperative Dairy* was set up in the Hjedding with the initiative of a young dairyman 'Stilling Anderson' in 1882 in ***Denmark***. Since then the continuous efforts have been made to develop the Cooperative Dairy Movement (Sehgal, 1990). In ***Turkey***, the first Cooperative society was established in 1867 in Pirot Town by "Mithat Pasha'. Since then, the Cooperative movement in Turkey has grown and the number of existing Cooperatives has reached to above 19,501 (Yardimici, 1995).

It was not until the National Grange promoted Cooperatives in the Nation's Agricultural Areas in the 1870s that Cooperatives began to emerge as a vital force in the economy of ***United States of America*** .The Cooperative League of the United States of America (CLUSA) and the National Milk Producer's Federation—both emerged in 1916 for actively marketing the produce of American farmers (Felder, 1980). The ***Swedish*** Movement was also started with a modest beginning more than a century ago and during this period; it also passed through many vicissitudes. Today, however, it has come to occupy a commanding position in the economy of Sweden. The most important landmark in the history of Swedish movement was the emergence of the Central Organization of the Cooperative Union and the wholesale Societies known as "KF'— 'Kooperative Forbundet' founded in 1899 (Kamat, 1978).

Cooperative development in ***Thailand*** was initiated by the Government in 1916 when the first Cooperative Society was established among the small paddy farmers in a village. It was known as a *Village Credit Cooperative* with unlimited liability, based on 'Raiffeisen Model' (National Cooperative Union of India, 1992). In the history of Cooperative movement in ***Sri Lanka***, 1911 to 1930 is regarded as the period of Cooperative Credit Societies development. The other types of Cooperatives developed during 1931 to 1941 (Prakash, 1992). Consumer Cooperatives of the ***Moscow*** region has catered above two million people. Over its 100 years, the regional Cooperative system has become economically the mightiest consumer union in the USSR. These days, when market relations are taking shape, the USSR's Consumer Cooperatives are facing a difficult situation (National Cooperative Union of India, 1991).

In ***Hungry***, about 94.2 per centof agrarian land was at the disposal of 1350 Cooperatives in 1981, where 6,50,000 people were employed by Cooperatives (Jammu and Kashmir Cooperative Union, 1981). In ***Japan***, Cooperatives emerged in the second half of the 19th century when Japan entered the modern world. These Cooperatives were strongly oriented towards Western Models. But it was not until 1900 that the large number of already existing Cooperatives could be based on National Cooperative Legislation by adopting the 'Industrial Cooperative Act' which was drawn up in the line with the German Cooperative Act (Burkner, 1998) .The Japanese Consumer's Cooperative Union (JCCU) started the *Tokyo Consumer's Cooperative society* in 1969(Nakabayashi, 1976). In ***Bangladesh***, village-based Cooperative Societies were organized in 1960 at South Rampur and Monsasan and in 1963; the *Bangladesh Cooperative College* was located on the *Academy Kotbari Campus* (Raper, 1970). ***African*** Cooperatives were started from the marketing end. Though there are *Craft men's Cooperatives*, the movement is dominated by marketing only. It is quite natural that in a number of mono-crop economics of Africa, Cooperative history is replete with battle between the movement and crop authorities, especially on the returns to farmers. This is true in case of ***Uganda, Nigeria, Zambia, Ghana, Kenya and Tanzania***, where the movement have been 'hard done by' Governments (Ramanujam, 1998).

The Nationals where the Cooperative Movement has shown much strength are the United States of America, Britain, Germany, New Zealand, France and Japan and with that there have been found signs of new efforts to spread the movement in a number of other countries (Sarojini, *et al.* 1997).

## Cooperatives in India

The overriding reason for the establishment of Cooperatives in India was the dire need for improvement in the conditions and quality of life of the rural masses, most of who were very poor. The first sustained growth in Cooperatives occurred around the turn of the century in respect of Credit Cooperatives, primarily because the village money-lender greatly exploited the poor when providing credit. Although some efforts at establishing Cooperatives had been made earlier, they were not very successful. In 1895, the Government of Madras deputed Sir Fredrick Nicholson to look into the possibility of introducing Land and Agricultural Banks in the province. However, the first Cooperative society was started in Punjab in 1891 for controlling the common land of the village. But this functioned till 1922. A real beginning of the Cooperative movement in India was the passing of the Cooperative Credit Societies Act of 1904, which was largely modelled on the lines of 'English Friendly Societies Act'1793. It was, however, soon found that the act of 1904 was insufficient to cope with the expanding movement. It did not allow central and non-credit Societies to be organized. These short comings were removed by a new Cooperative Societies Act, passed in 1912. On the basis of 'Maclagam Committee Report' in 1915, a Mont Ford Act was passed in 1919. In 1925, Bombay Government passed a separate Cooperative Societies Act. In 1927, the 'Royal Commission on Agriculture' stressed the importance of Cooperatives. In 1929, the Central and Provincial Banking Enquiry Committee made suggestions for its improvements. In 1935, the Reserve Bank of India (RBI) was established and its Agricultural Credit Department was given the task of studying the problems faced by the Cooperative movement. In 1937, the Reserve Bank on India recommended the establishment of multipurpose Cooperative Societies. The Cooperative movement picked up momentum after the Second World War. In 1945, there were 1,72,000 Cooperative Societies with a membership of 9.16 million persons and a working capital of Rs.164 crore. But the real impetus to the Cooperative Movement had to wait the dawn of Independence (IGNOU, 1997).

In the post Independence period, between 1947 and 1954, the various states either adopted the Act of 1912 or other such Act as was in force in other states. In 1949-50, the old Mysore state was having 51 *Primary Weavers Societies* and an *Apex Cooperative society* (Heggade, et al. 1993). For the first 50 years of the Cooperative Movement in India, i.e. from 1904 to 1954, the dominant pattern had been to recognize village as the basic unit for organization of *Primary Agricultural Cooperative Societies*. This pre-occupation with *'Villagism'* was adversely commented upon by the *Rural Credit Survey Report*, which was published in 1954 (Puri, 1992).

Dissemination of Cooperative Education particularly the principle of Cooperation amongst the masses has not received the desired attention during the post-Independence period. As such, there is a lot of perceptual gap among the people with regard to the principle of Cooperation as enunciated by the International Cooperative Alliance (ICI). In the face of the latest enactment, this area is going to assume paramount and with a fair amount of seriousness and concern (International Cooperative Alliance, 2001).

## Cooperatives Under Five Year Plans

Following the establishment of Planning Commission in 1950, the policy frame of Cooperative development was incorporated in the planning documents of the various Five-Year Plans. This policy frame was based on the recommendation based on the report of 'All India Rural Credit Survey Committee' (Misra, 1999).

**First Five Year Plan (1951-56):** The First Five Year Plan described Cooperative forms of organization as an indispensable instrument of planned economic action in a democracy (Suresh and Joseph, 1990). The Reserve Bank of India conducted an 'All India Credit Survey' in 1951, whose report was published in 1954. In consequence to its recommendations, an integrated scheme of 'Rural Credit' was executed in this plan. In this plan, 130 crore were distributed through Cooperative Credit Societies (Sehgal, 1990). The number of Cooperative Societies rose from about 1,80,000 to about 2,40,000 and the number of members from 14 to 17.62 million. At the end of the Plan, there were 9000 Primary Marketing Societies, 2000 Marketing Federations and 16 State Marketing Societies in the country.

**Second Five Year Plan (1956-61):** During the second plan, 1869 primary Marketing Societies were assisted through the National Cooperative Development and Warehousing Board. About 1,670 Godowns at Mandi Centre had been set up. At the end of the Second Plan, about 4,100 rural Godowns had been set up. By 1960-61, 30 Cooperative Sugar Factories, out of a total of 41; were in production. In 1959-60, there were 7,168 Primary Stores with a membership of about 1.4 million and a total paid of capital of Rs.2.4 crore. By the end of this plan, there were 3.32 lakh Cooperative Societies all over India, with membership in Primary Societies as 342 lakh and share capital of Rs.221 crore. Steps were taken during the Second Plan to strengthen the State Cooperative Departments, for such functions as audit, supervision and inspection.

**Third Five Year Plan (1961-66):** For the development of cooperation, the Third Plan provided Rs. 80 crore as against the estimated expenditure of Rs. 34 crore in the Second Plan (Suresh and Joseph, 1990). The 'National Agricultural Cooperative Marketing Federation (NAFED) of India Limited' was set up during 1961-62 (Amarchand and Varadhara, 1979). Programmes for the Third Plan provided for assisting 50 Whole-Sale Stores and 2,200 Primary Consumer Stores. Conditions for the development of Consumer Cooperatives in the Third Plan were generally favourable. The number of Industrial Cooperatives in the Third Plan increased from 30,000 to 40,000, their membership raised from over 2 million to about 3 million and their share capital from about Rs.10 crore to about Rs. 20 crore.

**Annual Plans (1966-69):** During 1967-68, the total plan outlay on Cooperation was Rs. 47.26 crores. This was inclusive of a provision of Rs. 10 crore for the Agricultural Refinance Corporation. As against this outlay, the actual expenditure was Rs. 38.29 crore. The membership of the Primary Agricultural Credit Societies increased during 1967-68 from 2.67 million to 2.83 million, covered about 90 per centof the villages in India (Suresh and Joseph, 1990). One of the notable developments of the period was the organization of a network of Consumer Cooperatives in urban areas. Indian Farmer's Fertilizer Cooperative Limited (IFFCO) was registered on 3rd November 1967; as a Multi-Unit Cooperative Society with a primary objective of production and distribution of fertilizers. The United States of America's Cooperatives through the Cooperative Fertilizer International (CFI) provide a million dollar aid besides technical know-how to the newly born Indian Farmer's Fertilizer Cooperative Limited (Prakash and Shotriya, 1999).

**Fourth Five Year Plan (1969-74):** During this period, the outlays on Cooperative Development Programmes were Rs. 78.57 crore, along with Rs. 90 crore separately for Land Development Banks (LDBs). The value of agricultural produce marketed by Cooperatives in 1972 reached Rs.844 crore. At the end of this period, in the sector of Consumer Cooperation, there were 13,913 Primary Consumer Cooperatives, 387 Central/ Wholesale Stores with 2,647 branches and 80 Departmental Stores, 14 State Federation of Consumer Cooperative Stores and a National Cooperative Consumer's Federation (NCCF) at apex level (Suresh and Joseph, 1990).

**Fifth Five Year Plan (1974-79):** There were 1,76,943 Credit Cooperatives at the end of this Plan period comprising of 47 State Level Societies, 349 Central Level Societies and 1,76,547 Primary Agricultural Credit Societies. The membership in such Societies was 55,981 thousand with the share capital of Rs. 87,029 lakh. The loans advanced for the Primary Credit Societies; during this period, was Rs.1,80,432 lakh (Reserve Bank of India, 1979).There were 1.16 lakh Primary Agricultural Credit Societies including Large Adivasi Multipurpose Cooperative Societies (LAMPS), Farmer's Service Society (FSS), etc. in 1978-79, with a membership of 5.18 crore. A four tier system comprising the National Federation, State Federations, Central Society at the District and Primary Societies at the Base Level, had been operating in the field of consumer activity. In 1979, this structure consisted of a National Federation, 14 State Consumer Federations, 8 State Cooperative Marketing-cum-Consumer Federations, 481 Central/Wholesale Consumer Societies at the district Level and 16,348 Primary Consumer Cooperatives at the Base Level. In the rural areas, the total value of consumer articles sold by the Cooperatives was estimated at Rs. 800 crore in 1979-80 (Suresh and Joseph, 1990).

**Sixth Five Year Plan (1980-85):** During 1980-81, there were 1,23,687 Credit Cooperatives with the membership of 83,313 thousand, Rs. 1,64,727 lakh share capital and Rs. 4,27,432 lakh of loan advanced in such Societies (National Bank for Agriculture and Rural Development, 1981). A major development in the field of credit during the sixth plan period was the setting up of National Bank for Agriculture and Rural Development (NABARD) in 1982 (Suresh and Joseph, 1990). At the end of this period, there were 32,753 Cooperative Societies in Andhra Pradesh with membership of 13,139 thousand, and Rs. 33,538 thousand as paid up share capital (Government of Andhra Pradesh, 1985). But there were only two Women Cooperative Societies in India (in Arunachal Pradesh); comprising membership of only 113 (National Bank for Agriculture and Rural Development 1985).

**Seventh Five Year Plan (1985-90):** The target of Rs.5,552.65 crore was laid for the marketing of agricultural produces through Cooperatives during this period (Government of India, 1987). Maharashtra Cooperatives made the major development. Till 1985, nearly 100 Sugar Cooperatives were registered with the membership of 6,080 hundred; 11,108 Dairy Cooperatives with membership of 9,596 hundred; 1,106 Fisheries Cooperatives with 1,450 hundred members; 21,195 Primary Cooperative Housing Societies with membership of 7,295 hundred and 14 Cooperative Consumer Societies with 294 hundred members existed in the Maharashtra State (Government of Maharashtra, 1986). In 1987-88, the total number of Cooperative Societies in India were 0.348 million with the membership of 150 million and working capital of Rs. 5,38,804.9 million. The Seventh Plan aimed at strengthening the Primary Marketing Societies and making their activities broad based. Out of 94,000 Primary Agricultural Credit Societies, 43,296 Societies were covered under the rural Consumer Cooperative Programme during this period (Suresh and Joseph, 1990).

**Annual Plans (1990-92):** At the end of march 1991, there were 2,646 Large Adivasi Multi-Purpose Cooperative Societies (LAMPS) in the country organized essentially to serve the tribal population. Of these, only 1,201 Societies constituting 45.4 per centwere viable. At the end of march 1992, the net work of the Short-Term Cooperative Credit Structure comprised 88,977

Primary Agricultural Cooperative Societies (PACS), 351 District Central Cooperative Banks (DCCB) with 10,775 branches and 28 State Cooperative Banks (SCB) with 651 branches .The owned funds of the structure rose by 8.7 per centand stood at Rs.4,303 crore (National Bank for Agriculture and Rural Development, 1993). During 1991-92, there were 4,653 Women Cooperatives, with 5.3 million members and Rs. 108.2 millions share capital (National Resource Centre, 1993).

**Eighth Five Year Plan (1992-97):** During 1994-95, there were 7,195 Women Cooperative Societies all over India, with the membership of 5,91,704; out of which 3.6 per cent members were scheduled caste .The share capital in such Societies was Rs.150.5 million, out of which Government had contributed 24 per cent (National Resource Centre, 1997).The advances borrowed to women through National Cooperative Agriculture and Rural Development Bank's Federation Ltd., was Rs. 68.98 crore in 1995-96 and Rs. 75.97 crore in 1996-97(National Cooperative Agricultural and Rural Development Bank's Federation,1997).The National Cooperative Consumer's Federation of India Limited had 22 state level federations,101 Large Sized Wholesale/Primary Societies, 2 National Level Federations, National Cooperative Development Corporation and Government as its members till the end of 1997,with the paid up capital of Rs.11.33 crore (National Cooperative Consumer's Federation Ltd., of India ,1997).During 1995-96,there were 8,171 Women Cooperative out of total 4,52,657 Cooperatives all over India, with 6,92,649 members in Women Cooperative(National Resource Centre, 1998).

**Ninth Five Year Plan (1997-2002):** The Ninth Plan took the country forward to the next millennium with emphasis upon Cooperatives as an important component (Srinivasan, 1999). This Plan gave top priority to agriculture and rural development with a view to generate adequate productive employment and eradication of poverty(Ahmed and Haque,1997). Efforts were made in the ninth plan to involve more and more Cooperative organizations in the processing of agriculture produce (Sharma,1998). Cooperatives employed 1,38,000 people, besides benefiting 19.28 crore members . Hence in both employment generation and rural development, the Cooperative sector offered immense potential that was tapped in the Ninth Plan period (Srinivasan,1999). The advances borrowed to women during 1997-98 through National Cooperative Agricultural and Rural Development Bank's Federation Limited, was Rs. 93.38 crore (National Cooperative Agricultural and Rural Development Bank's Federation, 1997). During 1997-98, there were 4,88,158 Cooperatives in India with 207.577 million members and Rs. 1,16,555 million share capital (National Resource Centre, 1999). Out of this, 8,714 were Women Cooperatives with 8,97,780 members and Rs. 204.23 millions share capital (National Resource Centre, 2001). During 1999-2000, the number of Cooperatives in India increased to 5,28,249 with 228.767 million members and Rs. 1,66,495.1 million share capital. This number included 8,393 Women Cooperatives with 8,42,327 members and Rs. 160.419 million share capital. The 45$^{th}$ 'All India Cooperative Week' (14-20 Nov.), 1998, recommended the creation of Women Cell in the Cooperative business federations and in the National Cooperative Organizations to handle gender issues (National Resource Centre, 1998). Till 1999, the Housing Cooperatives constructed 1.5 lakh dwelling units against the target of one lakh units under the two million housing Programme (Krishna, 1999). The number of Primary Housing Cooperatives increased at a faster rate in Delhi, Gujarat, Haryana, Maharashtra, Uttar Pradesh and West Bengal; although even in other states and union territories, there had been definite up-trends (Khurana, 1992). In Tamil Nadu, a scheme namely the Cooperative Micro-Credit to women vendors was implemented and 24,102 women were benefited to an extent of Rs. 47.50 lakh till 1999 (Khurana, 1999). During 2001, there had been 1,10,000 Primary and District Level Wholesale and Retail Consumer Outlets and Fair-Price Shops in India, playing a significant role in consumer Sector (Sehgal, 2001).

**Tenth Five Year Plan (2002-2007):** The Plan lays great emphasis on agriculture since growth in this sector is likely to lead to the widest dissemination of benefits, especially to the rural poor including agricultural labour. Also, since the majority of women workers are engaged in agriculture, investments in this sector have enormous implications for gender equality. Incidentally, the first generation of reforms in the industrial economy and reforms in the agricultural sector were neglected but this trend would change in the Tenth Plan (General Studies Manual, 2004).Emphasis is laid on the establishment of Women Cooperative Banks in various states of India especially in Jammu and Kashmir.

The Cooperative movement in different states is in varying degrees of development. Some states could be termed as cooperatively well-developed whereas others are not. It is observed that the attitude and approach of the Government machinery also is generally better in states where Cooperatives are strong. The movement has, therefore, a very difficult task of convincing the Governments of the cooperatively less developed states to be partners in development activities rather than having negative influence (Sisodia, 1999). Nevertheless, the 21$^{st}$ century seems poised to see Cooperatives in their new incarnation, carved specifically to suit the new economy. This would be reflected not only in the coming into being of insurance Cooperatives, Cooperative Producer Companies and the like, but also in the new legal environment created by amendments of the old Cooperative Laws facilitating the Cooperatives to breathe in a free atmosphere (Sud, 2001).

## Need For Agricultural and Consumer Cooperatives

The main purpose in organizing a Cooperative is to lead the Society towards a cooperative society—a society that is free from all types of exploitation, a society that provides full opportunities to an individual to grow and develop and a society that enables each individual to live a life of dignity and purpose (Taimni, 1981). Agriculture is the back bone of the Indian economy contributing about 45 per cent of the National Income, providing employment to about 70 per cent of the working population and accounting for sizeable share of the country's foreign exchange earning. The Agriculture

Marketing through Cooperatives needs high priority because it is an essential pre-requisite for the large expansion of Cooperative Credit. Cooperatives aim at improving the socio-economic status of agricultural community by rendering farm services like the supply of seed, fertilizers, farm implements, pesticides, etc. to boost up production. Cooperatives also help the farmers to secure remunerative prices by providing non-farm services like transportation, storage, processing and grading facilities (Kumar, 1983).

Living conditions of the population will be affected adversely whenever there is a price hike of goods and services. In order to arrest the price hike, the development of Consumer Cooperatives is found to be suitable remedy for the consumer protection against the malpractices in the market (Himachalam, 2001). In India, Cooperative Stores have an important role in the public distribution system. The main objective is to provide essential consumer commodities at fair prices to the general public (Daver, 1977). The Consumer Cooperatives are equally important for rural areas also. Because of frequent aroughts and famines, cultivators have to by their requirements of food grains in the open market when their crops fail. Lack of competition has also made the prices of many non-food items higher in rural areas than in urban areas (Umre, 1980). In a village, a consumer shop should not only sell food grains and sugar but simply other basic needs of villagers. Under the present arrangements, whereas the distribution of consumer goods in the urban areas is entrusted to the Urban Consumer Cooperatives separately organized for the purpose; in the rural areas, the Marketing and Village Service Cooperatives undertake the work (National Cooperative Development Corporation, 1974).

## Development Through Cooperative

Cooperatives meet their capital needs through various sources, viz. share capital contributed by members, any entry fees that may be charged, retention of surpluses from profitable operations, by the use of deferred pay-out for produce delivered, for goods sold and patronage refunds, by member's deposits of various types and borrowing from external sources including banks, government and government agencies and donations (Taimni, 1998). In a planned economy, pledged to the values of socialism and democracy, Cooperation can become progressively the principle basis of organization in many branches of economic life (Dev, 1992). Cooperative institutions deal with people at social and economic level. Strong Cooperatives not only create higher surplus but also provide greater and better services to the members (Prakash, 1989). Cooperatives are said to be poor man's organizations. Since self-help is the best help, the social thinkers and reformers have evolved the concept of Cooperation which means not merely working together but working together for a purpose (satisfaction of need of those who associate) by adopting certain principles, philosophy and procedures commonly known as Cooperative Principles (Desmukh, 1986). The Cooperatives have taken up multi-purpose activities and they attempt to coordinate diversified interests of the community. It has been accepted that since the Community Development Programme is concern with every aspect of rural life, it is not only inevitable but desirable that Cooperatives should involve themselves in different lines of business as far as possible (Kamat, 1974).

Cooperatives provide sufficient infrastructure to carry out the programme of economic development. The aim of any developmental programme is to achieve rapid growth, reduction of disparity in income and wealth, removal of poverty and achievement of egalitarian society based on social justice. The Cooperative Organization is an effective means in realizing all these objectives. All most all types of economic activities can be organized through the Cooperatives. The Cooperatives play a vital role in bringing together all economically non-viable units and help in the development of rural areas (Kumar, 1982). The most important aspect of Cooperative Development Programme in tribal areas is strengthening of Large Adivasi Multi-Purpose Cooperative Societies (LAMPS), so that they could effectively meet the three fold needs of tribal i.e. production requirements, marketing of tribal produce and distribution of agricultural inputs and consumer articles (Sharma, 1988). Among the institutional agencies providing credit for agricultural purpose, the Cooperative agency is acknowledged as the best suited for Indian conditions. Besides its main objective of providing credit especially for agriculture, the Cooperative Credit Structure plays an important part in mobilizing the savings of the community in the rural areas ((Rehman, 1982). Agricultural Cooperatives can significantly increase their output and growth if the State Governments fully exempt them from state-level taxes (Pandya, 1998).

The Cooperative Movement offers numerous opportunities to the youth who are backbone as well as future hope of the society in a very country. Cooperative's many fold activities and self-employment schemes could go a long way to help unemployed youth to run their own ventures instead of running after the white collar jobs (Gupta, 1982). Opportunity can be provided to youth by their involvement in the actual working of various types of Cooperative Institutions at various levels. They could be nominated, associated and appointed on the managing committees of Cooperative Societies (Khurana, 1981).

Housing is a primary need of all human being. The housing situation in India, indeed, is very depressing. Housing shortage is increasing every year. But Cooperative Sector aims to provide houses to their members or help them construct their housing units by providing financial assistance or construct houses for their members (Khurana, 1992). The Cooperative Sector of the sugar industry has also played a significant role in the overall development of rural areas. Sugar Cooperatives have made much impressive progress and it now occupies the top position both in respect of number and capacity of sugar units (Gogoi, 1992). The problem of equitable distribution of water can also well be tackled by the Cooperative Societies of the irrigation users. It is in this area that Cooperative Movement can involve itself intensively by taking over the administration of water-supply below the outlet level by forming *'Kulaba Cooperatives'* (Khan, 1991).

Cooperative Stores and Outlets are established in the rural as well as urban areas with special emphasis on the sale of essential commodities of life, whose demand is highly inelastic, despite rise in prices. The Cooperative Institutions play important role in holding the price line by supplying essential goods at the doorsteps (Sharma, 1991). At the same time, the Consumer Stores in Cooperative have to deal with the same form of work as in private sector (Majid, 1990).

The main reason for the non-resilience of the Cooperative Sector is interference and over-regulation of the movement by authorities, especially at the state level (Khurso, 1992). State governments are interfering in the internal managements of Cooperative Institutions and in many states; government has appointed administrators in key institutions (Kurien, 1993). Cooperatives being democratic institutions, efforts should be made to nurture and strengthen their democratic contents (Shah, 1990). Cooperative Education only can prepare the members to run their Cooperatives as service institutions on democratic lines (Bhave, 1982). Cooperative Organizations cover all most all activities of our economic life and they, therefore, need leadership for all tires of management in different areas of their operations (Joshi, 1981). Development of leadership should be stresses, ideally between values, ethos, ideas, socio-economic objectives and competitive strengths of the Cooperatives (Srinath, 2002). A regular and expanded programme of seminars and conferences planned and executed by the State and District Cooperative Unions with imagination can go a long way in enabling the leaders in learning from each other, in giving them orientation regarding changes in Cooperative Policies and Programmes and in discussing the common problems and devising strategies for solving them (Gopalkrishan, 1981).

## By-Laws or Articles of Association

It means the regulations of a Cooperative as originally framed or as amended from time to time. Every Cooperative must have its By-Laws or Articles of Association on the basis of which it is registered. It carries with it legal, administrative frame work, power, functions and liabilities of members and constitution of appointment of management organs like the general body, the board of directors, sub-committee, chairperson, chief executive and others. It also deals with financial implications like raise of funds through share capital or equity share, borrowing and other sources and creation of various funds. It facilitates management in the process of decision-making on various important aspects related to the functioning of the organization.

### Registration of Cooperative

Registration of a Cooperative Society is compulsory. Subject to the provisions of 'The Jammu and Kashmir Cooperative Societies Act,1960', and 'The Jammu and Kashmir Self Reliant Cooperatives Act, 1999', a Cooperative society or a Cooperative, which has as its object the promotion of the economic interests of its members in accordance with Cooperative Principles may be registered. It may be registered under Section 4 of the 'Jammu and Kashmir Cooperative societies Act 1960' and Section 3 of 'Jammu and Kashmir Self Reliant Act', 1999. Registrar of Cooperative societies (RCS) is a foundation of the Cooperative Movement by virtue of the statute under the provision of both these Acts. The State Government has been empowered to appoint the Registrar and the person to assist him and the State Government may by general or special order confer the power of registration to any person appointed to assist the Registrar. So the registra-tion authorities under general order by 'Jammu and Kashmir Cooperative Societies Act, 1960' lies under the hands of Additional Registrar Cooperative Societies(ARCS), Joint Registrar Cooperative Societies (JRCS), Deputy Registrar Cooperative Societies (DRCS), Assistant Registrar (AR) and under special order, Directors of concerned directorates like Animal Resources, Fisheries, Tribal Welfare, Industries, Handlooms, Cane Commissioner, Milk Commissioner etc. But, the Registration Authority as per the 'Jammu and Kashmir Self Reliant Act 1999' lies only under Registrar of Cooperatives.

## Membership in Cooperatives

The membership in Cooperatives is open to all irrespective of caste, colour, religion, race, sex, etc. However, membership may be restricted to homogeneous groups in some cases, e.g. the membership of farmer's Cooperatives may deny membership with those who are not farmers. Similarly, the members of the Women Cooperatives may deny membership with men. The members make the necessary contribution to the share capital and other financial contribution under the provisions of the By-Laws. However, members may be active or inactive. Active members are those who initiate share in the assets/liabilities and profit/Loss of the Cooperative and have live participation in the functioning of the Cooperative, as a result do not hold any share from profit/loss or assets/liabilities of the Cooperative. The members educate themselves about the Cooperative principles and business methods. The members are responsible to elect, suspend or remove members of managing committee. They receive the committee report of the preceding years' workings of the Cooperative together with the statements showing the receipts and payments; assets and liabilities and profit and loss of the year.

## Amalgamation of Cooperatives

In Cooperative Sector, 'Amalgamation' means combination of two or more Cooperatives for the interest of the members of the particular Cooperative, Cooperative movement and general public. Section 14 and 14-A of the 'Jammu and Kashmir Cooperative Societies Act, 1960', and Section 12 of 'Jammu and Kashmir Self Reliant Cooperatives Act, 1999', prescribe the procedure for voluntary and involuntary amalgamation of the Cooperatives to form the new Cooperative. Cooperatives may voluntarily or involuntarily transfer its assets and liabilities to another or may amalgamate themselves and form new Cooperatives. In order to amalgamate Cooperatives, general body meeting is called, where a resolution must be passed by two-third majority of members present in the meeting. The resolution comprises of all particulars about the proposed amalgamation. Once the resolution is passed, a notice in writing is given to all members and creditors of the Cooperative concerned. If any member or creditor does not agree for amalgamation, he/she has the option of withdrawing his/her shares, deposits or loans. It is important to exercise this option within a period of one month as per 1960's act and only within a period of 15 days as per 1999's act from the date of service of notice.

### Amendment of By-Laws in Cooperatives

By-Laws or Articles of Association concerning particular Cooperative can be amended for the betterment of Cooperatives. Under Section 12 and 12-A of 'Jammu and Kashmir Cooperative Societies Act, 1960' and 'Jammu and Kashmir Self Reliant Act, 1999'. Both these Acts, prescribe the procedures to be followed by a Cooperative for getting an amendment of By-Laws or Articles of Association passed. The essential requirement therein are as:

- A general body meeting shall be called to pass such amendment.
- A notice in accordance with the By-Laws or Articles of Association of Cooperative shall be given to all members for considering the proposed amendment.
- Two-third majority of the members present in the meeting shall vote in favour of resolution for proposed amendment.
- A copy of resolution along with the certificate as signed by the presiding authority in the meeting shall be furnished to the Registrar of Cooperatives.
- The application for amendment should be prescribed to the Registrar within 14 days as per 1960's Act and within 30 days as per 1999's Act, from the date of the general body meeting where such amendment is passed.
- In exceptional cases, Registrar of Cooperatives may condemn the delay if there is sufficient cause for such delay.

On receipt of application, the Registrar of Cooperatives approves the amendment of By-Laws or Articles of Association, only if he/she is satisfied that the proposed amendment—

- Is not contrary to the provisions of the act under which the Cooperative is registered.
- Does not conflict with Cooperative principles.
- Satisfies the requirements of sound business.
- Will promote the economic interests of the members of the Cooperative.
- Is not inconsistent with the principles of social justice.

## Financial Assistance Through Cooperatives

The capitals required to purchase and hold stocks for sale; maintain receivables; meet direct expenses towards transport, loading and unloading of goods, etc. is called working capital. Cooperatives require the capital in order to make its viable functioning, the capital of a Cooperative is provided by its members by purchasing shares. One member cannot subscribe to more than 10 per cent of the total share capital. Share contribution by members called, as 'Individual Share Capital' constitutes a small part of total capital. The major part of capital is raised by way of loans from Government or from the Apex Cooperative Institutions. Cooperatives may also receive grants and assistance from the government in the form of Government Share Capital, Managerial Assistance, Interest Free Loan, Specialized Loan, and Interest Subsidy etc.

## Credit Facilities Through Cooperatives

One of the major functions of the Cooperatives is to advance loans to its members. Through Cooperatives, need-based loan facilities are preferably given to those members who are progressive in their entrepreneur behaviour and borrow money only when really needed. Such loans include Short-Term loan, Medium-Term Loan and Long-Term Loan, through which profitable economic activities of members can be introduced.

(A) ***Short-Term Loans*** are preferably crop loans issued to the farmer members of Primary Agricultural Cooperative

Societies (PACS) for the purpose of meeting the expenditure connected with raising a particular crop in a season. These include basic cultivation expenses of crops like seeds, fertilizers, pesticides, etc. and cost of labour, fuel, irrigation and other over-head expenses. The loan consists of cash and kind component, which are called as Component 'A' and Component 'B' respectively. *Kind Component* is usually disbursed in kind and includes chemical fertilizer, improved variety of seeds and pesticides. The issue and recovery period of loans are fixed with reference to the period of sowing and harvest seasons of the crop respectively. Such Short-Term Loan encourages the small and marginal farmer members of Cooperatives, who cannot afford working capital from their personal savings as compared to big farmers who have the capacity and surplus to reinvest in crop production. This, however, does not mean that big farmer members of Cooperatives are not eligible for such loans. Moreover, consumption loans are also provided by Cooperatives mostly against the pledge of jewellery or hypothecation of articles financed. These loans are for meeting the expenses on social functions, medical need, purchase of consumer items, etc.

(B) ***Medium-Term Loans*** are given for the period of three to five years. Farm mechanization, minor irrigation, minor land improvement, animal husbandry activities and certain non-agricultural activities are the purpose for which Medium-Term Loans are given. Mortgage, hypothecation and pledge are the securities, differing as per the size of the loan, purpose and member borrower's income.

(C) ***Long-Term Loans*** are provided generally by the Long-Term Credit Structure. These loans, given for a period ranging from nine to twenty years, aim at increase in production and income of the member borrower. Mostly, Long-Term Loans are given against the mortgage of land. Till seventies, these loans were given mostly for redemption of prior debts. Later, they were meant for land improvement. They are listed as:

- *Minor irrigation*—construction of new wells, deepening of old wells, drilling, electrical or diesel pump sets, pump house construction, pipe line distribution and storage tanks.
- *Land development*—land levelling, bench terracing, contour bunds, renovation of old earthen bunds, contour trenching, earth filling, reclamation of marshy lands, field drainage, vertical drains and fencing.
- *Plantation and horticulture*—cardamom, pepper, clove, cashew nuts, bee-keeping, sericulture, etc.
- *Animal husbandry*—cows, buffaloes, cost of sheds, goats, work bullocks, carts, rabbits, poultry, ducks, etc.
- *Fisheries*—catamaran, trawlers and prawn-farming etc.
- *Biogas*—construction of biogas plantation.
- *Farm mechanization*—tractors, trailers and power tillers.
- *Vehicle*—good's vehicle etc.
- *Non-farm sector*—printing, bookbinding, chemical products, sports goods, stationery items, etc.
- *Housing*—construction of houses in rural as well as in urban areas.
- *Integrated loans*—construction or building materials, hostels, restaurants and miscellaneous.
- *Jewellery loans*—consumption purposes against the pledge of gold jewellery.

## Cooperative Godowns

Storage of produce is not merely an operation to avoid theft or fire of produce during the period between receipt and dispatch. Storage, in Cooperative Godowns, is primarily concerned with the safety and preservation of stored produce and its handling i.e. in and out movements of the produce in the most economic manner. It is also concerned with the suitability in terms of convenience and cost, storage facility in a particular situation and its ability to protect the products from theft and fire. Godowns of Cooperatives help its members not only in improving the storage methods of fertilizer etc, but also in the efficient marketing of potatoes and other perishables, like fruits and vegetables. National Cooperative Development Corporation (NCDC) assists the viable or potentially viable Primary Agricultural Cooperative Societies (PACS), Large Adivasi Multi-Purpose Cooperative Societies (LAMPS) and Farmer's Service Societies (FSS) working at the village level and Marketing Cooperatives functioning at Mandi, State and National levels, for the construction of Godowns. Assistance is available to the village level Cooperatives (PACS, LAMPS and FSS) for construction of rural Godown complexes together with the facilities of mini-bank counter (office room), consumer shop and residence for the manager. This is intended at developing Godown complex as rural growth centre. Moreover, owned Godowns comprise the valuable assets of Cooperatives.

### Audit in Cooperatives

The financial position of Cooperatives can be ensured through its audit. It ascertains the actual financial condition and earning of the Cooperative and also access how far the Cooperative has been able to carry on business on sound Cooperative lines and secure the economic benefits of its members. Income and expenditure, profit and loss, and assets and liabilities accounts are prepared during annual audit through verification of books, vouchers and other records of the Cooperative. This procedure brings about accurate and suitable recordings and summarizing of authorized financial transactions. Auditor can be appointed by the Registrar of Cooperatives to audit the Cooperatives as per the Act of 1960. While a Chartered Accountant can be appointed by the concerned Cooperative for audit purpose, as per the Act of 1999. The auditor utilizes proper and reasonable skills while examining the records of the Cooperative. However, he/she must confine himself/ herself to records to ascertain that the By-Laws of the concerned Cooperative have been duly carried out in business transactions.

2

# INDIAN COOPERATIVE MOVEMENT AND WOMEN PARTICIPATION

Cooperative movement in India is one of the largest movements in the world. Initially it was started with a limited spectrum of activities or dispensation of rural credit has now entered in all fields of economic activity with social content. The movement has covered 100 per cent villages and 75 per cent rural households. It has been playing a significant role in disbursing agricultural credit, distribution of agricultural inputs, providing market support, processing, etc. Over the last more than hundred years (1904-2007), cooperatives have made substantial contribution to the country, particularly to the rural poor. Notwithstanding their achievements and phenomenon growth, cooperatives are beset with several issues and confront with challenges in the era of economic reforms. The cooperative sector in India has more than 5.49 lakh societies of various types with membership of more than 22.95 million and working capital of about Rs. 3,827,496,000 thousand as on 31st March 2003. The membership in cooperatives has risen from 142.1 million in 1984-85 to 229.4 million in 2002-2003. The employment generated through cooperatives is 15 per cent at national level, in addition to 14.79 million self employed persons via cooperatives.

Anjaria (1968) identified factors that are conducive to development and efficient working of Cooperative Marketing

Societies and also those that hinder their growth. The overall assessment of performance of the selected Societies on the basis of certain indicators like membership, amount of pledge advances, volume of marketing activity, progress in respect of interlinking of credit with marketing, volume of distribution activities, etc. show that they can be classified in to three categories. The first category include good working Societies, second include generally satisfactorily Societies and third category comprises poor Societies. The major factors that contribute to the successful and efficient working of Societies include a substantial area in the jurisdiction of the selected Marketing Societies, better yields per acre due to favourable soil conditions and availability of irrigation facilities. Lack of educate development of Cooperative credit and continued dependence of cultivators on creditor-traders with the consequent loss of freedom to sell to an agency of choice are the factors which made the second category lower than those in the first category. In respect of the Societies included in the third category, the factors responsible are small size of land-holding, poor financial position and weak management.

Krishnaswami (1976) conducted empirical research to study the influence of socio-economic factors on democratic control in Societies and to identify the factors that promote or retard democratic practice in Societies. The extent of member's participation in the democratic process has been found very small. Only 1.3 per cent of the ordinary members and 5.1 per cent of the committee members are activists. The majority of both categories (56.8 per cent and 84.6 per cent respectively) are medium participants and as high as 41.9 per cent of the ordinary members and 10.3 per cent of the committee members are low or non-participants. About 14 per cent of the ordinary sample members have never attended any general meetings and 91 per cent of ordinary members who have attended meetings and 85 per cent of committee-men have never been participated in any discussions in meetings. This finding leads to the conclusion that education, social participation, member's stake, a longer period of membership, knowledge of co-operation, knowledge of own Society, member identification, business participations, and member satisfaction promote democratic participation and that illiteracy, caste, hierarchy, occupational heterogeneity, socio-economic disparity, lack of enlightenment, lack of identification, lack of loyalty and lack of satisfaction consequent on inefficient service retard democratic participation of members in Cooperative Societies.

Desai (1978) after considering the records of the Cooperative Credit Movement analysed the failure of village Cooperatives and found that the conclusion that *Primary Cooperative Society* has taken root in India, was premature and would be perhaps still premature nearly for 40 years. The failure of Cooperative Credit is explicable in terms of the total impracticability of any attempt to combine the very weak in competition with the very strong and expect them by themselves to create conditions; firstly, for their emancipation from the interests which oppose them; and secondly, for their social and economic development in the context of the severe disadvantages historically imposed on them by a structure of the type described. The forces of transformation have to be at least as powerful as those that are sort to be counteracted. Such forces can be generated not by cooperation alone but by cooperation in conjunction with the state.

Ganesan (1982) recapitulated the *'Mulakanoor Cooperative Rural Bank'* in *Andhra Pradesh,* which has been registered in 1956. One of the objectives of this Cooperative is to purchase quality consumer articles locally and at fair price, thereby providing consumer services. This bank runs consumer stores at *Mulakanoor* and at *Kotchkonda* through which it tries to supply members as well as the general public with essential household requirements, such as food grains, sugar, cloth, refined oil, toilet and washing soaps, hair oil, blades, tooth paste, spices, condiments, kerosene, etc. at a reasonable price. Controlled cloth, too, is made available to members through the Multi-Cooperative's sale counters.

Goel (1983) selected *Punjab* to study the role of Cooperatives in agricultural development. It is found that only 8.7 per cent of households are within the ambit of Cooperatives and can market only 0.9 per cent of the total produce. All the sampled beneficiaries do not make use of Society for disposal of their marketable surplus. About 57.4 per cent value of the stocks is realized through sources other than Cooperatives. Besides, leaving aside paddy and wheat, all other food grains are preferred to be sold by the beneficiaries either through *arhtias* or other sources. These findings are an indication that all is not well with Cooperatives in promotion of agricultural development. Cooperatives have failed to attain even a partial success and their organizations have become a mere formality.

Bedi (1984) took the case study of *'Mudialy Fishermen's Cooperative Society Limited'*, of *Calcutta*. This Cooperative Society was formed in November 1961, with its area of operation extending to *Mudialy* and *Garden Reach Municipality* with an initial membership of 55 and a share capital of Rs. 550. The State Government contributed a share capital of Rs. 4000 that was later raised to Rs. 7000. The Society is the finest example of a successful Cooperative among one of the most backward communities. The outstanding feature of the Society includes a very strong financial base which it has built over the years, very good benefits which the Society is providing to the members, progressive outlook of the Society and management towards fish culture, a market-system free from exploitation and, above all, a democratically elected management.

Sathyanarayana (1984) conducted a micro-level study of *Chittoor* district of *Rayalaseema, Tirupati* and evaluated the working of *'Credit Cooperatives'*. The source-wise borrowings indicate that the percentage participation of the institutional agencies in the total credit requirement of the farmers is satisfactory in the central region of the district; while in the other regions, it is far from being satisfactory. With regard to repayment of loans, the study reveals that they are influenced by farm-size and farm-business income. Therefore, efforts have to be made to improve the farm-business income of the farmers by re-organizing the structural and institutional facilities.

Attwood and Baviskar (1987) singled out *'Cooperative Sugar Factories'* of Western India, *Maharashtra,* for showing their remarkable successful performance that is not found in case of other Cooperative/Private/Public organizations. In a comparative sociological analysis, organizational factors have been found to be crucial for the success of a Cooperative unit. The ability of the Cooperative Sugar Factories to generate a stable alliance among the small, medium and large-scale cane growers, who are the shareholders, is the main reason of their success. This alliance is made possible by two sets of factors: internal ones which are specific to the technical requirements of production and external ones which are rooted in the agrarian system of the region where these Cooperatives have flourished. Comparisons with other types of Cooperatives in other regions of the country show remarkable divergence in these factors. Detailed comparisons with the successful *Dairy Cooperatives* of *Gujarat* have revealed that Cooperative Alliances between small and large-scale farmers may take different organisational form under different regional conditions and hence variations on their success.

Goel and Pandey (1987) investigated the *'Cooperative Banks'* in *Hissar* district of *Haryana*. It took into account such variables as operated size of holding, total amount of outstanding loans, percentage of consumption expenditure to total expenditure, per capita income from crop production, repayment capacity and percentage of earning adults to total adults. Only three variables, viz. total amount of outstanding loans, percentage of consumption expenditure to total expenditure and percentage of earning adults to total adults are found to be the most significant factors responsible for affecting the over-dues of Primary Agricultural Cooperative Societies and Cooperative Service Societies.

Pawan (1987) studied the functioning of an *'Apex Cooperative Federation'* in the state of *Punjab*. The study has undertaken various management aspects such policy-making and direction, organisational structure, human resources, and some of its substantive operations like marketing, processing and distribution. The organisational structure has developed in a zigzag way. Functional growth has generally preceded structural modifications. The federation, under the multi-agency approach adopted by the government, is required to maintain huge stocks of chemical fertilizers, including un-popular ones, much in advance of the sowing season, in spite of the fact that their consumption is confined to few months only. Cooperative Marketing Societies are becoming dormant and non-viable because of the managements policy of withdrawing the distribution of fertilizers through them. In view of the importance of chemical fertilizers in the matter of improving the agricultural productivity, it is pertinently important to keep its prices low.

Singh *et al.* (1987) looked for '*Ludhiana Primary Cooperative Land Mortgage Bank*', to examine the economic rationale of the Long-Term Cooperative Credit advanced for various purposes on some selected farm situations. The borrowings for underground water channels, purchase of tractors, installations of tube wells, and purchase of land have been selected for study. Return tests, re-paying test and risk bearing ability test are worked out. The test of adequate additional returns except in one case of tractor purchase and the test of re-paying capacity justify the loan to be obtained for different types of long term investments. Most of the cases disqualify the test of risk bearing ability.

Chahal and Gill (1988) endeavoured to examine the role of Cooperatives in the rural development in *Punjab*. It is highlighted that with the commencement of Cooperative Marketing of milk, the dairy farmers have been saved from the clutches of private milk vendors. The consumers are also provided with better quality of milk at reasonable prices. The Milk Cooperatives have also encouraged farmers to rear the cows, specially the exotic cross-breeds. The setting up of milk plants has not only provided competitive market for milk but has also opened new avenues of employment to the rural people because the collection, transportation, processing and re-distribution of milk involve a big infrastructure. Moreover, the farmers have become quality conscious as the milk is marketed on quality basis. Thus, the dairying has not only increased the income of rural milk producers but also raised the standard of living of rural farmers in *Punjab*.

Verma and Pathania (1988) assessed the regional disparities in the performance of Cooperatives in *Himachal Pradesh*. In the wake of modern technology and increasing education, the Society is under going tremendous changes. The government policy of uplifting the poor must be carried with strong political will and people's involvement which can come only with the Cooperative Movement. The cultural solidarity among different sections of society can be utilized through Cooperative in furthering the transformation process.

Khusro Committee (1989) in its report of the 'Agricultural Credit Review Committee' (ACRC) states, *'in respect of the economically weaker sections of the community, and only in respect of them, we appreciate the role of concessionary finance of low interest rates, of limited, well-focused subsidies to specified target groups among the poor and of promotional measures to bring up the economics of low-income farmers, and weaker sections of rural people, mostly first generation entrants in to the fold of credit. We believe that bringing them into credit system will itself benefit them by inculcating discipline and offering productive opportunity and that they need special help in entering that system. And, we are also clear that this special help to the weaker sections of society is not just a welfare- promoting measure but will, if administered judiciously, graduate these weaker sections into productive and profit making functionaries'.*

Gound (1992) studied *'Cooperative Electricity Supply Society'* (CESS), *Sircilla* in *Karim Nagar* district of *Andhra Pradesh*, which has been established in 1970, as one of the first pilot projects in India. It is found that backward *Sircilla* region has developed much due to the Cooperative bored power supply systems, bringing dry lands into wet and subsistence farming to commercial farming, having so much of individual potential, absorbing only 6,000 labour force directly in power looms and 8,000 labour force mostly women in *Beedi* rolling daily. Meanwhile, the life style or standard of living of the poor has improved lot off.

Kapoor (1992) observed that there have been 87,805 *Primary Agricultural Credit Societies*, 349 *District Central Cooperative Banks*, and 28 *State Cooperative Banks*, in India during 1991-92, supplying short-term and medium-term agricultural credit. Their coverage extends even to remotest parts of India. However, the high delinquency rate in recovery of loans has depressed the growth of borrowing membership and will continue to so affect it till the channels of credit recycling are unclogged by better recovery performance. Data also reveals that there has been a significant shift of borrowers from non-institutional to institutional sources of credit; while there has been no significant enlargement in the proportion of borrowers.

Kanitkar (1994) designed a study on *'The Narmada Group Cooperative Fruit and Vegetable Society Limited', Panetha* (NGCFVS), which was registered as a Cooperative Society in 1989. Since its establishment till 1993, the membership has increased from 20,200 to 67,410, membership deposits Rs. 4,42,441.25 to 3,36,369.10 and reserve fund Rs. 1,390 to 72,225.96. The net profit as per the audited accounts of 1993 has reached up to Rs. 40,672.24 and the assets of the Cooperative are worth Rs. 25,26,682.61. The society charges two per cent commission on the sale of produce made on behalf of the members which goes towards the Society's income.

Subramamyam (1994) reported that there have been 91,592 *Primary Agricultural Cooperative Societies* (PACS) in India during the year 1993-94; out of which 60,647 have been fully viable, 28,262 potentially viable, 2,401 dormant, 274 defunct, in addition to other 8 Primary Agricultural Cooperative Societies. The total membership in such Cooperatives have been 88,989 thousand; comprising 14,011 thousand scheduled caste; 12,535 thousand scheduled tribe; 29,216 thousand small farmers; 3,833 thousand rural artisans and 29,392 thousand marginal farmers and others.

Srivastava (1995) tried to find the impact of *'The Student Consumer Scheme'* upon the members in *Maharashtra.* The objectives of the *'Student Consumer Scheme'* has been by and large achieved with reference to stabilization of prices of student consumer articles i.e. stationary, books, etc. The membership coverage has been more or less satisfactory, though only one or two stores have achieved the target of enrolling hundred per cent students as members of stores. Out of a sample of thirty stores, it was encouraging to observe that twenty-nine stores have been audited. Seventy-seven of the selected sample stores have had elections to the board of management. But majority of the stores are very poorly staffed. It needs to be ensured that the margin money assistance is used to raise working capital in order to make the cash operating cycle optimally efficient, the margin money itself should not be used as working capital.

Roy (1998) evaluated the *'Kushmandi Cooperative Marketing Society'* situated in South *Dinajpur* district of *West Bengal.* During the year 1965-66, this Society started with a meagre share capital of Rs. 6,340 i.e. beginning with zero. Now, the Society has become hero of Agricultural Cooperative Movement in *West Bengal,* as their share capital for 1997-98 has swelled to Rs. 31.42 lakh. The Society has not restricted its area of operation in the West Bengal State only, but it works throughout India. The main activities involve procurement and sale of agricultural commodities produced in their area which are paddy, wheat, *urad, arhar,* mustard seeds, raw jute, garlic etc. The Society has a consumer shop for selling various kinds of shirting/suiting clothes, sari, bed sheet, woollen garments, etc. which is running profitably; besides, the Society sells fertilizer to the local farmers with bare minimum margin. The Society is authorized dealer of *Konark Cement* and sells cement to local consumers. 'Indian Oil Corporation' has set up a diesel-cum-petrol pump of the Society that is running successfully. It encourages the local students by providing financial assistance regarding to the meritorious poor students.

Selvaraju (1998) studied the general working of *'Tiruvarur Cooperative Land Development Bank'.* The study reveals that Cooperative Banks especially this Land Development Bank has help a lot to rural credit. *'Tiruvarur Cooperative Land Development Bank'* is the first bank in *Tamil Nadu* that has introduced the supervised credit system and its service in rural credit is more commendable and the farmers in the area of operation of bank are benefited on a large scale.

Sundar (1998) emphasized on an urgent need for revitalizing the *Industrial Cooperatives* engaged in the traditional skills of rural artisans. The study has undertaken eight units of *Cuddalore* district, *Chennai,* engaged in coir-making, toy-making, cashew-crushing, metal-making etc. Fifty-two per cent of respondents have adduced futility of attending meetings as the reason for their non-attendance thereby indicating the inferiority complex of the respondents that they could not do anything worthwhile in the meeting. All the respondents have expressed total ignorance about member education. Government should spare no efforts to arrange for member education periodically and observe behavioural change in the members of the Society. If Industrial Cooperatives are facilitated to function efficiently and successfully, they should be helped to shed their old moorings and style of functioning, they are certain to ring the bell of hope for rural India where unemployment stalks.

Bandna (2000) commented that many Cooperative ventures have failed because of the lack of managerial competences and suggested that *Community Polytechnics* can provide the support by way of helping villagers to organize Cooperatives for overall rural development, which includes economic development, improvement in life style, beautification of the environment and enrichment of social and cultural life. One such attempt was made by *'Ramgariah Polytechnic', Phagwara,* which has promoted one multi-purpose Cooperative Society for undertaking integrated development of a village. The attempt for integrated development could not be further pursued for lack of policy support, although it has tremendous potential.

Bachute (2000) analysed the human resource or manpower available in *'Non-Agricultural Cooperative Credit Societies'* in *Wai Taluka* of district *Satara, Maharashtra.* The average number of member per Society is about 540.The average members per employees Cooperative Credit Society is very less due to limited area of operation. However, the average member per Urban Cooperative Credit Society is comparatively high viz. 750. Though females consist of more than fifty per cent of the population in *Wai Taluka,* only 22.08 per cent females are members of these Societies. The per centage of female directors is only 15.62. The female chairmen and secretaries are only in two Urban Cooperative Credit Societies. The number of females appointed in the staff is negligible. However, the number of females working as collection agents is sizeable mainly due to sincerity and honesty of work.

Bisht (2000) attempted to evaluate the existing system of providing term loans to farmers by *'Land Development Bank'* in *Uttar Pradesh.* The major finding of the study is that most of the farmers are hesitant to approach the *Land Development Bank* for loan because of the strict steps taken by the *Bank* when the farmers became unable to make payment at the time of recovery. The small and medium holding groups of farmers have to face problem of delay in obtaining loan. The study stressed that the right cooperative spirit behind every Cooperative effort is key to the success of the Cooperative Movement. Bank can play a more significant role by providing adequate long-term finance to the farmers for strengthening rural economy.

Kodag (2000) conducted a case-study of *Sangli* district in order to assess the Indian Grape *Export* through Cooperatives. Some leading grape growers started the Cooperative Societies in the region for developing the infrastructural facilities, such as roads, fast transportation, and supply of export packaging materials, grape guard paper and cold storages. It is observed that the total export from *Sangli* district is above 6,000 tones every year. But the Cooperative Societies are having export around 2,000 tones per year that is thirty per cent share in total grape export. Farmers are getting Rs. 16-20 per kilogram because of export quality of grapes. It appears from the data collected that from 1991 so many farmers are taking interest in cultivating the quality grapes more particularly for export.

Rao (2000) presented a success story of *'Cooperative Tea Industry'* in *Tamil Nadu—INCOSERVE;* which is the apex body for the seventeen *Industrial Cooperative Tea Factories* in the *Nilgiris,* serving 21,326 acres of tea gardens through the *Industrial Cooperative Tea Factories.* The annual production of the tea factories attached to *INCOSERVE* is about 167 lakh kilograms. It is the largest *Tea Cooperative* in India functioning under the control of Government of *Tamil Nadu*. Its major weakness is that tea growers are having small-holdings and there is absence of technical field staff to render technical adviser to the tea growers. In order to encourage the tea farmers, tea board should develop basic infrastructural facilities and financial support to the tea factories through *INCOSERVE*. Government should extend financial support in respect of promotion of packet tea sales through reasonable advertising budget.

Salve (2000) undertook the overall picture of *'Warna Bazar'* and *'Shetkari Sahakari Sangh Limited'* in *Kolhapur* district as per annual reports of these Consumer Cooperatives. The studies have shown that 77 per cent (7,481) of members in *'Warna Bazar Consumer Cooperative'* are females and 23 per cent (2,214) are males. The proportion of female members is more than male members. It is mainly because of developing other Women's Cooperative activities in this Society, like *Warna Bhagini Mandal, Shri Warna Mahila Udyog, Warna Poultry, Dairy, Warna Cooperative Bank, Warna Mahilas' and Credit Society*. The value of one share is generally Rs. 501 for male and Rs. 251 for female membership. The *'Shetkari Sahakari Sangh Limited'* has hundred branches. Most of the branches are concentrated into rural and semi-urban areas. The membership of the Society has increased and is open to the entire public residing in rural and urban areas. This Society has come to occupy an important place in the Consumer's Cooperatives' map of India. However, Consumer's Cooperative Movement has not been developed in rural areas. It is necessary to set-up Consumer's Cooperative Society for each village of *Gram Panchayat* Level.

Patil et al. (2000) studied the 'Kolhapur *Zilla Dudh Utpatak Sangh Limited'* which is one of leading Cooperative organisation which has set an example for transfer of technology in animal husbandry and dairy. *'Gokul'* is favourite trade/brand name of various milk products sold by the *Sangh*. *'Gokul Gram Vikas Yojana'* has been implemented since 1990. This programme has covered women education, member education, management committee training, secretary training, procurement training, youth group discussion, women group discussion, leadership development, refresher courses etc. Due to these multi-spectrum dairy extension activities, awareness regarding importance of this business has been created and consequently farmer members are inclined to take up dairy as a business in the *Kolhapur* district.

Singh (2000) made a case-study of '*Kongba Bazar Consumer Cooperatives Society Limited*', which has been registered on October 26th, 1960, as a Primary Consumer Society. The Society has been established to make available the daily essential goods to the people of the area at low price. It had 37 members, holding 101 shares, and the paid-up share capital of Rs.1,010 initially. It operates in 12 villages. In the year 1964, the Society was renamed as the '*Kangba Primary Consumer Cooperative Society Limited*'. The Society's main activities are the purchase and sale of various consumer goods and non-controlled cloths. The Society purchases goods from the *Imphal* Market and sells these in the local area. The Society's business turn-over is found decreasing during the past 5 years. The Society is facing the problems of lack of working capital and non-availability of goods from wholesale and the 'Manipur State Cooperative Consumer Federation Limited'. So the Society cannot sale goods at fair price.

Sharma (2000) commented that the Cooperatives in *Gujarat* and *Maharashtra* are laying great emphasis on developing infrastructure facilities in the form of schools, hospitals, entertaining centres, rural roads, drinking water facilities for the common masses. Social forestry programmes are being arranged by *'Indian Farmers Fertiliser Cooperative Limited'* (IFFCO) for protecting the rural environment. The interest of the weaker sections of society like unskilled labour, illiterate fishermen and landless labourers are also being promoted through setting up of Cooperatives for weaker sections. The latest innovation of Farmers Credit Card in the field of rural finance is helping the farmers in getting working capital for enabling them to purchase inputs like fertilizers, seeds etc. All these efforts are a pointer towards the positive role of Cooperatives in the empowerment of people in India.

Singh (2000) showed the status of *'Nongpok Muster Cooperative Thrift Society Limited,' Nongmeibung, Imphal,* which was started only with 39 members; but at the end of 1998, it had 464 members. The main objective of the Society is to encourage thrift by enabling members to save part of their income in a safe and convenient way with the prospect of a fair incoming profit, so as to accumulate a decent promotion for themselves for old age or for their families on their death and to prevent indebtedness by making loans on reasonable terms. Each member is getting loan benefit up to Rs.3,000 and it may be enhanced up to Rs.5,000 at the rate of 21 per cent per annum against their share-value and Rs. 10,000 against the gold ornaments and charged at the rate of 24 per cent per annum. They are also allowed recurring deposits and fixed deposits by giving interest as per the bank norms. The Society has raised their fund by subscription and shares. They have also raised funds by taking donations and admission fees, loans and deposits. The normal value of each share shall be Rs.100. At present, there is lot of scope for improvement in financial position of this Society.

Dash (2001) selected the *'Nav Nirman Cooperative Bank', Ahmedabad,* for a case-study and studied the role of human assets in contributing to the growth and development of the bank. *'Navnirman Cooperative Bank'*, as the name symbolizes re-building, has occupied an important place in the urban banking sector. From a sinking bank 20 years ago, it has come up to the rank of the 79th among 1,800 old Urban Cooperative Banks in India. The combined efforts of dedicated staff, enlightened members and visionary leaders have brought laurels for the Bank. The success can fairly attributed to the attempts of the human assets. Employees' knowledge, skill and attitude need to be sharpening for a better result.

Inamdar *et al.* (2001) attempted to determine the comparative economics of paddy processing. The findings indicate that the private sector rice mills tend to be relatively more efficient in acquiring land and undertaking building construction at lowest cost as compared to their co-interprets in the Cooperative Sector. It is noticed that all the indicators are on higher line in the case of private sector rice mills than Cooperative rice mills. It indicates that the private sector rice mills perform well than Cooperative Sector.

Kalamlkar et al. (2001) investigated the progress of *'Agricultural Credit Societies and Non-Agricultural Credit Societies'* in *Vidarba*. The study reveals that the number of Societies increased by 3.64 and 14.60 per cent during 18 years period registering a growth rate of 0.36 and 5.87 per cent for *'Agricultural Credit Cooperative Societies and Non-Agricultural Credit Cooperative Societies'* in *Vidarbha* respectively. The membership has increased by 49.46 and 32.39 per cent during the study period registering a growth rate of 2.23 and 8.24 per cent for *'Agricultural Credit and Non-Agricultural Credit Cooperative Societies'*, respectively. Growth in advances accompanied by poor recovery have kept the over dues at significantly high level. This increase in over dues shows poor performance of the Credit Societies.

Codag (2001) presented a case-study of *'Shree Warana Vibhag Sahakari Grahak Mandal Limited', Warannagar, Maharashtra*. This is the first Cooperative Department Store in rural India, started in 1978. Its area of operation is two districts i.e. *Kolhapur* and *Sangli* covering 78 villages. It is found that the main aim of the Society is to protect the consumers from adulteration. This is an organization supplying quality goods to their members. They also provide goods at reasonable price. Their distribution channel is very strong which helps them for the increasing trend of sale from last ten years. All the business activities are conducted properly and purchases are done through the committee. This is only one organization in Western *Maharashtra,* having such success in departmental stores. Reason behind the success of *Warana Bazar* is proper planning, proper location selection, good coordination and due control.

Patil (2001) purposively selected the *Miraj* region of *Sangli* district to find the effectiveness of short-term (crop) loan in *'Primary Agricultural Cooperative Societies'* (PACS). The percentage of short-term loan amount borrowed by the selected farmers is comparatively higher in irrigated (wet) area. It is but natural, because the credit worthiness of the wet area farmers is higher due to cash crops, mainly sugar cane. A few big farmers enjoy large share of the total loan disbursement, while small farmers have got very small share of the total short-term loans. The causes of defaulters are different in different areas. In non-irrigated area, scarcity of rain and increase in family expenses are the main reasons of defaults. While increase in family expenses, marriages and investment in land, building, agricultural implements, etc are the reasons of defaults in irrigated area.

Kulkarni et al. (2001) examined the growth of *'Lead Bank Credit'*. Growth parameters of the total deposit, total advance and total branches showed highly significant and positive growth rate. The growth rates of total priority sector advance, agricultural advance, small-scale industry advance, other priority sector advance, and 'Integrated Rural Development Programme' (IRDP) advance are positive and significant at 5 per cent level. The growth rates of total deposits, total advances, agricultural advance and small-scale industry advance reveal more than 10 per cent during 11 years. There is positive and considerable correlation between total advance of the lead bank and moderate correlation between total advance and advance to agricultural sector and negative correlation with other priority sector advances of the lead bank. There is moderate correlation between total advance of all institutions except lead bank and advance to small scale industry and the correlation between total advance of all institution except lead bank and advances to total priority sectors, agriculture, other priority sector and IRDP are non significant.

Behera and Dash (2001) assessed the district-wise growth of Cooperative Societies, i.e. *'Primary Agricultural Cooperative Societies'* (PACS), *'Large Adivasi Multi-Purpose Cooperative Societies'* (LAMPS) and *'Farmers Service Society'* (FSS), over the period of 1984-85 to 1996-97, covering all the districts (undivided) in *Orissa*. In *Orissa,* in the year 1996-97, the number of *Primary Agricultural Cooperative Societies* including *Large Adivasi Multi-Purpose Cooperative Societies* and *Farmer Service Societies* stood at 2,806 with a total membership of 34.44 lakh and a working capital of Rs.371 crore. It is found that there exists inter-district variations in the growth rate of different selected indicators, namely, number of Societies, number of members, number of borrowing members, working capital, share capital, deposits, loan advanced (short-term loan and medium-term loan), total loan outstanding, total over due and amount of consumer goods sold. In certain cases, as the development of Cooperatives has been in a negative direction, this hampers the Cooperative Movement in the state. Share capital per member has significant impact in the net earning per Cooperative Society, whereas, loan advanced per member has no significant impact on the net earnings per Society. Hence, in order to increase the net earnings per Cooperative Society, which includes *Primary Agricultural Cooperative Societies, Large Adivasi Multi-Purpose Cooperative Societies* and *Farmers Service Society,* in *Orissa,* advancement of loan to borrowing members, deposits of the member and total loan outstanding of the Cooperative Societies have to be decreased.

Pitchai et al. (2001) presented a case-study of *'Madurai Medical College Students Cooperative Stores'.* The 1959 *'Madurai Medical College Students Cooperative Store'* was started with 559 members. Its share capital at that time was only Rs.2,795. In the year 2000, the members' strength has been found increased to 8,137 and its share capital is Rs.1,52,457. Initially, its sale was to the tune of only Rs.25, 000 but at the end of the year 1999-2000, its purchase has been Rs.1.65 crore and a sale has crossed Rs.1.73 crore. The members of the stores are the students and the faculty members of the *'Madurai Medical College'.* In the beginning, it was started to cater to the needs of medical college students. Now, the faculty members and the people in and around the college have also benefited out of this store. Its main aim is to provide quality products at reasonable price mainly to the students' community. The store is running on its own-money. It has no borrowing from external sources. Every year two branches of store distribute 14 per cent dividend. The store is now planning its own building for its functions.

Salve (2001) highlighted the educational problem of Seasonal Migrant Worker's Children in the *'Cooperative Sugar Factories'* in the *Maharashtra*. There are 190 sugar factories in the *Maharashtra* state. Contract basis seasonal workers migrate from their villages to sugar factories for seasonal jobs in the sugar factories. They migrate along with children and families. Children in the age group of 7-14 years, discontinue their education due to seasonal migration of labour and other causes such as financial condition, failure in school, household chores. However, drop out rate at the primary and middle level schools is much higher among children of seasonal migrant workers. Therefore, it is suggested that *'Cooperative Sugar Factories'* should organize *'Migrant Labour Camp Seasonal Schools'* for children of Seasonal Migrant Workers. The working of seasonal schools should harmonize with the environment of seasonal labour camp, age group of children, crushing season, etc, of the sugar factories. Games and extra- curricular activities may be organized to infuse sustained interest among children in seasonal schools. Incentives like uniforms, textbooks, free slates, mid-day meals and milk etc, free of cost should be provided to them through Cooperative Sugar Factories.

Chander (2001) indicated the resource mobilization by *'Primary Agricultural Cooperative Societies'* in *Himachal Pradesh*. It has been found that the *'Primary Agricultural Cooperative Societies'* of *Hamirpur* district have distinguished in every sphere of working, may that be membership coverage, share capital, deposits and profit; whereas, in the *'Primary Agricultural Cooperative Societies'* of *Bilaspur* district such working is lacking. The Government stake in the form of share capital is very less in *Hamirpur* district and very high in *Bilaspur* district, but the working of *'Primary Agricultural Cooperative Societies'* is outstanding in *Hamirpur* district. Similarly, per member resource mobilization is very high in *Hamirpur* district as compared to the *'Primary Agricultural Cooperative Societies'* of *Bilaspur* district. It is concluded that due to the high stake of members in the *'Primary Agricultural Cooperative Societies'* of *Hamirpur* district, these institutions have excelled. The business composition proves that the *'Primary Agricultural Cooperative Societies'* of *Hamirpur* district have developed more scientific and business oriented approach than the *'Primary Agricultural Cooperative Societies'* of *Bilaspur* district resulting very high profit in *Hamirpur* district and very low in the *'Primary Agricultural Cooperative Societies'* of *Bilaspur* district.

Dharmarujan (2001) undertook a case-study of *'Kerala Dinesh Beedi Workers Central Cooperative Society'* that was organized and registered in February 1969. At the time of unit's inception, the total number of members stood at 3,000. But, gradually the Society increased the membership to 39,000 and by the year 1998, it reached to 42,185. The structure of the Society is two tiers in nature. At the top 'Central Society' is functioning and at the bottom level, there are 22 'Primary Societies', operating with 42,000 beedi workers, 50 per cent of them are females. The 'Central Society' purchases beedies made by the 'Primary Societies' every week on an agreed price, after adjusting the advances the 'Central Society' purchases the beedies and besides the advances, they are not allowed to make any outside borrowings. The future vision of this Cooperative enterprise will have to be based on the efficient management in strategic way of functioning with some parameters relating to management excellence, business diversification, improvement of operational efficiency, cost reduction and cost control, productivity development and strengthening of financial resource base.

Duggal (2001) made an attempt to study *'Cooperative Marketing'* in *Uttar Pradesh*. In *Uttar Pradesh*, Cooperatives play a vital role in distribution of agriculture inputs like fertilizer, pesticides, and seeds agriculture implements. During 1997-98, Cooperatives' network of *Uttar Pradesh* distributed 10.30 lakh tones of fertilizer, in nutrient from which is around 23 per cent of total fertilizer distribution by the Cooperatives in the country i.e. around 45 lakh tones in nutrient form. In *Uttar Pradesh*, the marketing of fruits and vegetables is done in haphazard manner and is mostly controlled by the private party. There are three Apex Federations in the Cooperative

Sector; these are: 'Apple and Fruit Federation', *Haldwan;* 'Potato Federation', *Ferukhabad;* and 'Uttar Pradesh Horticulture Marketing and Processing Federation', *Luckhnow.* Besides, there are more than 200 Societies registered in the state, but very few of them are doing marketing of fruits and vegetables successfully. As a result, during 1997-98, the Cooperatives in *Uttar Pradesh* marketed fruits and vegetables worth Rs. 5.8 lakh only. Therefore, farmers should be motivated to organize Cooperatives and confederation of Cooperatives is Apex Federation should ensure remunerative price to the horticulture produce of the farmers.

Kakade and Bagade (2001) examined the socio-economic condition of the milk production and the impact of Cooperative Sector on milk production in *Solapur* district of *Maharashtra.* Dairying has provided more employment to the youngsters. About 56 milk producers belong in the age group of 31-45 years among 100 milk producers. Illiteracy rate is very low among all milk producers. Thirty-one milk producers belong to marginal farmers' category. Insurance scheme awareness is very less among all types of milk producers. Semi-medium milk producers profit is very high among the other milk producers and large farmers' milk production going in loss.

Kumar (2001) analysed the working of '*Palani Cooperative Urban Bank Limited', Palani* in *Tamil Nadu.* The trend of giving loans and advances by the bank has showed increasing trend. But the credit deposit ratio reveals that it has reduced during the ten years from 1980-90; and in 1998-99, this ratio has been below 50 per cent. It indicates that the bank could not utilize the deposits to the maximum extend for giving loans and advances. So the bank keeps more surplus funds. The analysis of recovery performance of the bank has also shown that it is not so satisfactory. It is also one of the reasons for low profit of the bank. This is one of the major reasons for the reduction in profit of the bank. The bank should take initiative to assess the needs of the people in its area of operations and frame need based loan schemes instead of conventional methods of loans, to attract more and more people to take loans and advances from the bank.

Ramesh (2001) enumerated 13 milk unions of *'Karnataka Milk Federation' (KMF)*, throughout the state. The *KMF* also have 'Mother Dairy' at *Yelahanka, Bangalore*; 'Nandini Milk Products', *Bangalore;* 'Four Cattle Feed Plants' at *Rajankunte, Gubbi, Dharwad* and *Hassan; 'The* Bull-Breeding Farm' and 'Frozen Semen Bank' at *Hassaraghatta, Bangalore;* 'The Central Training Institute' at the KMF complex in *Bangalore* and 'Centralized Testing and Quality Control Laboratory' at the *KMF, Bangalore.* The *KMF* is playing pivotal role in both rural and urban milk marketing by propelling tough competition to the private milk traders. On the other hand, it is acting truly as an apex body for the promotion of milk unions. In spite of an impressive growth of the Dairy Cooperative Movement in the state, there is need to strengthen the Milk Cooperatives further so as to make milk production activity a successful venture by eliminating the malpractices committed by private milk traders. This will go a long way in helping the dairy farmers to realize better prices for their produce and in turn consumers will be benefited by way of getting quality milk at reasonable prices.

Singh (2001) ensured the trend in recovery of loan in *'Primary Agricultural Cooperative Societies'* and identify the various causes for overdue problems faced by *'Primary Agricultural Cooperative Societies'* of *Manipur.* It is found that recovery is very low in the hill areas, possibly by law and order problems and ethnic conflict. The other factors responsible for overdue are failure of bank machinery to recover the dues effectively, improper utilisation of loan by the borrowers, misappropriation of loan by the office bearers, bad law and order situation, too much political interference and poor working condition of *'Primary Agricultural Cooperative Societies'*. The bank should introduce quality lending system. Giving more funds to achieve viability norms should strengthen the working condition of the *'Primary Agricultural Cooperative Societies'* and other type of Societies. The legal authority should dispose off the pending cases quickly so that recovery can be affected by execution of decrees.

## COOPRATIVE LEADERSHIP

Cooperation as a form of organisation was statutorily introduced in India, as back as 1904, by the then British Government as an institutional means to help our agriculturists to obtain easy finance on reasonable terms. Though the policy direction came from foreign officials, but in common with the rest of the administrative structure the main responsibility for organisation of cooperatives fell on local officials who had to implement it through local non-official people, called honorary organisers (HO). The primary task of the HOs was to interpret the opportunities and responsibilities of association to the farmers who were exhorted to form cooperative societies. Thus, in the initial stage of our cooperative sector, the leadership was philanthropic. With the progressive horizontal and vertical expansions of the sector, both in the rural and the urban areas, it has emerged as a powerful force in our social, economic and political life and social, political and communal leaders and even sophisticated vested—interests entered the field and captured, to a greater extent, key positions in cooperative institutions operating at different levels—primary, district, state and national. The element of professional leadership hardly finds a place in the top level managerial structure of cooperatives.

As a democratic organization, a cooperative enterprise has been managed by the Board of Directors or the Managing Committee, elected by its members at its general meeting. In some experiences nominated, with full or restricted powers, by the financing institutions to which they are indebted, their federations and/or the concerned state government. But, in any case, the elected members enjoy the position of a majority segment in the Board or the Committee which takes all major policy decisions that are to be implemented by the other tiers of management. While in a large-sized cooperative enterprise, well-structured top, middle and lower levels of management and operational level employees—skilled, semi-skilled and unskilled—do exist, small-sized cooperative—mostly primaries—function with a managing committee and one or a few full-time and/or part-time operational level employees. A top level management comprises two tiers:

(a) Tier I having Board of Directors/Managing Committee/ Management Board/Governing Body, and

(b) Tier II with top executives like Managing/Functional/ Operational Directors/General Manager, Departmental Managers. In middle level management are grouped middle executives like assistant managers and other offices in higher executive cadres and in the lower level supervisory executives such junior executives as head clerks, superintendents, senior clerks and inspectors who may be in charge of office assistants, junior clerks and such other operational level employees are grouped.

## Participation of Women in Cooperatives

Majority of women workers, in India, are dependent on agriculture. A disturbing trend in women's participation in agriculture is the progressive shift from the cultivators to the agricultural labour's status. In the Indian context, women's use of economic opportunities has not increased relative to that of men in spite of legislation designed to improve women's status in the economic sphere. The women of the land owing classes had largely withdrawn from most kinds of out-door agricultural work before the advent of 'Green Revolution'. Punjab is the richest agricultural state in India and also has the lowest participation of women in its rural labour force. For the rural women in the third world, today, survival is a daily question and almost all activities are subsistence activities. Women's increased participation in agricultural production was related to decreasing farm size and rural poverty.

Cooperatives have the potential to offer opportunities to women to increase their earning, thus raising their status in the society and improve their economic condition. The fundamental concept of women's participation in Cooperative Movement is that they should join Cooperatives as members/ directors and extend their support to these Societies and also utilize services provided by them. Such participation should be effective and lead to improvement in the working of the

Societies as well as in their own living conditions. For this, it is necessary to develop the general awareness and cooperative conscious in women. This will shape their ideology and they would be motivated to join and adopt Cooperatives as a way of life. Today, women are members of *Agricultural Credit Cooperatives,* although their per centage is negligible. Although women contribute in agricultural operations and undertake various types of jobs during sowing and harvesting seasons, generally they are not the members of Cooperatives, and even if enrolled as members, they do not actively participate in the affairs of the society. In the previous study, conducted on Agricultural and Consumer Cooperatives in Srinagar district, it has been found that *Women Consumer Cooperatives* are more viable than men's *Consumer Cooperatives* (Jan, 1999).

Women's participation in Consumer Cooperatives is in two ways—there are Consumer Cooperatives with males and female membership and also Women's Consumer Cooperatives exclusively with female membership. The Consumer Cooperatives and Super Bazaars exclusively with female membership are also functioning in country. These Cooperatives besides the retailing business in day-to-day consumption article deal in essential commodities under public distribution system and own ration shops. Women members actively participate in these Societies and meet from time-to-time to review the sales and operation of these institutions.

Women are playing important role in *Urban Credit Cooperative Banks* and *Salary Earner's Thrift and Credit Societies.* In most of the Urban Cooperative Banks/Societies quite a considerable percentage of total membership comprises of women. The women's Urban Cooperative Banks are doing commendable job. These banks are not only dealing with credit business but are also assisting unemployed women and youth in setting up their business on individual or Cooperative basis. There is Cooperative conscious among the members of these banks who are generally well educated and well placed in the society and are keen on the development of women masses.

Dairy is another field in which rural women take keen interest. Women do almost all the basic jobs relating to dairy viz. milching, taking care of animals etc. There is quite a considerable percentage of female membership in *Dairy Cooperatives* especially in Gujarat, Karnataka and Andhra Pradesh (Sharma, 1987). Six thousand of the 70,000 *Dairy Cooperative Societies* in India are Women Societies. Though the percentage of women members on Cooperative Management Committees has increased, it still represents a very small start compared to what women can achieve.

As more women organize themselves into *'Thrift and Credit Cooperatives'*, the family economic condition is expected to improve, followed by significant changes in the health, literacy standards and education of women and girls, leading eventually to arise in the status of the women in the family to an equal partner (Mudda, 1998).

Heggade (1983) observed that in certain states exclusive Societies have been organized for women, for encouraging thrift, providing subsidiary occupations like knitting, cloth printing, dye making, leather goods manufacturing, cleaning and preparing condiments etc. Some Women's Cooperatives have also running their nursery schools, spinning and tailoring classes, cookery and painting classes. The members of such Societies are generally the women of lower middle class families living in towns. Such Societies have made good progress in *Punjab.* In *Tamil Nadu,* Industrial Cooperatives and Milk Societies organized by women engaged in tailoring and in making leave plates, have been organized in *Andhra Pradesh.* Women's Cooperatives have been organized in *West Bengal* for rehabilitation of displaced persons. In *Uttar Pradesh,* such Societies have been engaged in activities relating to the promotion of thrift, health and general welfare. The Voluntary Service Organizations (VSOs) shall play a very vital role in motivating and educating women regarding Cooperation. They also assist the concerned type of Cooperatives to enroll and educate women in Cooperative business and management.

Shah (1985) conducted field studies in *Kaira* and *Haryana* to evaluate women's participation in *'Dairy Cooperative'.*

About 48 per cent women have been involved in *'Dairy Cooperatives'* in case of *Kaira* and 40 per cent in case of *Haryana*. Women participate generally remains lower in the case of higher income level of the households. In case of the landless labour households, about 40 per cent of total time spent on dairy enterprise is contributed by family labour. In small farmers' households, women contribute one-third of total requirement of labour in dairy enterprise. Large farmers, however, put great reliance on hired labour, as their female members do not participate much in the dairy activity. All this goes to show that dairy activity has a large potential for gainful employment of under-employed and unemployed female labour especially belonging to weaker sections in rural areas.

Mathew and Nair (1986) surveyed the *'Women Cooperatives'* in *Kerala* to analyse the growth pattern of Women's Cooperatives and to examine how the interests of the dominant class have influenced them. This has been done in terms of an analysis of aspects such as, structure and organization, financial performance, production and marketing linkages, distribution of income among members and their participation. There have been 116 registered Women Industrial Cooperative, out of which only 86 have been functioning. There have been 28 Women Cooperatives sponsored by the Khadi and Village Industrial Board (KVIB). The survey has shown that 41.17 per cent of the Cooperatives have been running at a loss and the remaining ones at profit. While the units engaged in match-making incurred heavy losses; but fifty per cent of the candle-making units have been running on profit .The major problems faced by both types of Cooperatives remain cut-throat competition in the market, undue escalation in costs and limited availability of raw materials. The survey reveals that 'Women Cooperatives' have two important roles to perform i.e. creation of a spirit of cooperation among working women and provision of employment. The poor economic performance of majority of the Cooperatives has been reflection of the poor way in which they perform the social role. Unless politicization and concretization of the Cooperators take place at the base levels, these organizations will only remain as economic entities, ultimately serving the interests of the dominant classes.

Mathias (1987) reported about the affairs of the *'Nippani Wadgaon Credit Society', Maharashtra,* which has a share capital of Rs. 2.6 lakh and which has so far disbursed loans to its members for cattle breeding, laying of water pipelines, starting horticultural and dairy enterprise, besides running a fair price shop of its own. There are, of course, many examples of many Cooperatives formed and run exclusively by women for the making and marketing of products. But, this is perhaps the first time in *Maharashtra* that the predominantly male members of Credit Cooperatives have chosen to entrust their financial affairs in the hands of an *'All-Women Committee'*. The society has only 39 women members against 340 men. But frustrated with the mismanagement of the Society by its male committees in the past, the villagers this time preferred to vote in an all-women panel, in preference to the rival all-men candidates.

Rao (1987) overviewed *'All Women Cooperatives'* in *Andhra Pradesh* to encourage women's participation in dairying. A pilot project with financial assistance from the 'Ford Foundation' has been launched in *Nalgonda, Krishna* and *Chittor* districts. Under this scheme, 60 *'All Women Milk Producers Cooperative Societies'* have been organised and a total of 2,000 new members enrolled. In *Cuddupha* district, 8 Societies have been formed with 600 women as members, where the *'Milk Products Factory'* at *Proddutur* has been handed over to the *'Cuddapah* District Cooperative Milk Producers' Union Limited', under Operation Flood-II. The success of these *'All women Societies'* have lead to the formation of more such Cooperatives. In *Krishan* district, with a view to develop Women Cooperatives, the Societies have been formed with 1,000 women producers as members.

Verulkar (1989) approached *'Mahila Sahakari Banks'* in the country. It is realized that with the passage of time, the role of women in social and economic life has changed completely. The *'Mahila Sahakari Banks'* have to keep pace with this change and in fact, for future times, they have to be the pace setters in bringing women in the main stream of economic development of the nation. For fulfilling this objective, the managements of these have to be more professional and forward looking particularly while identifying prospective borrowers and assessing loan applications managements of these banks have to adopt altogether new approach. Unless there is a change at the top i.e. at the management level, the *'Mahila Cooperative Banks'* cannot assume a significant role in economic and social uplift of women.

Subudhi and Padhi (1991) recapitulated Indian Women in Cooperative Management. It is found that 48.4 per cent women members belong to *Industrial Cooperatives*, 37.6 per cent to *Textile Cooperatives*, 6.1 per cent to *Consumer Cooperatives* and 7.9 per cent to other Cooperatives. In urban areas, with highly qualified women, Cooperatives are expanding both by length and breadth. There are considerable number of women in the management of *Credit Cooperatives* and *Cooperative Banks*. Some *Credit Cooperatives* are set exclusively with female membership.

Bhatt (1992) presented the efforts made by *Self Employed Women's Association* (SEWA) to federate Women's Cooperatives. *SEWA* has organised hundred Women Cooperatives so far. The federation provides technical and managerial assistance in production, storage, acquisition of raw materials, product design, marketing of goods and services etc. *SEWA* Cooperatives in 1995 created 2,856 new employments worth Rs. 11,21,400 crore, put addition cash income of Rs.2,09,82,290 in the hands of 17,354 women; built assets worth Rs.1,52,29,412 for 13,725 women, both collectively and individually; 49,903 women benefited from *SEWA's* support services viz. health care, child care, training, housing, legal aid as per their need. All the members are covered under the group insurance. Each year, these statistics keep increasing, with the expansion of *SEWA*, its members and its Cooperatives. The Dairy Cooperative of the women in village namely *Rual*, have a severe fight to the land grabbers (men), who wanted to usurp the Cooperative's fodder farm. *'Vanraji: The Women's Tree Growers Cooperative'* fought the *Bharwads* (shepherds) in court, retained the waste land acquired from the government for collective plantations. *'Haryali: The Vegetable Vendor Cooperative'* managed their Cooperative so well that from their surplus, they gifted a building to the *SEWA* Union. The *'SEWA Cooperative Bank'* brings the illiterate, poor women workers and producers in the mainstream, formal banking systems, which are able to deal with the Bank of India at par with other Cooperative Nationalized Banks.

Rose (1992) found that women who have traditionally made wool blankets on pit looms, have formed Cooperatives under *SEWA* and members are constantly acquiring new skills, undergoing training at the 'National Institute of Design' in weaving shawls and dress materials and in the process moving from one room huts to two roomed housing with large pedal loom. Women block printers, who earlier worked on very low price rates stamping dye on to cloth, have sought training in how to make dyes, design blocks, prepare cloth and make more sophisticated designs and garments.

Dabir and Bora (1996) collected information on the entire Women's Cooperatives in *Mumbai* and its Suburbs. The findings of the study reveals that Woman's Cooperatives in *Mumbai* are catering to the women from low socio-economic backgrounds who are engaged in a limited number of activities. The total number of members in the Credit Cooperative Societies is found to be much higher (325-1,500) as compared to those in the Industrial Cooperative Societies (less than 200 in most of the cases). The contribution of members in the form of share capital is the main fund for all the Cooperatives. The value of share varied from Rs.10-50. Minimum contribution per member is Rs.100 in most of the cases. Only 27 per cent of the Industrial Cooperatives and 15 per cent of the Credit Societies have received some grant, loan or subsidy from the Government. More than 75 per cent of the Women's Cooperatives are engaged in production activities. Only 18 per cent of the Cooperatives are running a credit programme and the remaining 7 per cent are having production as well as credit activities.

Beena and Sharma (1997) made a case-study of Cooperative Movement among neo-literate women of *Durg* district. The favourable impact of Cooperative Movement is found on women and their family. All neo-literate women are identified as progressive women within tribal community. Home management related decisions are wholly in the hands of women and 60 per cent of the respondents get their daughters married after 18 years of age. Decisions related to Cooperative Society are taken through participative consensus. Development of strong leadership qualities could be seen among members. About 40 per cent women are in constant touch with block headquarter and dare to speak for justice.

Gopu (1997) stated the role of Cooperative Society in South *Arkat* district among the members of the Women Cooperatives. Out of the 200 members surveyed, as many as 83 members have been between 26 and 35 years. The next largest group of members amounting to 76 has been between 18 and 25 years. This reveals that majority of them have been young women. None of the surveyed members have any permanent position or occupation. So, it becomes necessary to find out the occupation of the member's husband or guardian. Further, 96 persons have agricultural as their occupation and 41 persons are daily wage earners. This shows that majority of the members are from farm families. It is evident that the income derived from the agricultural activities is not enough to support the family and so the women are also forced to seek opportunities for earning additional income. The Society should explore the possibility of obtaining work from private educational institutions and other establishments also so that the role-played by this Women Cooperative will be more effective.

Rao and Hasalkar (1997) identified entrepreneurship qualities among members of Women Cooperatives in *Dharwad* region. Cooperation has been the quality present in 40 per cent of the members. The main reason of this has been that the like-minded and similar professional women form these Women Cooperatives and the members are relatives of each other. These Cooperatives do not have any leader, but every one have equal scope for participation and decision-making. Sporadic efforts are being made through both Government and Voluntary Organisations to encourage women entrepreneurship through Cooperatives. Cooperatives can play an important role in exploring the entrepreneurial qualities of rural women and thereby increase the income of these women.

Sexena and Tripathi (1998) evaluated entrepreneurship among milk producers in *'Women Dairy Cooperative Societies'* of *Bareilly* district in *Uttar Pradesh.* Family education status, income generation, milk production, milk marketing, income from dairy enterprise and extend of facilities available are found to have significant and positive effort on achievement motivation of farmwomen. Income from dairy enterprise and high extent of facilities available in the village help in improving entrepreneurial attributes due to the existence of *'Women Dairy Cooperatives'.*

SEWA Academy (2000) reported that in *Madhya Pradesh* in 1985, forty per cent of the women workers involved in *beedi-rolling* had identity cards. These identity cards were in the name of the male head of the family and not that of the women, who had been actually rolling the *beedies* and out of the total sample households, more than fifty per cent depended exclusively on *beedi-rolling* and average daily earnings of *beedi- rolling* families was Rs.6 per day. In 1987; 1,300 women *beedi-workers* have got identity cards from the labour commissioner, through *Self Employed Women's Association (SEWA).* In 1989, *'Credit Cooperative Society of Beedi-Workers'* has been registered by *Self Employed Women's Association.* In 1990, eight training camps have arranged for 335 *beedi-workers* and *'Housing Cooperative'* consisting 302 *beedi-workers* have been registered. In 1996, the *beedi* rates per 1,000 *beedies* have increased in *Chhatarpur* town, due to *SEWA's* negotiations. About 3,361 *beedi-workers* have got identity cards in 1997. In 1998, a meeting of 1,000 *beedi-workers* with the labour commissioner as the chief guest has been held, where he has been presented with a memorandum depicting the problems of the *beedi-workers.* In 1999, *SEWA* has launched a state- wide campaign demanding a minimum wages of Rs.51 per 1,000 *beedies.*

Women's Cooperative Mobilization Project (2000) organised Cooperatives comprising women belonging to scheduled castes and economically weaker sections of *Rewari* sub-division of *Mohendragarh* district in *Haryana* and *Agra* city of *Uttar Pradesh.* These Cooperatives are of durry weaving, leather/shoe embroidery, leather goods manufacturing, spice grinding, tailoring, cotton ply making and dairying. These Cooperatives have been proven successful in bringing about a change in the socio-economic status of project target. The women organized into Cooperatives Societies are now able to earn an income of Rs. 8-10 on an average per day per head, working for about 4-5 hours per day. This surely has elevated their status and has developed self-confidence among them. Their personal bank accounts help them at the time of urgent need.

Junare (2001) studied the status of *Women Cooperatives* in *Gujarat* State. The State has 460 *Women Cooperative Societies* working for the economic and social empowerment of women, which constitute less than one per cent of the total Cooperative Societies in the State. Out of the total Women Cooperative Societies, about 67 per cent (314 Cooperative Societies) are the *Milk Cooperative Societies,* 15 per cent (73 Cooperative Societies) are *Consumer's Cooperative Societies* and 10 per cent (46 in numbers) are *Employees Cooperative Credit Societies.* Apart from these, there are 9 *Women Urban Cooperative Banks* working in the State, out of which, 3 *Women Urban Cooperative Banks* are located in *Ahmedabad* city only. Out of total Women Milk Cooperative Societies, 94 per cent are situated in *Vassed* district and six per cent Societies are located in *Baroda* and *Surat* districts. But, the success in such Women Cooperatives is not up to the expectation in number, progress, management etc. as compared to male dominated Cooperative Societies. The causes of less development of Women Cooperatives in *Gujarat* are illiteracy, lack of confidence, lack of training and guidance, lack of intensive and motivation, lack of leadership, social pressure etc.

Kohli (2001) assessed the role of *Women's Urban Banks* in the economic development of backward classes (*Dalits*) in the city of *Kolhapur.* All the members asserted that they do not face discrimination in treatment from the bank on credit grounds. Hundred per cent respondents have desired to continue their relationship with the bank in future too. Fifty per cent respondents are found to have savings with the bank in the form of pigmy deposits or fixed deposits. Five per cent members are saving as members of Self-Help Groups. The bank has cultivated saving habit among the Members. Of course, the total amount of savings of each respondent with the bank is less than Rs.10,000. Thirty- five per cent of the respondents are in over dues so far and the reasons are domestic problems, lack of sufficient income and illness. But no bitter experience is faced in recovering loan from them. The overall study shows that the bank has helped the women, cultivating savings habit and women are getting equal treatment in their day-to-day dealing with the bank. Therefore, it is advocated that development of separate Cooperatives for *Dalit* women and if that is not possible, they should be encouraged to join Cooperatives with mixed membership.

The overall review of the various studies concludes that women play an active role in promoting the economic status of the country. Social aspect of women's development is much more influenced by their economic development and visa-versa. But the economic activities of women do not necessarily lead to a change in their work patterns at home. Cooperatives have proven an important sector of economy in India. Cooperative movement has provided opportunities to women to organize their economic activities with small capital. There is a tendency of more and more women to come out of their homes to participate in Cooperative Movement. Women are capable and confident of entering into Cooperative Movement. This is possible because of two reasons, viz. capital need is small and know-how of the business is available without difficulty. Though women are participating in Cooperative activities, but their participation is very less. Utilization of women labour for productive purposes under Cooperative Movement can increase the gross national income and this can help to achieve our objective of socio-economic development. Cooperatives provide many varied opportunities for women participation. No doubt, their standard of living is improved by the income they earn from Cooperatives and their quality of life is enhanced due to social awareness, entrepreneurship, development of skills, increased participation in the affairs of Cooperatives leading to better understanding and utility. Though most of the Women Cooperatives in India have proven very successful, but they face cut-throat competition in the market. Women Cooperatives also suffer undue escalation of costs and limited availability of raw materials.

Thus, Cooperatives promote mutual cooperation among people and serve as a means of community development. Reviewing the literature available regarding Agricultural and Consumer Cooperatives, it is found that although several studies have been conducted on such Cooperatives but study made from the stand point of community development and women empowerment by Cooperatives are limited. Even if they are, their scope is limited and no study has been made to assess the role of women in Cooperatives at the corporate and membership level. Thus, the present study was undertaken to evaluate the role of women in Agricultural and Consumer Cooperatives.

The sample group consisted of 50 per cent (n=266) of the total of Agricultural and Consumer Cooperatives in Kashmir, which has been selected through *Disproportionate Stratified Random Sampling Technique,* comprising 1,51,659 members, out of 3,03,317 members. The sample was selected at the district level by using the *Random Number Table,* given by ***Miller***; in 1996 (*Annexure 1.1 and 1.2*). This table allowed the collection of data from each and every block in districts of Kashmir. However, the Women Cooperatives in the valley were few in number. As such, all Women Cooperatives in Kashmir valley were purposively included in the sample (the total number of such Cooperatives being only 15). Thus, this number of sample was excluded from the sample selected through the *Random Number Table.* Checklist and anecdotal Record list was prepared to collect information from the cooperatives in Kashmir (*Annexure 2*).

The study also covered cooperatives' officials and officers selected through multi stage sampling. Out of 100 Officers/

Officials working in Cooperative Sector, 50 respondents were selected from rural areas and 50 respondents from urban areas. These urban as well as rural Officers/Officials were covered from all districts of the Kashmir valley. Furthermore, 25 respondents were male and 25 respondents were female in both (i.e. rural and urban) areas. Data selected by this method, ensured the greater accuracy and eliminate the possibility of personal bias. It covered the advantages of both random and stratified sampling. A Structured questionnaire was administered on them in order to get clear cut information (*Annexure 3*). Scale regarding 'Attitudes of Cooperative Personnel towards Cooperative Movement' (ACPCM) was prepared and administered on Cooperative Officials/Officers *(Annexure 4).* The scale included 22 general items regarding Cooperative Movement in Kashmir. All these items were responded either in positive or negative. The positive responses were scored as one; whereas, negative responses were scored as zero. The scores of positive responses were summed up and the level of attitude of the Cooperative Personnel was ascertained. This scale was administered to find out if Cooperative Personnel themselves were devoted towards the Cooperative Movement, so that the efforts for the establishment of Women Cooperatives could prove fruitful. The following criteria were taken into consideration for the selection of sample:

i. The study was confined to Agricultural and Consumer Cooperatives only.
ii. Samples from rural as well as urban areas were included in the research, considering men and women respondents and Cooperatives separately.
iii. The sample was taken from middle socio-economic group.
iv. The women respondents' age, particularly, in case of Group-III, must be above 18 years, i.e. they must be competent to contract under section II of the Jammu and Kashmir Contract Act Samvat, 1977.

The study was confined to Agricultural and Consumer Cooperatives because:

i. It has a major contribution in Cooperative Movement in the State.
ii. It is a voluntary association of people who can organise a Cooperative with their limited resources.
iii. It can be easily established.
iv. Cooperative is the only institution of its kind in the State that provides higher self-employment opportunities in groups to literate, semi-literate, as well as illiterate adults.
v. Women in Kashmir have a good say in Agricultural and Consumer activities.

3

# COOPERATIVES FOR POOR WOMEN

Cooperatives have been playing an important role in improving the economic condition of Indian women by providing them with full or part-time employment. With the diversification of the cooperative movement and the growing needs of daily life, women gradually started taking interest in cooperatives. Women in India have organised many industrial cooperatives to create part-time employment opportunities for themselves, to supplement their family incomes. These societies are generally of two types, viz., workshop-type societies, which have their own workshops or factory sheds, where women assemble to carry on production and for which they earn monthly or weekly wages depending on the amount of work produced. In some cases marketing of their products is also undertaken by the cooperatives. The second type of Women Industrial Cooperatives is Service-cum-Sales Societies, through which raw materials are supplied by the cooperatives to the members, the processing and production is done by the members in their houses, with the help of members of the family. The cooperative collects the finished products sells them in the market and members are paid wages.

In India, there were 4,653 Women Cooperatives, with 5.3 million members and Rs. 108.2 million share capital during 1991-92. During 1994-95, there were 7,195 Women Cooperative

Societies all over India, with the membership of 5,91,704; out of which 3.6 per cent members were scheduled caste .The share capital in such Societies was Rs. 150.5 million, out of which Government had contributed 24 per cent. The advances borrowed to women through National Cooperative Agriculture and Rural Development Bank's Federation Ltd., was Rs. 68.98 crore in 1995-96 and Rs. 75.97 crore in 1996-97. The number of women cooperatives in India rose from 11,374 in 2000-2001 to 11,662 in 2001-2002. And the membership of women rose from 999,673 to 1,024,709 during the same period. The share capital of Rs. 295.256 million contributed 13.07 per cent government share in 2001-2002.

## Capital Investment in Women Cooperatives

In Srinagar district, there were 144 Cooperative Societies with 91,250 members in 1993-94. This number excludes 401 Handicrafts and Handloom Cooperatives, which comprised 15,226 members during the same year. The Jammu and Kashmir Cooperative Union conducted 10 women development courses during 1997-98, in which 100 women participated, in order to acquaint them with the techniques and education of cooperative enterprise. The Agriculture Credit disbursed by the Cooperatives increased from Rs. 0.59 lakh (in 1950) to Rs. 24.05 crore as on ending December 1997. About 1,200 Cooperative Retail Outlets for distribution of fertilizers were handled around 52,387 quintal fertilizer during 1997-98. During 1998, the total number of all types of Cooperative Societies was 1,101 comprising 637 Societies in Jammu division and 464 Societies in Kashmir division, with share capital of Rs. 854.15 lakh comprising of Rs. 502.51 lakh in Jammu division and Rs. 351.64 lakh in Kashmir division; with working capital of Rs. 4,92,058 lakh both for Jammu and Kashmir division. The loans advanced for Kharief and Rabi crops by Cooperative Banks during 1999-2000 were Rs. 30.96 lakh in Jammu and Kashmir.

The resolution for the Self-Reliant Act, 1999 was passed in the Jammu and Kashmir State Cooperative Conference on 11th October 1999. Up to 2001-02, there have been 1,393 Cooperative

Societies in the state with a total membership of 6.02 lakh. The total share capital of these Societies has been Rs. 35 crore, of which Government Share is Rs. 27 crore. In order to boost the farming/consumer activities in Cooperative Sector and to rejuvenate the cooperative structure at different levels, the Department of Cooperatives, Jammu and Kashmir Government, has initiated the series of measures to promote institutionalization of essential/perishable commodities like vegetables, milk, fruit, mutton, eggs and chicken and other commodities of daily use.

Capital Investment includes the extent of Government share capital, financial assistance like managerial assistance, special assistance, interest free loan and other assistances, exemption from taxes etc. and bank borrowings in Women Cooperatives in relation to Men Cooperatives. The influence of all these investment on the physical condition of Cooperatives has also been found out.

**Levels of Privileges to Cooperatives (Table 3.1)**

Overall, 85.34 per cent Cooperatives have received Government share capital. About 79.04 per cent Cooperatives have also been provided financial assistances in one form or another. Among these, 89.88 per cent have received managerial assistance, followed by 49.38 per cent Cooperatives which have got special assistance, 30.63 per cent Cooperatives have received interest free loans and 10.63 per cent Cooperatives have been provided other types of financial assistances. Moreover, 95.49 per cent Cooperatives have received other borrowings from Cooperative banks.

Highly significant differences are found ($p<0.01$) between Cooperatives which are provided Government share capital, managerial assistance, interest free loan, bank borrowings, exemption from taxes, fee and duties and other types of financial assistances. But special assistances provided to Cooperatives have been found insignificant ($p>0.05$) in difference.

**Privileges to Cooperatives (Table 3.2)**

Government share capital has been provided to 66.66 per cent Women Cooperatives, but 86.45 per cent Men Cooperatives

**Table 3.1**
**Leves of Privileges to Cooperatives**

(n = 266)

| Variables | Levels (In Nos.) | | p-Value |
|---|---|---|---|
| | Not-Provided | Provided | |
| Government Share Capital [a] | 227(85.34) | 39(14.66) | <0.01 |
| Financial Assistance [b] | 159(79.04) | 68(29.96) | <0.01 |
| Managerial Assistance [b i] | 139(89.88) | 21(13.13) | <0.01 |
| Special Assistance [b ii] | 79(49.38) | 81(50.63) | >0.05 |
| Interest free loan [b iii] | 17(10.63) | 143(89.38) | <0.01 |
| Other Assistances [b iv] | 49(30.63) | 111(69.38) | <0.01 |
| Exemption from Taxes, etc. [c] | 254(95.49) | 12(4.51) | <0.01 |
| Bank Credit [d] | 116(43.61) | 150(56.39) | <0.01 |

Row per centage in parentheses

have also received the same. Thus, 33.33 per cent Women Cooperatives have been deprived from Government share; while only 13.54 per cent Men Cooperatives have been deprived from such share.

Out of the Cooperatives holding Government membership, 80 per cent Women Cooperatives have received financial assistance; whereas, only 70 per cent Men Cooperatives have been provided financial assistance by Government. Among financial assistances, maximum number of Women Cooperatives, holding Government membership, have been provided managerial subsidy; but 86.18 per cent Men Cooperatives with Government membership have also been provided the same assistance.

Special assistance has been given to 37.50 per cent Women Cooperatives and 62.50 per cent Women Cooperatives have been deprived from such assistance; whereas, 50 per cent Men Cooperatives have got special assistance, leading Women Cooperatives by 13 per cent. No Women Cooperative has been provided interest free loan; while 11.18 per cent Men Cooperatives have got the same kind of loan from Cooperative Banks. Most of the Women Cooperatives i.e. 87.18 per cent have received other types of financial assistances from Government like specialised assistance for Women Cooperatives etc; as compared to only 27.63 per cent Men Cooperatives who have got other assistances like loan for Godown construction, interest subsidy etc.

**Table 3.2**
**Privileges to Cooperatives**

*(n = 266)*

| *Variables* | *Types of Cooperatives* | | |
|---|---|---|---|
| | *Women Cooperatives* | *Men Cooperatives* | *p-Value* |
| ***Government Share Capital*** | | | |
| Provided | 10 (66.66) | 217 (86.45) | <0.05 |
| Not-Provided | 5 (33.33) | 34 (13.54) | |
| Total | 15 (100.00) | 251 (100.00) | |
| ***Financial Assistance*** | | | |
| Provided | 8 (80.00) | 152 (70.04) | |
| Not-Provided | 2 (20.00) | 65 (29.95) | >0.05 |
| Total | 10 (100.00) | 217 (100.00) | |
| ***Managerial Assistance*** | | | |
| Provided | 8 (100.00) | 131 (86.18) | |
| Not-Provided | - | 21 (13.81) | >0.05 |
| Total | 8 (100.00) | 152 (100.00) | |
| ***Special Assistance*** | | | |
| Provided | 3 (37.50) | 76 (50.00) | |
| Not-Provided | 5 (62.50) | 76 (50.00) | >0.05 |
| Total | 8 (100.00) | 152 (100.00) | |
| ***Interest Free Loan*** | | | |
| Provided | - | 17 (11.18) | |
| Not-Provided | 8 (100.00) | 135 (88.81) | >0.05 |
| Total | 8 (100.00) | 152 (100.00) | |
| ***Other Assistance*** | | | |
| Provided | 7 (87.50) | 42 (27.63) | |
| Not-Provided | 1 (12.50) | 110 (72.36) | <0.01 |
| Total | 8 (100.00) | 152 (100.00) | |
| ***Exemption from Taxes/Fee/Duties*** | | | |
| Provided | 15 (100.00) | 239 (95.21) | |
| Not-Provided | - | 12 (4.78) | >0.05 |
| Total | 15 (100.00) | 251 (100.00) | |
| ***Bank Credit*** | | | |
| Provided | - | 116 (46.21) | |
| Not-Provided | 15 (100.00) | 135 (53.78) | <0.01 |
| Total | 15(100.00) | 251(100.00) | |

Column percentage in parentheses.

All Women Cooperatives are exempted from taxes, fees and other duties pertaining to their functioning under 'Jammu and Kashmir Cooperative Societies Act, 1960' and 'Jammu and Kashmir Cooperative Societies Act, 1989'. Same case applies with 95.21 per cent Men Cooperative; while 4.78 per cent Men Cooperatives have been registered under 'Jammu and Kashmir Self Reliant Cooperative Act, 1999', which has no provision for exemption of taxes, fee or duties. None of the Women Cooperative has any bank borrowing, but 46.21 per cent Men Cooperatives have more or less bank borrowing. About 53.78 per cent Men Cooperatives have no cash credit or bank borrowing. The borrowings borne by such Cooperatives are usually from the Cooperative Banks.

However, no significant differences have been observed among Women Cooperatives and Men Cooperatives with financial assistance provided by Government, managerial assistance, special assistance, interest free loan and exemption from taxes, fee or duties ($p>0.05$). Significant difference ($p<0.05$) is seen between Government share capital and Men and Women Cooperatives. Moreover, highly significant differences ($p<0.01$) are seen between other types of financial assistance and bank borrowings in Women Cooperatives and Men Cooperatives.

**Levels of Capital Investment in Cooperatives (Table 3.3)**

Most of the Cooperatives (46.62 per cent) have contributed least individual share capital i.e. below Rs. 10,000; whereas, 20.30 per cent Cooperatives have contributed above Rs. 40,000 as their individual share, followed by 18.42 per cent Cooperatives contributing Rs.10,000-20,000; 7.89 per cent between Rs. 20,000-30,000 and only 6.77 per cent contributing Rs. 30,000-40,000 as their individual share capital. Government has contributed its share above Rs. 40,000 in case of 70.04 per cent Cooperatives. Thus Government has contributed lion's share in the Cooperatives of the State. About 9.69 per cent Cooperatives have received Government share between Rs. 30,000-40,000. About 7.49 per cent have got Rs. 20,000-30,000 Government share and the same percentage (7.49 per cent) have also got up to Rs. 10, 000 as share from Government. Only 5.29 per cent Cooperatives receive Rs. 10,000-20,000 as Government share.

Managerial subsidy has been provided up to Rs. 10,000 to 48.20 per cent Cooperatives, followed by 20.14 per cent which are provided Rs. 10,000-20,000; 13.67 per cent receiving Rs. 20,000-30,000; 10.07 per cent receiving above Rs. 40,000 and 7.91 per cent receiving between Rs.30,000-40,000. Equal percentage of Cooperatives (40.51 per cents) have been provided special assistance up to Rs.10,000 and between Rs. 10,000-20,000. About Rs. 30,000-40,000 as special assistance, is provided to least percentage of Cooperatives i.e. 30.80 per cent; while 8.86 per cent Cooperatives have been provided above Rs. 40,000 as special assistance, followed by 6.33 per cent Cooperatives (with Rs. 20,000-30,000 for same type of assistance).

**Table 3.3**
**Levels of Capital Investment in Cooperatives**

*(n = 266)*

| *Levels (in Rs.)* | *Individual Share Capital* | *Government Share Capital* | *Managerial Assistance* | *Special Assistance* | *Interst Free Loan* | *Other Assistance* | *Bank Credit* |
|---|---|---|---|---|---|---|---|
| Up to 10000 | 124 (46.62) | 17 (7.49) | 67 (48.20) | 32 (40.51) | 2 (12.50) | 8 (16.33) | 30 (25.86) |
| 10000-20000 | 49 (18.42) | 12 (5.29) | 28 (20.14) | 32 (40.51) | 3 (18.75) | 17 (34.69) | 34 (29.31) |
| 20000-30000 | 21 (7.89) | 17 (7.49) | 19 (13.67) | 5 (6.33) | 4 (25.00) | 6 (12.24) | 13 (11.21) |
| 30000-40000 | 18 (6.77) | 22 (9.69) | 11 (7.91) | 3 (3.80) | 1 (6.23) | 4 (8.16) | 1 (0.86) |
| Above 40000 | 54 (20.30) | 159 (70.04) | 14 (10.07) | 7 (8.86) | 7 (41.18) | 14 (28.57) | 38 (32.76) |
| Total | 266 (100.00) | 227 (100.00) | 139 (100.00) | 79 (100.00) | 17 (100.00) | 49 (100.00) | 116 (100.00) |
| p-Value | <0.01 | <0.01 | <0.01 | <0.01 | >0.05 | <0.01 | <0.01 |

Column percentage in parentheses.

Around 41.18 per cent Cooperatives have been given interest free loan by above Rs. 40,000; followed by 25 per cent Cooperatives receiving Rs. 20,000-30,000. The least percentage of Cooperatives provided interest free loan are by 6.25 per cent. They have been provided this loan between Rs. 30,000-40,000. Moreover, 12.50 per cent Cooperatives have received the same loan up to Rupees 10,000 and 18.75 per cent have got it up to Rs. 10,000-20,000.

Other types of assistances are provided to 34.69 per cent Cooperatives between Rupees 10,000-20,000; followed by 28.57 per cent Cooperatives as above Rs. 40,000; 16.33 per cent up to Rs. 10,000; 12.24 per cent between Rs. 20,000-30,000 and 8.16 per cent between Rs. 30,000-40,000. Majority of Cooperatives (32.76 per cent) have bank borrowing more than Rs. 40,000. But negligible percentage of Cooperatives (0.86 per cent) has borrowed between Rs. 30,000-40,000; whereas, 29.31 per cent Cooperatives borrow Rs. 10,000-20,000; followed by 25.86 per cent Cooperatives having borrowing up to Rs. 10,000 and 11.21 per cent Cooperatives Rs. 20,000-30,000.

The differences between the amounts of individual share capital, Government share capital, managerial assistance, special assistance, bank borrowings and other types of assistances are highly significant where p-value is less than 0.01; but the difference within interest free loan is found insignificant, as p-value is more than 0.05.

### Capital Investment in Cooperatives (Table 3.4)

The maximum number of women members in 86.66 per cent Women Cooperatives have contributed their share capital up to not more than Rs. 10,000. Only 6.66 per cent women Cooperatives have contributed their individual share capital in the cohort of Rs.10,000-20,000. The same percentage of Women Cooperatives has also contributed their share above Rs.40, 000; whereas, in case of 44.22 per cent Men Cooperatives, only up to Rs.10,000 has been contributed as individual share capital, followed by 21.11 per cent Men Cooperatives, which have contributed above Rs.40,000 as individual share capital; 19.12 per cent Men Cooperatives contributing Rs. 10,000-20,000; 8.36 per cent contributing Rs. 20,000-30,000 and 7.17 per cent Men Cooperatives contributing Rs. 30,000-40,000 as their individual share capital.

**Table 3.4**
**Capital Investment in Cooperatives**

(n = 266)

| Variables | Types of Cooperatives | | |
|---|---|---|---|
| | Women Cooperatives | Men Cooperatives | p-Value |
| ***Individual Share Capital*** | | | |
| Up to 10,000 | 13 (86.66) | 111 (44.22) | |
| 10,000-20,000 | 1 (6.66) | 48 (19.12) | |
| 20,000-30,000 | - | 21 (8.36) | <0.05 |
| 30,000-40,000 | - | 18 (7.17) | |
| Above 40,000 | 1 (6.66) | 53 (21.11) | |
| Total | 15(100.00) | 251 (100.00) | |
| ***Government Share Capital*** | | | |
| Up to 10,000 | 1 (10.00) | 16 (7.37) | |
| 10,000-20,000 | - | 12 (5.52) | |
| 20,000-30,000 | 2(20.00) | 15 (6.91) | >0.05 |
| 30,000-40,000 | - | 22 (10.13) | |
| Above 40,000 | 7(70.00) | 152 (70.04) | |
| Total | 10(100.00) | 217 (100.00) | |
| ***Managerial Assistance*** | | | |
| Up to 10,000 | 5 (62.50) | 62 (47.32) | |
| 10,000-20,000 | - | 28 (21.37) | |
| 20,000-30,000 | 2 (25.00) | 17 (12.97) | >0.05 |
| 30,000-40,000 | - | 11 (8.39) | |
| Above 40,000 | 1 (12.50) | 13 (9.92) | |
| Total | 8(100.00) | 131 (100.00) | |
| ***Special Assistance*** | | | |
| Up to 10,000 | 2 (66.66) | 30 (39.47) | |
| 10,000-20,000 | - | 32 (42.10) | |
| 20,000-30,000 | 1 (33.33) | 4 (5.26) | >0.05 |
| 30,000-40,000 | - | 3 (3.94) | |
| Above 40,000 | - | 7 (9.21) | |
| Total | 3(100.00) | 76(100.00) | |
| ***Other Assistance*** | | | |
| Up to 10,000 | - | 8 (19.04) | |
| 10,000-20,000 | 2 (28.57) | 15 (35.71) | |
| 20,000-30,000 | 3 (42.85) | 3 (7.14) | >0.05 |
| 30,000-40,000 | - | 4 (9.52) | |
| Above 40,000 | 2 (28.57) | 12 (28.57) | |
| Total | 7(100.00) | 42(100.00) | |

Column percentage in parentheses.

An equal percentage of men and Women Cooperatives i.e. 70 per cent have received above Rs. 40,000 as share capital by Government. No Women Cooperative has received Government share capital between Rs. 10,000-20,000 and Rs. 30,000-40,000. However, 20 per cent Women Cooperatives have received Government share between Rs. 20,000-30,000, but only 6.91 per cent Men Cooperatives have received the same amount. Similarly, 10 per cent Women Cooperatives have got Government share up to Rs.10,000; but only 7.37 per cent Men Cooperatives have received the same Government share. About 5.52 per cent Men Cooperatives have been provided Rs. 10,000-20,000 Government share and 10.13 per cent Men Cooperatives have received Rs. 30,000-40,000 as the same share. Thus, the amount of Government share capital has been provided more to Men Cooperatives than to Women Cooperatives.

In case of managerial subsidy and special assistance, 62.50 per cent and 66.66 per cent Women Cooperatives respectively have been assisted up to Rs. 10,000. While only 47.32 per cent and 39.47 per cent Men Cooperatives respectively, have also received the same assistance with equal amount. No Women Cooperative has received managerial subsidy between Rs. 10,000-20,000 and Rs. 30,000-40,000 in addition to special assistance in same cohorts and above Rs. 40,000. About 25 per cent Women Cooperatives have received managerial subsidy between Rs. 20,000-30,000 and 12.50 per cent of same Cooperatives have received above Rs. 40,000 as same assistance. But, in case of Men Cooperatives, 21.37 per cent of them have received same assistance between Rs. 10,000-20,000, followed by 12.97 per cent receiving Rs. 20,000-30,000; 9.92 per cent receiving above Rs. 40,000 and 8.89 per cent receiving Rs. 30,000-40,000 as same assistances. Men Cooperatives have also been provided special assistance between Rs. 10,000-20,000 by 42.10 per cent. Only 33.33 per cent Women Cooperatives have got Rs. 20,000-30,000 as special assistance; while, 9.21 per cent Men Cooperatives have got same assistance by above Rs. 40,000. About 5.26 per cent and 3.94 per cent Men Cooperatives have also received the same assistance between Rs. 20,000-30,000 and 30,000-40,000 respectively.

Other types of financial assistances have been provided to 42.85 per cent Women Cooperatives between Rs. 20,000-30,000; followed by 28.57 per cents of Women Cooperatives receiving between Rs.10,000-20,000 and above Rs. 40,000 respectively. Same percentage of Men Cooperatives (28.57 per cent) have also received assistance above Rs. 40,000; followed by 35.71 per cent Men Cooperatives receiving Rs. 10,000-20,000; 19.04 per cent receiving up to Rs. 10,000; 9.52 per cent receiving Rs. 30,000-40,000 and 7.14 per cent Men Cooperatives receiving Rs. 20,000-30,000.

The differences between Government share capital, managerial subsidy, special assistance and other types of assistances among Women Cooperatives and Men Cooperatives are found statistically insignificant ($p>0.05$); but in case of individual share capital, significant difference is observed ($p<0.05$) between Men and Women Cooperatives.

**Difference between Women Cooperatives and Men Cooperatives per their Capital Investment (Table 3.5)**

The average share capital contribution by Women Cooperatives is less than Men Cooperatives. The mean score of Men Cooperatives as per their individual share capital is Rs. 32,375; while in case of Women Cooperatives, it is only Rs.9,430. The wide difference is also obvious between Government share contribution in Men and Women Cooperative. Again, the mean score of Men Cooperatives (Rs.1,34,739) is more than Women Cooperatives (Rs.93,200). But in case of managerial subsidy, the difference is reversed, as Women Cooperatives have mean score more than the Men Cooperatives. This means that State Government has provided managerial subsidy more to Women Cooperatives than to Men Cooperatives. But special assistance and other types of financial assistances are again led by Men Cooperatives than Women Cooperatives. However, the differences between Men and Women Cooperatives as per working capital i.e. individual share capital, Government share capital, managerial subsidy, special assistance and other types of financial assistance are not found statistically significant ($p<0.05$).

**Table 3.5**
**Difference between Women Cooperatives and Men Cooperatives as Per their Capital**

| *Working Capital* | *Mean* | *S.E* | *F-Value* |
|---|---|---|---|
| ***Individual Share Capital*** | | | |
| Women Cooperatives | 9430 (15) | ± 4324 | 1.40 |
| Men Cooperatives | 32375 (251) | ± 4719 | |
| ***Government Share Capital*** | | | |
| Women Cooperatives | 93200 (10) | ± 30260 | 0.42 |
| Men Cooperatives | 134739 (217) | ± 13604 | |
| ***Managerial Assistance*** | | | |
| Women Cooperatives | 27250 (8) | ± 9492 | 1.90 |
| Men Cooperatives | 18444 (131) | ± 1474 | |
| Special Assistance | | | |
| ***Women Cooperatives*** | 12667 (3) | ± 7667 | 0.34 |
| Men Cooperatives | 18812 (77) | ± 2046 | |
| ***Other Assistances*** | | | |
| Women Cooperatives | 30714 (7) | ± 6882 | 0.17 |
| Men Cooperatives | 1993946 (41) | ± 1950219 | |

Sample in parentheses.
S.E denotes Standard Error of Mean.

### Correlation Analysis of Capital Investment with External Dimensions (Table 3.6)

Individual share capital is positively and highly significantly ($p<0.01$) influenced by total Godowns including own Godowns of the Cooperatives; whereas, no other variable is significantly ($p>0.05$) affected by individual share capital. Trained employees have no influence on individual share capital. Trained employees have no influence on individual share capital; whereas hired Godowns as well as their intake capacities are least influenced by individual share capital. Branches of Cooperatives, their employees and total Godown capacity including own Godown capacity are almost equally influenced (5-6 per cent) by individual share capital. All variables are positively influenced by Government share capital. Branches of Cooperatives, number of employees therein, trained employees, total Godowns including own Godowns as well as their capacity have highly significant ($p<0.01$) and have positive relation with Government share capital. Hired Godowns as well as their capacities are influenced by Government share capital only by 6 per cent and this influence is insignificant (p>0.05).

**Table 3.6**
**Correlation Analysis of Capital Investment with External Dimensions**

*(n = 266)*

| *Variables* | *Working Capital* | | | | | | |
|---|---|---|---|---|---|---|---|
| | *Y i* [r] | *Y ii* [r] | *Y iii* [r] | *Y iv* [r] | *Y v* [r] | *Y vi* [r] | *Y vii* [r] |
| Branches | 0.06 | 0.19** | -0.02 | 0.08 | -0.22 | -0.01 | 0.04 |
| Number of Employees | 0.05 | 0.64** | 0.26** | 0.01 | -0.01 | -0.12 | 0.07 |
| Trained Employees | 0.00 | 0.52** | 0.17* | 0.09 | 0.09 | -0.05 | 0.04 |
| Hired Godowns | 0.02 | 0.06 | 0.01 | -0.14 | -0.13 | 0.01 | 0.06 |
| Own Godowns | 0.19** | 0.32** | 0.21** | 0.00 | -0.17 | -0.16 | 0.08 |
| Total Godowns | 0.18** | 0.30** | 0.07 | -0.14 | -0.28 | -0.04 | 0.12 |
| Hired Godown Capacity | 0.02 | 0.06 | 0.01 | -0.14 | -0.13 | 0.01 | 0.06 |
| Own Godown Capacity | 0.06 | 0.49** | 0.08 | -0.10 | -0.10 | 0.01 | 0.03 |
| Total Godown Capacity | 0.05 | 0.37** | 0.12 | -0.10 | 0.16 | -0.07 | 0.05 |
| | *Individual Share Capital* | *Government Share Capital* | *managerial Assistance* | *Special Assistance* | *Interest Free Loan* | *Other Assistance* | *Bank Borrowings* |

* Significant at 0.05 level.
** Significant at 0.01 level.

Managerial subsidy is insignificantly and least negatively influenced by branches of Cooperatives and hired Godowns of Cooperatives. Their intake capacity are insignificantly but least positively influenced by managerial subsidy (p>0.05). Significant relation is seen only with number of employees including trained employees and own Godowns. Employees of Cooperatives and own Godowns of Cooperatives have highly significant positive relation with managerial subsidy (p<0.01). Trained employees of Cooperatives have also shown positive and significant (p<0.05) effect on managerial subsidy provided to Cooperatives. Total number of Godowns and intake capacity of own Godowns are almost equally and insignificantly positive (7-8 per cent) in relation with managerial subsidy.

Special assistance, interest free loan, bank borrowing and other assistances are found statistically insignificantly ($p>0.05$) related with external dimensions of Cooperatives. Interest free loan provided to Cooperatives have positive relation only to trained employees and total Godown capacity of Cooperatives; whereas, branches of Cooperatives, total Godowns of Cooperatives including own and hired Godowns and intake capacity of own and hired Godowns are negatively influenced by interest free loan. The number of employees in Cooperatives are least effected by interest free loan provided to Cooperatives. Bank borrowings are seen positively influenced by the number of Godowns constructed by Cooperatives; whereas, all other variables are not seen much effected by bank borrowings. Other types of financial assistances are least positively influenced by hired Godowns, their capacity as well as own Godown capacity. Similarly, trained employees and total number of Godowns are least negatively influenced by hired Godowns. Number of employees in Cooperatives and own Godowns constructed by Cooperatives are considerably and negatively affected by other types of financial assistances provided to Cooperatives.

4

# EMANCIPATION OF COOPERATIVE SECTOR

The National Cooperative Union of India (NCUI) is an apex promotional Organization of Indian Cooperative movement, established in the year 1929. Today it has 226 member federations, out of which 17 are national level federation 176 are state level federations, National Dairy Development Board and 32 Multi State Cooperative Societies. NCUI implements cooperative education and training programmes on a nation wide scale. There are some education and training programmes exclusively for women, but they are also at liberty to make use of the general programmes.

NCUI launched a pilot project for women's cooperative education in 1964 in Delhi. In 1965, the programme was evaluated and found to be useful and effective. On the basis of evaluation report, it was recommended that the programme be expanded to cover the whole country. Under this programme, women's wings were set up in most of the states under the state cooperative unions, consisting of one officer and four educational instructors, all women. Women's Advisory Committees were also formed in each state.

In order to focus attention on the need and importance of involving women in cooperative movement and to formulate need-based programmes for their education and training, the NCUI convened three conferences for women cooperative workers in 1965, 1968 and 1978. The conference on Women and cooperative held in 1965 stressed the organization women's wings in every state and intensification of women's education programmes for educating and motivating women to join cooperatives. The conference of Women's Industrial Cooperative held in 1968 recommended that arrangements should be made for the marketing of the products of women's cooperatives. The conference of 1978 recommended the introduction of a well-knit and wide spread education programme for the women members of cooperative societies and the provision of training facilities for women members and employees. The conference also recommended that the cooperative apex institutions and government should come forward to provide special facilities and guidance to these cooperatives in business matters and assist them to market their products.

In 1981, NCUI implemented cooperative education programmes exclusively for women in ten states, through women education officers/instructors. The women instructors organized classes of ten days' duration for housewives and prospective mms. Exclusive classes are also being conducted for managing committee members. I addition to this, the women education personnel conducted study circle meetings for housewives, and short duration seminars and conferences, as well as classes for girl students and young women. In these classes for girls and women, various topics relating to cooperation, viz., principles, laws and management, were taken up for discussion. In many other states, Cooperative Education Programme for women members was undertaken as part of general cooperative education programmes.

The Government of India have been implementing a Central Sector Scheme for Cooperative Education and Training through the National Cooperative Union of India (NCUI) and the National Council for Cooperative Training (NCCT) since the 3rd five year plan. It is a continuing scheme. The programmes relating to cooperative Education are being implemented by the NCUI. The Government of India is providing 100 per cent financial assistance in the form of grants-in-aid to NCUI for implementing the Special Scheme of Intensification of Cooperative Education in Cooperatively Under Developed States and 20 per cent of the total expenditure for approved activities like monitoring of Cooperative Education Programmes being implemented by the State Cooperative Unions, publications, convening of conferences, congress etc for cooperative development, running of National Centre for Cooperative Education (NCCE), Cooperative Data Bank etc. During the year 2004-05, up to 31st December 2004, 12,15,358 persons were educated by the NCUI under various programmes.

The Cooperative Training Programmes are being conducted through the National Council for cooperative Training (NCCT) and its constituents, 5 Regional Institutes of Cooperative Management, 14 Institutes of Cooperative Management located in different states and the Vaikunth Mehta National Institute of Cooperative Management, Pune. The Government of India provides 100 per cent financial assistance in the form of grants-in-aid to NCCT for conducting cooperative training programmes. During the year 2004-05, up to 30th November 2004, VAMNICOM, Pune conducted 74 programmes with the participation of 3156 persons. RICMs and ICMs put together trained 27378 persons under 976 programmes during the above period.

The outlay earmarked for implementing the Cooperative Education and Training programmes during the year 2004-2005 is Rs. 45,07,00 thousand including Rs. 4, 50,00 thousand for the N.E. Region. (Rs. 18,00,00 thousand for the on–going programmes and Rs. 27,07,00 thousand for the Re-structured scheme). With the overall objective of bringing women in the cooperative fold from grass root levels by informal approach and to revitalize and develop women participation in group activities; and to improve the socio-economic condition of women of selected blocks, NCUI in 2004 run 4 exclusive women development projects located at Shimoga (Karnataka), Berhampur (Orissa) , Manipur (Imphal) and Bhopal (MP) under the Special Scheme of Intensification of Cooperative Education in the cooperatively under-developed States.

Besides, each field project has got a special women development component. Under this, women are organized into self-help groups and help them to develop thrift habits. Women are also given training to undertake income-generating activities with the help of their own resources or by borrowing from cooperatives. The projects personnel help them in marketing their produce in the local market and by organizing fairs or exhibitions.

The Cooperatives in Jammu and Kashmir State have been organised to provide relief to Members from indebtedness and perform the services such as supply of credit, distribution of inputs, marketing, supply of consumer goods and distribution of essential items. In order to accomplish all these activities successfully, the State Government has acted as an initiator, promoter and protector of the movement through policy, financial outlay and legislation. The Cooperative Department in Jammu and Kashmir State is headed by the Minister of Cooperatives. The Secretary and Commissioner for Cooperation is in charge of the Department and is assisted by one Additional Secretary, one Joint Secretary, two or three Under-Secretaries and three or four Section Officers in Government Secretariat.

The Registrar of Cooperatives is Head of the Department in the State. The Registrar of Cooperatives is generally a senior Indian Administrative Service (IAS) Officer appointed by the Government. The Institution of 'Registrar of Cooperatives' has been important since inception of Cooperative Movement in Kashmir and the success of the Cooperative Movement depends upon the role played by him/her in formulating and executing the policies. The Registrar of Cooperatives has three types of powers viz. Administrative, financial and statutory. He/she exercise all the powers which are conferred on him/her by the Cooperative Act. The Registrar of Cooperatives is assisted by a team of officials in the Department at Head Quarter as well as in the field to promote, regulates, supervise, audit and control the Cooperatives. The Registrar of Cooperatives has delegated theses powers to his/her team of officials so that they exercise these powers in their areas of jurisdiction.

The present chapter comprises the perception and role of Cooperative officials regarding scope for women in Cooperatives. This part of the study is conducted for preliminary preparation in order to organise an intervention programme to increase women's awareness about the role of Cooperatives in their economic development.

## Background Information

The background information of Cooperative personnel includes their personal characteristics, service carrier and job satisfaction. Respondents up to the age of 20-30 years have been categorised in the rank of *'Early'* age; those having 30-50 years of age are put under *'Middle'* age category; and those bearing more than 50 years of age, are ranked as *'Late'* age . Officials belonging to establishment staff e.g. clerks, accountants, assistants etc. are classified under *'Low'* designation. *'Medium'* designation belongs to field workers i.e. supervisors, inspectors and auditors; whereas, those officers having gazetted ranks like, assistant registrars, deputy registrars, joint registrars etc. are put under *'High'* category of designation. In context of qualification, those officials who have achieved formal education below graduation are classified under *'Less'* qualified; those officials who are graduates are put under *'Medium'* qualified; whereas, those being post-graduates, M.Phil and Ph.D are categorised as *'Highly'* qualified. Similarly, officials receiving salary up to Rs.5,000 have been ranked under *'Low'* salary. Pay scale between Rs.5,000-10,000 is classified under *'Average'* salary and more than Rs.10,000 is categorised under *'High'* salary. Finally, officers/officials residing up to 5 kilometres from their posted place are put under the category of *'Short'* distance; 5-10 kilometres as *'Average'* distance and more than 10 kilometres are ranked as *'Far'* distance.

### Levels of Personal Characteristics of Cooperative Personnel (Table 4.1)

Most of the Cooperative personnel i.e. 76 per cent are middle aged. Only 5 per cent officials are late aged and 19 per cent bear early age. Majority of officials (43 per cent) have medium qualification, followed by high and less qualification by 30 per cent and 27 per cent respectively. In case of designation; medium and high posts are hold by 37 per cents respectively, than 26 per cent officials at low designations. Average salary is received by 42 per cent officials, followed by 39 per cent and 19 per cent officials with high and less salaries respectively. The per centage of officials who have to cover far distance from their posted areas to residential areas, fall as 47 per cent. While 29 per cent and 24 per cent officials have to cover less and average distances respectively.

The differences between the ranks of designation is found insignificant ($p>0.05$). However, between the levels of qualification, there is a significant difference ($p<0.05$); while categories of age, salary and distance covered, have shown highly significant differences at the levels of 0.01.

**Table 4.1**
**Levels of Personal Characteristics of Cooperative Personnel**
*(n=100)*

| *Variables* | *Levels* | | | *p-Value* |
|---|---|---|---|---|
| | *Early/Low* | *Middle/Medium* | *Later/High* | |
| Age | 19<br>(19.00) | 76<br>(76.00) | 5<br>(5.00) | <0.01 |
| Educational Status | 27<br>(27.00) | 43<br>(43.00) | 30<br>(30.00) | <0.05 |
| Designation | 26<br>(26.00) | 37<br>(37.00) | 37<br>(37.00) | >0.05 |
| Salary | 19<br>(19.00) | 42<br>(42.00) | 39<br>(39.00) | <0.01 |
| Distance | 29<br>(29.00) | 24<br>(24.00) | 47<br>(47.00) | <0.01 |

Row percentage in parentheses.

### Personal Characteristics of Cooperative Personnel (Table 4.2)

The table under observation reveals that in the urban areas, the male officials are at early age level (57.14 per cent) than male officials in rural areas (42.86 per cent). But middle aged officials are more in rural areas (51.28 per cent), than in urban areas (48.72 per cent). Late aged male Cooperative personnel are equally distributed in rural and urban areas by 50 per cents respectively. In contrast, female early aged officials are more in rural areas (66.67 per cent) than in urban areas (33.33 per cent).Whereas, in the urban areas, there are more females in middle age (56.76 per cent) than in rural areas (43.24 per cent). No urban female personnel in the department is late aged; whereas, only 2 female rural officials under study are in late age.

With regard to qualification of the officials, rural male are less qualified (75 per cent) than urban males (25 per cent). Urban and rural male officials hold equally medium qualification by 52 per cent and 48 per cent respectively; whereas, urban male officials are highly qualified by 58.82 per cent than rural male officials by 41.18 per cent. Similarly, female officials are less qualified in rural areas (78.95 per cent) than in urban areas (21.05 per cent). Double the number of female officials holds the medium level of qualification in urban areas (66.67 per cent), than in rural areas (33.33 per cent). Moreover, urban females are highly qualified (69.23 per cent) than rural female officials by 30.77 per cent.

No male official under the study has low designation; whereas majority of rural females by 69.23 per cent and 30.77 per cent urban females have low designations in the Cooperative Department. Medium and high designations are equally distributed among rural and urban males (50 per cents respectively); while 69.23 per cent female officials in urban areas and 30.77 per cent in rural areas bear medium designations. Moreover, 72.73 per cent urban females have high designation as compared to only 27.27 per cent among rural females.

The salary of the officials is prescribed as per their designation and duration of service. Rural males and females (80 per cent and 85.71 per cent respectively) have low salary than urban males and females (20 per cent and 14.29 per cent respectively). Medium level of salary is received by urban males and females (60.87 per cent and 57.89 per cent respectively), than rural males and females (39.13 per cent and 42.11 per cent respectively). High salary is mainly obtained by urban female officials i.e. 70.59 per cent, followed by rural males (54.55 per cent), 45.45 per cent urban males and 24.41 per cent rural females.

In context to distance from residential to posted area; urban male and female have to cover short distance (60 per cent and 78.95 per cent respectively) than rural male and female officials (40 per cent and 21.05 per cent respectively). About 66.67 per cent officials in urban areas have to cover

**Table 4.2**
**Personal Characteristics of Cooperative Personnel**

*(n = 100)*

| | *Male* | | | *Female* | | |
|---|---|---|---|---|---|---|
| *Variables* | *Urban* | *Rural* | *p-Value* | *Urban* | *Rural* | *p-Value* |
| ***Age*** | | | | | | |
| Early | 4 (57.14) | 3 (42.86) | | 4 (33.33) | 8 (66.67) | |
| Middle | 19 (48.72) | 20 (51.28) | >0.05 | 21 (56.76) | 16 (43.24) | >0.05 |
| Late | 2 (50.00) | 2 (50.00) | | - | 2 (100.00) | |
| Total | 25 (50.00) | 25 (50.00) | | 25 (50.00) | 25 (50.00) | |
| ***Educational*** Status | | | | | | |
| Less | 2 (25.00) | 6 (75.00) | | 4 (21.05) | 15 (78.95) | |
| Medium | 13 (52.00) | 12 (48.00) | >0.05 | 12 (66.67) | 6 (33.33) | <0.01 |
| High | 10 (58.82) | 2 (41.18) | | 9 (69.23) | 4 (30.77) | |
| Total | 25 (50.00) | 25 (50.00) | | 25 (50.00) | 25 (50.00) | |
| ***Designation*** | | | | | | |
| Low | - | - | | 8 (30.77) | 18 (69.23) | |
| Medium | 12 (50.00) | 12 (50.00) | >0.05 | 9 (69.23) | 4 (30.77) | <0.01 |
| High | 13 (50.00) | 13 (50.00) | | 8 (72.73) | 3 (27.27) | |
| Total | 25 (50.00) | 25 (50.00) | | 25 (50.00) | 25 (50.00) | |
| Salary | | | | | | |
| Low | 1 (20.00) | 4 (80.00) | | 2 (14.29) | 12 (85.71) | |
| Medium | 14 (60.87) | 9 (39.13) | >0.05 | 11 (57.89) | 8 (42.11) | <0.01 |
| High | 10 (45.45) | 12 (54.55) | | 12 (70.59) | 5 (29.41) | |
| Total | 25 (50.00) | 25 (50.00) | | 25 (50.00) | 25 (50.00) | |
| ***Distance Covered*** | | | | | | |
| Short | 6 (60.00) | 4 (40.00) | | 15 (78.95) | 4 (21.05) | |
| Average | 8 (66.67) | 4 (33.33) | >0.05 | 9 (75.00) | 3 (25.00) | <0.01 |
| Far | 11 (39.29) | 17 (60.71) | | 1 (5.26) | 18 (94.74) | |
| Total | 25 (50.00) | 25 (50.00) | | 25 (50.00) | 25 (50.00) | |

Row percentage in parentheses.

average distance than rural males (33.33 per cent). Similarly, 75 per cent urban females need to cover average distance than 25 per cent rural females. Majority of rural male and female officials (60.71 per cent and 94.74 per cent respectively) have to cover far distance to reach their posting, than urban male and female officials who have to cover far distances by 39.29 per cent and 5.26 per cent respectively.

The differences between rural and urban male officials are not found to be significant ($p>0.05$) as per their age, qualification, designation, salary and distance covered by them from their residential areas to posted areas. Same case also applies to urban and rural female officials as per their age. But highly significant differences ($p<0.01$) are found between rural and urban female officials as per their qualification, designation, salary and distance covered.

**Service Career of Cooperative Personnel (Table 4.3)**

An equal per centage of urban and rural male officials (50 per cents respectively) have service duration up to 10 years and 15-20 years. No urban male official has service duration between 10-15 years. However, 57.89 per cent of urban males have more than 20 years' service duration, than rural males (42.11 per cent). No female official in rural areas has service career of more than 20 years; whereas equal per centage of rural and urban female officials by 50 per cents respectively have 15-20 years' service career. The per centage of rural female officials having up to 5 years' service only is double (66.67 per cent) than the urban female officials (33.33 per cent). Similarly, 36.36 per cent urban females have been working since 5-10 years' and 63.64 per cent rural females are also servicing since same period. While reverse is true in case of 10-15 years' service duration, where 63.64 per cent female officials belong to urban areas and 36.36 per cent belong to rural areas.

About 51.72 per cent urban males and 48.28 per cent rural males are satisfied with their jobs. But 47.62 per cent urban males and 52.38 per cent rural males are dissatisfied with their jobs. In case of females, 57.14 per cent in urban areas and 42.86 per cent in rural areas are satisfied with their jobs. But, 44.83

per cent urban females and 55.17 per cent rural females are dissatisfied with their jobs.

Among satisfied officials, achievement of economic independence through their service in Cooperative Department is true in case of 36.36 per cent urban males and 63.64 per cent rural males. While reverse is true in case with female officials, where 66.67 per cent in urban areas and 33.33 per cent in rural areas are satisfied with their jobs due to economic independence achieved by them. No urban female official feels that achievement of job in Cooperatives has made any improvement in their status. However, 61.54 per cent of them in urban areas feel that they are serving the nation through Cooperatives, along with 38.46 per cent rural female officials who also feel the same. Equal per centage of male officials in urban and rural areas (50 per cents respectively) feels that they have improved their status through Cooperatives. Whereas, 70 per cent urban male officials feel that they are serving the nation through Cooperatives, along with only 30 per cent rural male officials who also have the same feeling.

Among respondents being dissatisfied with their jobs, equal per centage of rural and urban male officials (50 per cents respectively) blames less salary as well as less chances of promotion in Cooperative Department. No encouragement for good performance is blamed mostly by rural males and urban females (53.85 per cent and 60 per cent respectively), than urban males and rural females (46.15 per cent and 40 per cent respectively). No rural female official has felt less chances of promotion as a factor responsible for their job dissatisfaction. However, 85.71 per cent rural female officials are dissatisfied due to less salary provided to them by the Cooperative Department, as compared to 14.29 per cent urban female officials who also feel the same. Equal per centage of urban and rural, as well as male and female officials (50 per cents respectively) are dissatisfied with their jobs due to other reasons like work load, bad treatment by higher authority and far distance to be covered from their residential to posted areas.

**Table 4.3**
**Service Career of Cooperative Personnel**

*(n = 100)*

| | *Male* | | | *Female* | | |
|---|---|---|---|---|---|---|
| *Variables* | *Urban* | *Rural* | *p-Value* | *Urban* | *Rural* | *p-Value* |
| ***Service Duration*** (Years) | | | | | | |
| Up to 5 | 9 (50.00) | 9 (50.00) | | 4 (33.33) | 8 (66.67) | |
| 5-10 | 2 (50.00) | 2 (50.00) | | 4 (36.36) | 7 (63.64) | |
| 10-15 | - | 3 (100.00) | >0.05 | 7 (63.64) | 4 (36.36) | >0.05 |
| 15-20 | 3 (50.00) | 3 (50.00) | | 6 (50.00) | 6 (50.00) | |
| More than 20 | 11 (57.89) | 8 (42.11) | | 4 (100.00) | - | |
| Total | 25 (50.00) | 25 (50.00) | | 25 (50.00) | 25 (50.00) | |
| ***Job Satisfaction*** | | | | | | |
| Positive | 15 (51.72) | 14 (48.28) | | 12 (57.14) | 9 (42.86) | |
| Negative | 10 (47.62) | 11 (52.38) | >0.05 | 13 (44.83) | 16 (55.17) | >0.05 |
| Total | 25 (50.00) | 25 (50.00) | | 25 (50.00) | 25 (50.00) | |
| ***Reason for Satisfaction Independence*** | | | | | | |
| Economic | 4 (36.36) | 7 (63.64) | | 4 (66.67) | 2 (33.33) | |
| Service to Nation | 7 (70.00) | 3 (30.00) | >0.05 | 8 (61.54) | 5 (38.46) | >0.05 |
| Improvement in Status | 4 (50.00) | 4 (50.00) | | - | 2 (100.00) | |
| Total | 15 (51.72) | 14 (48.28) | | 12 (57.14) | 9 (42.86) | |
| ***Reason for Dissatisfaction*** | | | | | | |
| Less Salary | 1 (50.00) | 1 (50.00) | | 1 (14.29) | 6 (85.71) | |
| Less Chances of Promotion | 2 (50.00) | 2 (50.00) | | 1 (100.00) | - | |
| No Encourage-ment | | 6 (46.15) | 7 (53.85) | >0.05 | 3 (60.00) | 2 |
| (40.00) | >0.05 | | | | | |
| ***Other Reasons*** | 1 (50.00) | 1 (50.00) | | 8 (50.00) | 8 (50.00) | |
| Total | 10 (47.62) | 11 (52.38) | | 13 (44.83) | 16 (55.17) | |

Row percentage in parentheses.

However, no significant differences are observed between rural and urban, male and female officials as per their service duration, job satisfaction and reasons for satisfaction or dissatisfaction in their jobs (p>0.05).

**Job Satisfaction of Cooperative Personnel as per their Personal Characteristics (Table 4.4)**

Early aged officials/officers are more dissatisfied with their jobs (52.63 per cent); whereas late aged officials/officers are more satisfied by their jobs (60 per cent). An equal per centage of middle aged officials are satisfied and dissatisfied with their jobs by 50 per cents respectively. Only 47.37 per cent early officials are satisfied with their service career and 40 per cent late aged personnel have got dissatisfied service career.

As per the qualification of Cooperative personnel, low qualified are more dissatisfied (66.67 per cent) and highly qualified are more satisfied (63.33 per cent) with their service. Again, almost equal per centage of Cooperative personnel with medium qualification, are satisfied and dissatisfied (51.16 per cent and 48.84 per cent respectively) with their services. Only 33.33 per cent low qualified officials are satisfied and 36.67 per cent highly qualified officials are dissatisfied with their jobs.

Officials having low designation are more dissatisfied by 69.23 per cent than those at high designations who are satisfied by 62.16 per cent. Only 30.77 per cent low designated officials are satisfied with their jobs. Similarly, only 37.84 per cent highly designated officials are dissatisfied with their service career. Moreover, 51.35 per cent officials with their medium designations are satisfied than 48.65 per cent officials at same level of designations, who are dissatisfied with their jobs.

In context of salary, officials obtaining low salary are dissatisfied with their jobs by 73.68 per cent than 26.32 per cent officials receiving same level of salary, but satisfied with their jobs. An almost equal per centage of officials receiving medium level of salary are satisfied by 52.38 per cent and dissatisfied by 47.62 per cent. Those officials receiving high level of salary are also more satisfied by 58.97 per cent. But 41.03 per cent officials enjoying high level of salary are dissatisfied with their jobs for other reasons.

The distance covered by officers/officials of Cooperative Department from their residential to posted areas, have put forth no considerable findings. Officials covering short as well as far distances towards their posted areas are satisfied with their jobs by 53.19 per cent and 41.38 per cent respectively. About 54.17 per cent officials with average distance towards their offices are also satisfied, than 45.83 per cent officials

**Table 4.4**
**Job Satisfaction of Cooperative Personnel as Per Their Personal Characteristics**

*(n = 100)*

| *Variables* | *Service Career* | | *p-Value* |
|---|---|---|---|
| | *Satisfied* | *Dissatisfied* | |
| ***Age*** | | | |
| Early | 9 (47.37) | 10 (52.63) | |
| Middle | 38 (50.00) | 38 (50.00) | >0.05 |
| Late | 3 (60.00) | 2 (40.00) | |
| Total | 50 (50.00) | 50 (50.00) | |
| ***Educational Status*** | | | |
| Less | 9 (33.33) | 18 (66.67) | |
| Medium | 22 (51.16) | 21 (48.84) | >0.05 |
| High | 19 (63.33) | 11 (36.67) | |
| Total | 50 (50.00) | 50 (50.00) | |
| ***Designation*** | | | |
| Low | 8 (30.77) | 18 (69.23) | |
| Medium | 19 (51.35) | 18 (48.65) | <0.05 |
| High | 23 (62.16) | 14 (37.84) | |
| Total | 50 (50.00) | 50 (50.00) | |
| ***Salary*** | | | |
| Low | 5 (26.32) | 14 (73.68) | |
| Medium | 22 (52.38) | 20 (47.62) | >0.05 |
| High | 23 (58.97) | 16 (41.03) | |
| Total | 50 (50.00) | 50 (50.00) | |
| ***Distance Covered*** | | | |
| Short | 12 (41.38) | 17 (58.62) | |
| Average | 13 (54.17) | 11 (45.83) | >0.05 |
| Far | 25 (53.19) | 22 (46.81) | |
| Total | 50 (50.00) | 50 (50.00) | |
| ***Service Duration(Years)*** | | | |
| Up to 5 | 17 (56.67) | 13 (43.33) | |
| 5-10 | 4 (26.67) | 11 (73.33) | |
| 10-15 | 8 (57.14) | 6 (42.86) | >0.05 |
| 15-20 | 10 (55.56) | 8 (44.44) | |
| More than 20 | 11 (47.83) | 12 (52.17) | |
| Total | 50 (50.00) | 50 (50.00) | |

Row percentage in parentheses.

covering same distance, but dissatisfied with their jobs. Moreover, 58.62 per cent officials covering less distance and 46.81 per cent officials with far distances are dissatisfied with their service career.

Officials working in the department since more than 20 years are les satisfied by 47.83 per cent, than 52.17 per cent who are dissatisfied by their service career. But those officials, who have been working between 15-20 years, are satisfied by 55.56 per cent than 44.44 per cent dissatisfied officials with same service career. Similarly, officials having less service up to 5 years are also satisfied with their jobs by 56.67 per cent; while 43.33 per cent officials working since same period are dissatisfied with their jobs. Moreover, only 26.67 per cent officials with their service career in the cohort of 5-10 years are satisfied; but majority of officials (73.33 per cent) in the same cohort are dissatisfied. Moreover, 57.14 per cent officials working since 10-15 years are satisfied with their jobs, than 42.86 per cent officials under the same cohort being dissatisfied with their jobs.

However, no significant differences are found between the satisfied and dissatisfied service career of Cooperative personnel according to their age, qualification, salary, distance covered and service duration; where the levels of significance are greater than 0.05. But a significant difference is seen between the designation and service status of Cooperative Personnel, where the level of significance is less than 0.05.

**Designation of Cooperative Personnel as per their Service Duration (Table 4.5)**

The table under observation has shown a highly significant difference between the Cooperative personnel and their service duration ($p<0.01$). Officials having only up to 5 years service, rank high designation by 40 per cent, followed by 36.67 per cent medium designations and only 23.33 per cent low designations under the same category. No high designation is held by the officials with the service duration of 5-10 years. While, 53.33 per cent low and 46.67 per cent medium designations are observed under the same group. Officials with

10-15 years service are mainly represented by medium designations (50 per cent), followed by 35.71 per cent low and 14.29 per cent high designations. About 38.89 per cent Cooperative personnel at high ranks have 15-20 years service, followed by 33.33 per cent low designations and 27.78 per cent medium designations with same service duration. No official with more than 20 years service, hold low designation; rather majority of them i.e. 69.57 per cent are holding high and 30.43 per cent are at medium designations. Overall, majority of officials by 30 per cent have been working in the Cooperative Department since 5 years only. But 23 per cent officials have more than 20 years service career, followed by 18 per cent officials with 15-20 years service; and 15 per cent and 14 per cent officials with 5-10 years and 10-15 years service respectively.

**Table 4.5**
**Designation if cooperative Personnels per their Service Duration**

*(n = 100)*

| *Service Duration (Years)* | *Designation* | | | *Total* |
|---|---|---|---|---|
| | *Low* | *Medium* | *High* | |
| Up to 5 | 7 | 11 | 12 | 30 |
| | (23.33) | (36.67) | (40.00) | (100.00) |
| 5-10 | 8 | 7 | - | 15 |
| | (53.33) | (46.67) | | (100.00) |
| 10-15 | 5 | 7 | 2 | 14 |
| | (35.71) | (50.00) | (14.29) | (100.00) |
| 15-20 | 6 | 5 | 7 | 18 |
| | (33.33) | (27.78) | (38.89) | (100.00) |
| More than 20 | - | 7 | 16 | 23 |
| | | (30.43) | (69.57) | (100.00) |
| Total | 26 | 37 | 37 | 100 |
| | (26.00) | (37.00) | (37.00) | (100.00) |

p-Value <0.01
Row percentage in parentheses.

### Designation and Salary of Cooperative Personnel as per their Qualification (Table 4.6)

Among Cooperative personnel with low designations, majority of them (57.69 per cent), are low qualified; whereas 26.92 per cent have medium qualification; and 15.38 per cent are highly qualified. Similarly, officials at medium designations are possessing medium qualification by 51.35 per cent, followed by 27.03 per cent highly qualified and 21.62 per cent with less qualification. As far as high posts in Cooperative Department are concerned, almost equal per centage of officials have medium and high qualifications by 45.95 per cent and 43.24 per cent respectively. But 10.81 per cent officials with less qualification are also ranking among high designation.

**Table 4.6**
**Designation Andsalary of Cooperative Personnel as per their Qualification**

*(n = 100)*

| *Variable* | *Qualification* | | | *Total* |
|---|---|---|---|---|
| | *Low* | *Medium* | *High* | |
| ***Designation*** | | | | |
| Low | 15 (57.69) | 7 (26.92) | 4 (15.38) | |
| Medium | 8 (21.62) | 19 (51.35) | 10 (27.03) | <0.01 |
| High | 4 (10.81) | 17 (45.95) | 16 (43.24) | |
| Total | 27 (27.00) | 43 (43.00) | 30 (30.00) | |
| ***Salary*** | | | | |
| Low | 8 (42.11) | 7 (36.84) | 4 (21.05) | |
| Medium | 14 (33.33) | 20 (47.62) | 8 (19.05) | <0.05 |
| High | 5 (12.82) | 16 (41.03) | 18 (46.15) | |
| Total | 27(27.00) | 43 (43.00) | 30 (30.00) | |

Row percentage in parentheses

Majority of less qualified officials are also receiving less salary (42.11 per cent), followed by 36.84 per cent officials with medium qualification and 21.05 per cent getting less amount of salary. Such difference in salary is seen due to their level of designation and service duration in Cooperative Department. Thus, majority of officials with medium qualification (47.62 per cent) are receiving medium level of salary. While 33.33 per cent less qualified officials and 19.05 per cent highly qualified officials are also getting medium level of salary. About 21.82 per cent less qualified officials are enjoying high level of salary; while 46.15 per cent highly qualified and 41.03 per cent officials with medium qualification are also enjoying high level of salary in the Cooperative Department. The difference between salary and qualification of Cooperative officials is found significant at 0.05 level. A highly significant difference ($p<0.01$) is observed between designation and qualification of Cooperative personnel.

**Difference between Various Characteristics of Cooperative Personnel as per their Sex (Table 4.7)**

The table under observation reveals that the mean age of male officials is more than the female officials. Similarly, mean salary obtained by male officials is more than the female officials and the mean distance covered by male officials is also more than the female officials in the Cooperative Department. Such difference between age and distance of male and female officials is insignificant ($p > 0.05$).

**Table 4.7**
**Difference between Various Characteristics of Cooperative Personnelas per their Sex (ANOVA)**

| *Characteristics* | *Mean* | *S.E* | *F-Value* |
|---|---|---|---|
| ***Age (Years)*** | | | |
| Male | 41.52 (50) | ± 1.12 | 7.46** |
| Female | 37.24 (50) | ± 1.10 | |
| ***Salary (Rs. per Month)*** | | | |
| Male | 10561 (50) | ± 769 | 1.91 |
| Female | 8966 (50) | ± 860 | |
| ***Distance (Kms)*** | | | |
| Male | 22.46 (50) | ± 3.91 | 6.24* |
| Female | 11.90 (50) | ± 1.62 | |

S.E. denotes Standard Error of Mean.
** Significant at 0.01 level.
Sample in parentheses.

The mean age of male officials is almost 42 years; female officials are on an average around the age of 37 years. The average salary received by the female officials is only Rs. 8,966 per month; while male officials receive around Rs. 10,561 as their monthly salary. Similarly, male officials cover around 22 kilometres' distance, but females cover almost only 12 kilometres distance from their residential to posted area.

**Difference between Various Characteristics of Cooperative Personnel as per their Residence (Table 4.8)**

The average age of urban and rural officials is almost equal i.e. 40 years and 38 years respectively. But the mean monthly salary received by urban officials is more (Rs. 11,442 per month) than rural officials (Rs. 8,085 per month). Moreover, urban officials have to cover less distance (10 kilometres) than rural officials (24 kilometres) from their residential to posted area. Such difference between the salary and distance covered by urban and rural officials is found highly significant at 0.01 level, but the difference between the age of urban and rural officials is found insignificant (p>0.05).

**Table 4.8**
**Difference between Various Characteristics of Cooperative Personnel as per their Residence (ANOVA)**

| *Characteristics* | *Mean* | *S.E* | *F-Value* |
|---|---|---|---|
| ***Age (Years)*** | | | |
| Urban | 40.14<br>(50) | ± 1.08 | 0.88 |
| Rural | 38.62<br>(50) | ± 1.20 | |
| ***Salary (Rs. Per Month)*** | | | |
| Urban | 11442<br>(50) | ± 892 | 9.07** |
| Rural | 8085<br>(50) | ± 669 | |
| ***Distance (Kms)*** | | | |
| Urban | 10.14<br>(50) | ± 1.36 | 11.67** |
| Rural | 24.22<br>(50) | ± 3.89 | |

S.E denotes Standard Error of Mean
** Significant at 0.01 level
Sample in parentheses

**Difference between Personal Characteristics of Cooperative Personnel as per various Levels (Table 4.9)**

The average age of early aged officials is 27 years. Middle-aged officials are around the mean age of 41 years and late aged officials fall around the mean of 54 years. Officials with less amount of salary have received only around Rs. 3,230 per month. While the average of medium salary includes Rs. 7,450 per month and high salary is averaged as Rs. 15,438 per month.

**Table 4.9**
**Difference between Various Characteristics of Cooperative Personnel as per Various Levesl (ANOVA)**

| *Characteristics* | *Mean* | *S.E* | *F-Value* |
|---|---|---|---|
| ***Age (Years)*** | | | |
| Early | 27.47<br>(19) | ±0.66 | |
| Middle | 41.40<br>(76) | ±0.62 | 80.88** |
| Late | 53.80<br>(5) | ±1.24 | |
| ***Salary (Rs. Per Month)*** | | | |
| Low | 3230<br>(19) | ±35 | |
| Medium | 7450<br>(42) | ±31 | 107.58** |
| High | 15438<br>(39) | ±74 | |
| ***Distance (Kms)*** | | | |
| Short | 3.65<br>(29) | ±0.30 | |
| Average | 8.37<br>(24) | ±0.34 | 22.85** |
| Far | 30.02<br>(47) | ±3.8 | |

S.E denotes Standard Error of Mean
** Significant at 0.01 level
Sample in parentheses

Similarly, the average nearby distance covered by officials is around 4 kilometres from their residential to posted areas. The mean score of 8 kilometres is ranked as average distance covered by officials and the far away distance covers the mean score of 30 kilometres. Such distance between the levels of age, salary and distance are observed highly significant at 0.01 level.

**Correlation Analysis between Socio-Personal Dimensions of Cooperative Personnel (Table 4.10)**

The positive and highly significant ($p<0.01$) influence of salary is found on age and favourable attitudes of Cooperative personnel towards Cooperative Movement. Positive effect of age is also seen on the favourable attitudes of officials towards Cooperative Movement. However, this effect is not seen statistically significant ($p>0.05$).

**Table 4.10**
**Correlation Analysis between Socio-Personaldimensions of Cooperative Personnel**

*(n = 100)*

| | *Socio-Personal Dimensions* | |
|---|---|---|
| *Variables* | *Y i* [r] | *Y ii* [r] |
| Age | - | 0.11 |
| Salary | 0.40** | 0.31** |
| Distance | 0.02 | 0.09 |
| | Age | Favourable Attitude Towards Cooperative Movement |

** Significant at 0.01 level.

The background information of cooperative personnel bring forth that most of the officers/officials are in medium level of age, qualification, designation and salary. The distance covered by majority of officials, from their residential to posted area is very high. Early aged male officials are mainly in urban areas than in rural areas. But in rural areas, middle aged male officials are more than in urban areas. Later age of Cooperative personnel are equally distributed in rural and urban areas. In contrast, early aged female officials are more in rural areas than in urban areas; whereas in urban areas, there are more female officials in middle age, than in rural areas.

In rural areas, male officials are less qualified than in urban areas. Same case is seen among female officials. Almost no difference is seen between male and female officials as per their designations. This means, women are, in no way, inferior in their employment status than men.

The salary of the officials is distributed as per their designation and duration of service. Those officials with low designation and duration of service; also enjoy low level of salary and vice-versa. In context to distance from residential area to posted area; urban male and female officials need to cover short distance, than rural officials. Further male officials have to cover more distance than female officials.

Most of the male officials have more than 20 years' experience in Cooperative Department; while female officials mainly in rural areas, have no such long experience. This depicts that in past, very few women were appointed in Cooperative Department, mainly due to lack of education among women. *Mohanan* (1989) found that a significant proportion of staff (60 per cent) in Cooperatives have put in long years of service of more than 15 years with their Cooperatives. Majority of them (80 per cent) had studied up to high school. However, only a few had (13 per cent) undergone Cooperative training and none possessed any professional qualification.

The present study shows that the per centage of rural and urban male officials being satisfied or dissatisfied with their jobs is almost equal. But most of the female officials in rural areas, are dissatisfied with their jobs. Their reasons for dissatisfaction are less salary and no encouragement for good work. Majority of female officials have other reasons for dissatisfaction in their jobs, like Bad treatment by officers, heavy workload and long distance to be covered from residential to posted area. The main reasons for those officials being satisfied with their jobs are economic independence, service to nation and improvement in status. However, no female official in urban areas feel that being employed in Cooperative Department, has contributed in improving her status. The age, qualification, salary, distance covered and service durations have seen not to be influenced on the service status of the Cooperative officials.

However, it is observed that officials at low designations are more dissatisfied with their jobs and vice-versa. But medium level of designation has influenced the satisfaction or dissatisfaction of Cooperative officials. Most of the officials with less service duration are at high ranks in Cooperative Department. This is due to direct recruitment in Kashmir Administrative Service (KAS) and Financial Analysts in Cooperative Department. This is due to departmental promotions due to them, in spite of being less qualified. However, most of the officials with high qualifications are also seen at medium and high designations.

Low level of salary is also received by less qualified officials, being at low designations. Rural officials receive average level of salaries; while urban officials enjoy high level of salaries, as per their designation. With the increase in the age of the officials; their salaries also raise high. Rise in salary has lead to the favourable attitudes of officials towards the Cooperative Movement.

## Perception Towards Cooperative Movement

The perception of Cooperative personnel in Kashmir has been analysed in relation to the goal accomplished by the Cooperative Movement, achievement of socio-economic aim by Cooperatives, functioning of Cooperatives and Community Development through Cooperatives. The coordination between the authority of Cooperative Department and the management of Cooperatives is also analysed along with their reasons for dissatisfactory coordination. The financial assistance has been prevented to Cooperatives since 1995 till the period of data collection for the study i.e. up to 2002. The reasons for such avoidance of financial assistance to Cooperatives have been put under analysis.

### Perception of Cooperative Personnel Regarding Cooperative Movement (Table 4.11)

Equal per centages of urban male and female officials (61.29 per cents respectively) are considering Cooperative Movement best for the economic uplift of masses. While 38.71 per cent rural male and same per centage of rural female also perceives the same concept. Majority of male officials in rural areas (77.78 per cent) and only 22.22 per cent urban male officials perceive mutual cooperation as a main aim of Cooperatives. Similarly, majority of female officials in rural areas (84.62 per cent) also perceive the same. But only 15.38 per cent urban female officials regard mutual cooperation as an objective of Cooperatives. Almost an equal per centage of rural male officials (60 per cent) and urban female officials (66.67 per cent) consider that Cooperatives are being established only to expand the Cooperative Movement; while 40 per cent urban male and 33.33 per cent rural female officials are also considering the establishment of Cooperatives just a formality to expand the Cooperative Movement in Kashmir.

About 53.33 per cent urban male officials have agreed that Cooperatives have been playing an important role in the social uplift of people, as compared to 46.67 per cent rural males. But, 51.43 per cent rural males, followed by 48.57 per cent urban male officials do not agree to this view. In case of female officials, majority of them in rural areas (60.87 per cent) perceive that social uplift of people can be achieved through Cooperatives. Similarly, 39.13 per cent urban female officials also consider the same. But 59.26 per cent urban female officials and 40.74 per cent rural female officials do not consider the same view.

The highest number of officials is dissatisfied with the functioning of Cooperatives. Urban male officials by 57.14 per cent and rural female officials by 57.89 per cent are highly satisfied with the functioning of Cooperative organisations. Similarly, 42.86 per cent rural male officials and 42.11 per cent urban female officials also feel the same. But majority of rural male (51.16 per cent) and urban female officials (54.84 per cent) have opposite perception of it. They feel that the functioning of Cooperatives in Kashmir is not satisfactory. Similarly, 48.84 per cent urban males, followed by 45.16 per cent rural female officials are also dissatisfied by the functioning of Cooperatives.

An equal per centage of female officials in rural and urban areas (50 per cents respectively) consider that making people self employed through Cooperatives, is a best means for community development. About 60 per cent urban male and 40 per cent rural male officials also consider the same view. An equal per centage of urban male as well as female officials (46.67 per cents respectively) regard Cooperatives as a measure for holding the price line. Similarly, an equal per centage of rural male as well as female officials (53.85 per cents respectively) have the same perception. Mutual cooperation through Cooperatives is perceived by 58.82 per cent rural male

**Table 4.11**
**Perception of Cooperative Personnel Regarding Cooperative Movement**

*(n = 100)*

| *Variables* | *Male* | | | *Female* | | *p-Value* |
|---|---|---|---|---|---|---|
| | *Urban* | *Rural* | *p-Value* | *Urban* | *Rural* | |
| ***Goal of Cooperatives*** | | | | | | |
| Economic | 19 (61.29) | 12 (38.71) | | 19 (61.29) | 12 (38.71) | |
| Mutual Cooperation | 2 (22.22) | 7 (77.78) | >0.05 | 2 (15.38) | 11 (84.62) | <0.01 |
| Expansion of Movement | 4 (40.00) | 6 (60.00) | | 4 (66.67) | 2 (33.33) | |
| Total | 25 (50.00) | 25 (50.00) | | 25 (50.00) | 25 (50.00) | |
| ***Achievement of Social Aim by Cooperatives*** | | | | | | |
| Agreed | 8 (53.33) | 7 (46.67) | | 9 (39.13) | 14 (60.87) | |
| Disagreed | 17 (48.57) | 18 (51.43) | >0.05 | 16 (59.26) | 11 (40.74) | >0.05 |
| Total | 25 (50.00) | 25 (50.00) | | 25 (50.00) | 25 (50.00) | |
| ***Functioning of Cooperatives*** | | | | | | |
| Satisfied | 4 (57.14) | 3 (42.86) | | 8 (42.11) | 11 (57.89) | |
| Dissatisfied | 21 (48.84) | 22 (51.16) | >0.05 | 17 (54.84) | 14 (45.16) | >0.05 |
| Total | 25 (50.00) | 25 (50.00) | | 25 (50.00) | 25 (50.00) | |
| ***Community Development Through Cooperatives*** | | | | | | |
| Self-Employment | 12 (60.00) | 8 (40.00) | | 12 (50.00) | 12 (50.00) | |
| Holding Price Line | 6 (46.67) | 7 (53.85) | >0.05 | 7 (46.67) | 8 (53.33) | >0.05 |
| Mutual Cooperation | 7 (41.18) | 10 (58.82) | | 6 (54.55) | 5 (45.45) | |
| Total | 25 (50.00) | 25 (50.00) | | 25 (50.00) | 25 (50.00) | |

Row percentage in parentheses

officials and is followed by 41.18 per cent urban male officials. About 54.55 per cent urban females and 45.45 per cent rural female officials also perceive the same concept.

However, insignificant differences ($p>0.05$) are seen between urban and rural male officials of Cooperative Department regarding the goal fulfilled by Cooperatives, achievement of social aim by Cooperatives, functioning of Cooperatives and community development through Cooperatives. The insignificant differences are also observed among the urban and rural female officials ($p>0.05$) as per the achievement of social aim by Cooperatives, functioning of Cooperatives and community development through Cooperatives. But a highly significant difference ($p<0.01$) is found between rural and urban female officials of Cooperative Department regarding the goals achieved by Cooperative Movement in Kashmir.

### Perception of Cooperative Personnel towards Relations between Cooperative Administration and Cooperative Management (Table 4.12)

The highest per centage of rural male (63.64 per cent) and female (61.90 per cent) officials are satisfied by the coordination between Cooperative Administration and Cooperative Management. While 36.36 per cent urban male and 38.10 per cent urban female officials are also satisfied by such coordination. But, 58.62 and urban female officials of Cooperative Department are dissatisfied by the coordination obtained between administration and Cooperatives, followed by 53.85 urban male officials, 46.15 per cent rural male officials and 41.38 per cent rural female officials.

Among the respondents assuming non-coordination between administration and management of Cooperatives, mainly 81.82 per cent urban male officials blame the communication gap between the two levels. About 66.67 per cent urban females, followed by 33.33 per cent rural females and 18.18 per cent rural male officials also feel that there is a communication gap between the two levels. Lost of confidence on the management of Cooperatives is perceived by urban male and female officials by 55.56 per cents respectively; and rural male and female officials by 44.44 per cents respectively. The management of Cooperatives has also lost its faith on administration according to majority of rural male officials (63.16 per cent), followed by equal per centage of urban and rural female officials (50 per cents respectively) and urban male officials (36.84 per cent) of the Cooperative Department.

Financial crunch in the State is justified by 52.94 per cent rural female officials for avoidance of financial help to Women Cooperatives, followed by 47.06 per cent urban females and 25 per cent rural male officials. However, 60 per cent urban female officials are blaming huge outstanding against the Members of Cooperatives and this is followed by 59.09 per cent rural male officials. An almost equal per centage of urban male (40.91 per cent) and rural female (40 per cent) officials are also claiming huge outstanding against the Members of Cooperatives. This is considered true by 66.67 per cent rural males, followed by 61.54 per cent rural females, 38.46 per cent urban females and finally by 33.33 per cent urban male officials/officers.

The differences between urban and rural male as well as female officials are not found significant (p>0.05) regarding coordination between administration and management, reasons for dissatisfactory coordination and avoidance of financial assistance to Cooperatives.

**Table 4.12**

**Perception of Cooperative Personnel Towards Relations between Cooperative Administration and Cooperative Management**

*(n = 100)*

| *Variables* | *Male* | | | *Female* | | *p-Value* |
|---|---|---|---|---|---|---|
| | *Urban* | *Rural* | *p-Value* | *Urban* | *Rural* | |
| ***Coordination Between Administration and Cooperatives*** | | | | | | |
| Satisfied | 4 (36.36) | 7 (63.64) | | 8 (38.10) | 13 (61.90) | |
| Dissatisfied | 21 (53.85) | 18 (46.15) | >0.05 | 17 (58.62) | 12 (41.38) | >0.05 |
| Total | 25 (50.00) | 25 (50.00) | | 25 (50.00) | 25 (50.00) | |
| ***Reason for Dissatisfaction*** | | | | | | |
| Communication Gap | 9 (81.82) | 2 (18.18) | | 8 (66.67) | 4 (33.33) | |

*Contd...*

(n = 100)

| Variables | Male | | | Female | | p-Value |
|---|---|---|---|---|---|---|
| | Urban | Rural | p-Value | Urban | Rural | |
| Lack of Confidence by Administration | 5 (55.56) | 4 (44.44) | <0.05 | 5 (55.56) | 4 (44.44) | >0.05 |
| Lack of Confidence by Cooperatives | 7 (36.84) | 12 (63.16) | | 4 (50.00) | 4 (50.00) | |
| Total | 21 (53.00) | 18 (46.15) | | 17 (58.62) | 12 (41.38) | |
| ***Avoidance of Financial Assistance*** | | | | | | |
| Financial Crunch | 12 (75.00) | 4 (25.00) | | 8 (47.06) | 9 (52.94) | |
| Huge Outstanding | 9 (40.91) | 13 (59.09) | <0.05 | 12 (60.00) | 8 (40.00) | >0.05 |
| Lack of Coordination | 4 (33.33) | 8 (66.67) | | 5 (38.46) | 8 (61.54) | |
| Total | 25 (50.00) | 25 (50.00) | | 25 (50.00) | 25 (50.00) | |

Row percentage in parentheses.

Basically, the purpose of Cooperation is to evolve a scheme of community organisation which touches upon all aspects of life within the rural economy in particular. It has become a primary means of raising the level of productivity, extending improvements in technology and expanding employments so as to ensure the basic necessities for every member of the community. The Cooperative form of organisation has advantages which neither the system of private enterprise nor that of state ownership can match. As an instrument of democratic planning, combining initiative, mutual benefit and social purpose, there is a vast field for the application of cooperation in the economic uplift of people. Such perception is more common among urban officials than rural officials. *Naresh* (1982) also observed Cooperatives as effective organisation in achieving rapid economic growth and reduction of disparity in income and wealth.

Majority of officials in rural areas consider promotion of mutual cooperation among Members, as the main goal of Cooperatives. Cooperative organisations are the voluntary associations of persons, in the sense that people can become its Members and they can leave it at their own will. No one is compelled to become or continue its membership. Persons having common interests and desirous of pursuing a common objective can form themselves into a Cooperative. That is why officials consider mutual cooperation as a main aim of Cooperative sector.

But there are few officials of Cooperative Department, under study, who think that Cooperatives have lost its importance in the present century and the establishment of Cooperatives have now become only a formality to expand the Cooperative Movement in Kashmir. Nevertheless, Cooperatives have been playing an important role in the social uplift of people. Such perception is mainly held by rural female officials and urban male officials.

The National Seminar on Cooperatives and population problems held in New Delhi in 1974, considered Cooperatives as an effective instrument for dealing with the problems of population. There is no doubt that Cooperative Organisation enjoys certain apparent advantages over any other agency in this respect. *Swaminathan* (1991) also suggested a programme for the organisation of 'Child Survival and Development Cooperatives' to achieve population stabilisation, promote female literacy and mother care, ensure child nutrition, health care and education, and promote environmental sanitation.

The highest number of officials, in the study, is dissatisfied with the functioning of Cooperatives in Kashmir. The perceptions of male and female officials, in this respect, are almost same. But there is a close link between cooperation and community development. Cooperative schools, Cooperative Agricultural Organisations, Cooperative Hospitals and Health Centres, Cooperative Consumer Stores, Milk-supply Cooperatives and Labour Cooperatives—all these can serve the objectives under-lying the Community Development Programme and they can contribute to the improved living standards of the community as a whole. This means, in other words, the Community Development Programme gets consolidated by the formation of Cooperatives and these both together go a long way in satisfying the socio-economic needs of the society.

*Kamat* (1974) accepted that since the Community Development Programme is concerned with every aspect of rural life, it is not only inevitable but desirable that Cooperatives should involve themselves in different lines of business as far as possible. He further stressed that *Panchayati Raj* should always bear in mind that the promotional role to be played by the local government should always help development and growth of the Cooperative Sector on sound lines.

The officials of Cooperative Department, under study, also think that Community Development Programmes can be held through Cooperatives. Female officials think the Cooperatives promote community development by providing self-employment opportunities to people. Officials, in rural and urban areas, consider Cooperative as best means to hold the price line and ensure mutual cooperation among Members of Cooperatives. There is hardly any competition in rural areas to hold the price line at reasonable level. A vast number of consumer sections in the rural areas fall below the poverty line and their educational background and bargaining power is very poor. Hence in terms of charging undue profits, this chunk of our population is badly exploited. In the cities also, unless the Cooperative Stores are run side by side with the private trade especially in the matter of selling essential commodities of life, the labour class and other poor sections of population who are educationally backward, are prone to be cheated by the unscrupulous element in the private trade. The Cooperative institutions can play an important role in holding the price line by supplying essential goods at the door step of each and every segment of population. *Sharma* (1991) emphasised on the establishment of 'Fair Price Shops', through the network of Cooperative institutions. He stressed that an effective beginning can be made to check the undue profit being made by the middlemen which is the order of the day in the entire length and breadth of our country through the network of Cooperative institutions.

The highest number of rural male and female officials is dissatisfied by the coordination between Cooperative administration and Cooperative management. They feel that there is a communication gap between these two levels. The directions and guidelines of administration are not being properly delivered to the management of Cooperatives, which creates confusion and conflicts between management and administration. Cooperatives are in constant need of information, instruction, opinions and counselling from the authority. Existence of business rules, processes and procedures of work, division of power and functions, compensation and availability of various facilities in written form and their understanding are vital areas in communicating with Cooperative management. Such communications are useful for Cooperative to ascertain their positions in the organisation in comparison to other organisations. Cooperatives set their plans and programmes, their work efficiency, productivity and performance. They know financial and non-financial benefits, safety and security of job, physical facilities available to do work, discipline, as well as rules and regulations of their Cooperatives so that they can accommodate themselves in them. Communication between authority and Cooperative management also paves the way for mutual understanding, better inter-personnel relationships, and setting right human behaviour at work by increasing their motivation, morale and changing the attitudes towards the work and organisation. The Cooperatives' formation universe is not confined only to Members, employees and beneficiaries; but it extends far beyond that. It operates under certain political, economic, social and cultural environment. These factors also affect its functioning considerably. The Government, suppliers, competing organisations, market and product, situation, pricing and a host of other factors have great bearing on its working. Hence, Cooperatives have to maintain information link with them.

The Department of Cooperatives in Kashmir has lost its confidence in the management of Cooperatives. On the other hand, the management of Cooperatives have also lost their faith on administration and this is accepted by majority of rural male officials. Most of the Cooperatives in Kashmir have not been provided any financial assistance during 1995-2000. The highest per centage of urban male officials justifies it by financial crunch in the state. Most of the urban female officials are claiming huge outstanding against the Members of Cooperatives, which is preventing further financial assistance to them. Lack of coordination between administration and management of Cooperatives is also responsible for the avoidance of financial assistance to Cooperatives.

## AUTHORITY ON COOPERATIVES

This includes control of State Government on the Cooperatives. The reasons of favour and un-favour by Cooperative personnel are also found along with the reasons of failure of most of the Cooperatives in Kashmir.

### Government Administration in Cooperatives (Table 4.13)

The highest per centage of rural male officials (58.82) favour Government control in Cooperatives. Such control is also favoured by 57.14 per cent urban females, followed by 42.86 per cent rural females and 41.18 per cent urban male officials. But majority of urban male officials (68.75 per cent) are against the favour of Government control on Cooperatives. Same perception is followed by 59.09 per cent rural females, 40.91 per cent urban females and 31.25 per cent rural male officials of Cooperative Department. Among the officials favouring the control of Government on Cooperatives, an equal per centage of rural male and urban female (60 per cents respectively) officials consider Government as a good guide for Cooperatives. The same perception is also held by equal per centage of urban male and rural female officials (40 per cents respectively). Similarly, 66.67 per cent urban female officials perceive that Government financial assistance provided to Cooperatives make it necessary to have its control on Cooperatives. Such reason for favour of Government control on Cooperatives is also put forth by 60 per cent urban male officials, followed by 40 per cent rural male and 33.33 per cent rural female officials. An equal per centage of rural male and female officials (66.67 per cents respectively) realise that Government membership in Cooperatives make it important to have an overlook on them. Same perception is also accepted by equal per centage of urban male and female (33.33 per cents respectively) officials.

Control of Government weakens the self reliance of Cooperatives according to 66.67 per cent urban female and 33.33 per cent rural female officials. Urban male officials also feel the same. Government control is considered undue hindrance by

**Table 4.13**
**Government Administration in Cooperatives**

*(n = 100)*

| *Variables* | *Male* | | | *Female* | | *p-Value* |
|---|---|---|---|---|---|---|
| | *Urban* | *Rural* | *p-Value* | *Urban* | *Rural* | |
| ***Government Control on Cooperatives*** | | | | | | |
| Favouring | 14 (41.18) | 20 (58.82) | | 16 (57.14) | 12 (42.86) | |
| Not-Favouring | 11 (68.75) | 5 (31.25) | >0.05 | 9 (40.91) | 13 (59.09) | >0.05 |
| Total | 25 (50.00) | 25 (50.00) | | 25 (50.00) | 25 (50.00) | |
| ***Reason for Favour*** | | | | | | |
| Guidance | 8 (40.00) | 12 (60.00) | | 6 (60.00) | 4 (40.00) | |
| Financial Assistance | 3 (60.00) | 2 (40.00) | | 8 (66.67) | 4 (33.33) | |
| Government Membership | 3 (33.33) | 6 (66.67) | >0.05 | 2 (33.33) | 4 (66.67) | >0.05 |
| Total | 14 (41.18) | 20 (58.82) | | 16 (57.14) | 12 (42.86) | |
| ***Reason for Unfavour*** | | | | | | |
| Weakens Self Reliance | 2 (100.00) | - | | 6 (66.67) | 3 (33.33) | |
| Undue Hindrance | 8 (88.89) | 1 (11.11) | <0.01 | 2 (40.00) | 3 (60.00) | >0.05 |
| Lacks Secrecy | 1 (20.00) | 4 (80.00) | | 1 (12.50) | 7 (87.50) | |
| Total | 11 (68.75) | 5 (31.25) | | 9 (40.91) | 13 (59.09) | |
| **Failure of Cooperatives** | | | | | | |
| Incompetent Management | 13 (46.43) | 15 (53.57) | | 14 (58.33) | 10 (41.67) | |
| Lack of Supervision | 7 (53.85) | 6 (46.15) | >0.05 | 4 (36.36) | 7 (63.64) | >0.05 |
| Limited Financial Resources | 5 (55.56) | 4 (44.44) | | 7 (46.67) | 8 (53.33) | |
| Total | 25 (50.00) | 25 (50.00) | | 25 (50.00) | 25 (50.00) | |

Row percentage in parentheses

88.89 per cent urban male officials, followed by 60 per cent rural females, 40 per cent urban females and only 11.11 per cent rural male officials. Government control also weakens secrecy of the Cooperatives as per 87.50 per cent rural female officials, followed by 80 per cent rural males, 20 per cent urban males and only 12.50 per cent urban females of Cooperative Department.

Incompetent management is considered the cause of failure of Cooperatives by 53.57 per cent rural male officials; and also by urban male and rural female officials by 46.43 per cent and 41.67 per cent respectively. Lack of supervision is blamed by 63.64 per cent rural female officials than 36.36 per cent urban female officials of the department. The urban male officials have also admitted the same by 53.85 per cent than 46.15 per cent by rural male officials. But 55.56 per cent urban male officials and 53.33 per cent rural male officials are blaming limited financial resources of Cooperatives as a basic factor responsible for its failure. Around 46.67 per cent urban female and 44.44 per cent rural male official also consider limited financial resource as a cause of failure of most of the Cooperatives. There are no significant differences ($p>0.05$) between urban and rural; male and female officials; as per their perception towards Government control on Cooperatives, reasons of favour or un-favour for such control and failure of Cooperatives in Kashmir.

State Government is interfering in the internal managements of Cooperatives. Jammu and Kashmir Government has also appointed administrator in key institutions. In this regard, Jammu and Kashmir Cooperative Societies Act 1960 is very strict giving most of the powers to the Cooperative Department. These powers are favoured by highest per centage of rural male officials and urban female officials. They favour such powers because Government provides guidance to Cooperatives for its efficient functioning. Most of the urban female officials perceive that Government financial assistance provided to Cooperatives, make it necessary to have its control on Cooperatives. Government implements various schemes and programmes through Cooperatives, for the economic uplift of its Members. That is why majority of rural officials realise that Government's membership in Cooperatives make it important to have an overlook on them. Being the Member of Cooperatives, their activities are regulated by Government even though they are voluntary in character.

But there is considerable per centage of officials, who do not favour the control of Government on Cooperatives. They think that it weakens the self-reliance of Cooperatives. Undue hindrances in the affairs of Cooperatives is the another factor for un-favouring of Government control on Cooperatives. An over-administered interference reduces the flexibility of day-to-day operations. Sometimes, political and other vested interests also dominate the working of Coöperatives. It lacks the secrecy of Cooperatives. As a corporate body, a Cooperative is required to submit its reports and accounts to the Registrar of Cooperatives. As a result, full disclosure and publicity of affairs make it very difficult to preserve the secrets of Cooperative business. That is why; such undue hindrance in the affairs of Cooperatives is opposed by most of the rural officials. *Kurien* (1993) also suggest the inclusion of Cooperative Societies under the Companies Act, so that they may get working freedom.

Most of the Cooperatives in Srinagar city have proven a failure as per the study conducted by *Jan* in 1999. Present study also shows the same results. Majority of urban female officials are blaming incompetent management of Cooperatives. At the primary level, a Cooperative generally cannot afford to employ professional managers. It has to depend on honorary managerial service by Members who often lack specialized training and experience in management. That is why; incompetent management is considered the cause of failure of Cooperatives by most of the rural male officials. Lack of supervision is another cause of failure of most of the Cooperatives. Cooperative officials being less enthusiastic in their work have resulted in delays of decision-making in Cooperatives. Such lack of supervision is blamed by most of the rural female officials. Moreover, as Members are drawn from a particular locality and they usually have limited means, the capital which a Cooperative can raise is very limited. Restrictions on dividend and the principle of 'one-member-one-vote' discourage large investment by Members. This has proven another cause of failure of Cooperatives in Kashmir.

## Suggested Strategy

The various strategies have been suggested by Cooperative personnel for the promotion of Cooperative Movement in the State. The revival of existing Cooperatives as well as establishment of new Cooperatives is put under analysis.

### Strategy for the Promotion of Cooperatives (Table 4.14)

Most of the rural male officials (75 per cent) are suggesting the strategy of organising new Cooperatives in Kashmir. The same view is also perceived by 57.14 per cent rural females, followed by 42.86 per cent urban females and 25 per cent urban male officials. About 68.42 per cent urban male officials and 58.82 per cent urban female officials think that the existing poor Cooperatives need to be revived. This perception is followed by 41.18 per cent rural female officials and 31.58 per cent rural male officials in Kashmir. But the fact is that Cooperative Movement can be promoted by the organisation of new Cooperatives as well as by revival of existing Cooperatives. Almost equal per centage of rural male (66.52 per cent) and rural female (53.85 per cent) are holding this view. Such strategy is also favoured by 46.15 per cent urban females and 43.48 per cent urban male officials.

For the organisation of new Cooperatives in Kashmir, 66.67 per cent urban male officials and 62.50 per cent rural female officials stress on the enforcement of new act in Kashmir i.e. Jammu and Kashmir Self Reliant Cooperatives Act, 1999. The emphasis is also given on same act by 37.50 per cent urban females and 33.33 per cent rural male officials. People should be motivated to join Cooperatives according to equal per centage of rural and urban male officials (50 per cents respectively). About 61.54 per cent urban female and 38.46 per cent rural female officials also consider motivation to people as an important factor to boost Cooperative Movement in Kashmir. Cooperative Education to people is favoured by 68.18 per cent rural male and 66.67 per cent rural female officials, followed by 33.33 per cent urban female and 31.82 per cent urban male officials.

For the revival of the Cooperatives, amalgamation is considered a favourable step by 75 per cent urban male officials, followed by 57.14 per cent urban female officials, 42.86 per cent rural female officials and 25 per cent rural male officials. Financial assistance should also been provided to poor Cooperatives as per equal per centage of urban and rural female officials (50 per cents respectively), followed by 57.14 per cent urban male and 42.86 per cent rural male officials. The highest per centage of rural male officials i.e.75 per cent stress on the exposition of new technology to Members of Cooperatives. About 52.63 per

**Table 4.14**
**Strategy for the Promotion of Cooperatives**

*(n = 100)*

| *Variables* | *Male* | | | *Female* | | *p-Value* |
|---|---|---|---|---|---|---|
| | *Urban* | *Rural* | *p-Value* | *Urban* | *Rural* | |
| ***Strategy*** | | | | | | |
| Organisation of New Cooperatives | 2 (25.00) | 6 (75.00) | | 3 (42.86) | 4 (57.14) | |
| Revival of Existing Cooperatives | 13 (68.42) | 6 (31.58) | >0.05 | 10 (58.82) | 7 (41.18) | >0.05 |
| Both | 10 (43.48) | 13 (56.52) | | 12 (46.15) | 14 (53.85) | |
| Total | 25 (50.00) | 25 (50.00) | | 25 (50.00) | 25 (50.00) | |
| ***Strategy for New Organisation*** | | | | | | |
| Enforcement of New Act | 2 (66.67) | 1 (33.33) | | 3 (37.50) | 5 (62.50) | |
| Motivation | 3 (50.00) | 3 (50.00) | >0.05 | 8 (61.54) | 5 (38.46) | >0.05 |
| Cooperative Education | 7 (31.82) | 15 (68.18) | | 4 (33.33) | 8 (66.67) | |
| Total | 12 (29.26) | 29 (70.73) | | 15 (45.45) | 18 (54.54) | |
| ***Strategy for Revival*** | | | | | | |
| Amalgamation | 3 (75.00) | 1 (25.00) | | 4 (57.14) | 3 (42.86) | |
| Financial Assistance | 4 (57.14) | 3 (42.86) | | 2 (50.00) | 2 (50.00) | |
| New Technology | 2 (25.00) | 6 (75.00) | >0.05 | 10 (52.63) | 9 (47.37) | >0.05 |
| Continuous and Qualitative Supply | 14 (60.87) | 9 (39.13) | | 6 (46.15) | 7 (53.85) | |
| Total | 23 (54.76) | 19 (45.23) | | 22 (51.16) | 21 (48.83) | |

Row percentage in parentheses.

cent urban female officials also agree that Members of Cooperatives should be continuously exposed to new technology and business methods. The rural female officials by 47.37 per cent and urban male officials by 25 per cent also perceive the same view. About 60.87 per cent urban male officials, followed by 53.85 per cent rural female officials, 46.15 per cent urban female officials and 39.13 per cent rural male officials, stress that the activities or services for Cooperatives should be chosen on sound socio-economic reasons. Insignificant differences ($p>0.05$) are found between urban and rural; male as well as female officials; regarding strategy adopted for promotion of Cooperatives, including strategies for revival of Cooperative Societies and organisation of new Cooperatives.

Cooperatives are said to be poor man's organisations. The concept of Cooperation has originated out of the needs of the poor people, who because of their poor economic condition cannot resist or stop their exploitation by other stronger groups/individuals in the society and, therefore, need a support of institutional arrangement. The officials of Cooperative Department in Kashmir have suggested reviving the Cooperative Movement in Kashmir. Few officials are also favouring the organisation of new Cooperatives. But most of the officials have suggested revival as well as organisation of new Cooperatives simultaneously, in Kashmir.

For the organisation of new Cooperatives, most of the urban male officials and rural female officials stress on the enforcement of new Act in Kashmir, i.e. Jammu and Kashmir Self-Reliant Cooperatives Act, 1999. The Cooperative laws have been playing an important role to shape Cooperatives in Kashmir. These laws have been amended from time and again to meet the emerging need/situations, e.g. Jammu and Kashmir Cooperative Societies Act 1913; Jammu and Kashmir Cooperative Societies Act 1960 and Rules 1968; Jammu and Kashmir Cooperative Societies Act 1989; and now Jammu and Kashmir Self-Reliant Cooperatives Act, 1999. These amendments have been criticised favourably and unfavourably. An argument, of those who favour amendment, bring them before legislatures for approval and support them, so as to prove that these are necessary in the interest of sound and efficient functioning of the Cooperatives and eliminate mismanagement. Further, wherever, Cooperative do not voluntarily agree to admit to membership those who need and can use their services, provide them services and give share in the management to people who belong to weaker sections, are forced to do so through the process of Cooperative law. *Deshmukh* (1986) suggested that the Cooperative law need a radical change by incorporation of separate chapter on Cooperatives of weaker sections and by suitably amending general provisions giving favourable and special treatment to weaker section members in other societies. *Shah* (1990) also emphasised that the provisions of Cooperative law should go to strengthen the spirit of cooperation and should ensure observance of the Cooperative principles in the easiest form by the Members. Various Cooperative laws in Kashmir excluding Jammu and Kashmir Self-Reliant Cooperatives Act, 1999, have done infinite harm to the growth of the Cooperative Movement in the sense that these laws have not allowed the people to learn how to do things themselves, how to develop a spirit of self-reliance and self-dependence and even to make mistakes if they would have to make mistakes.

The Self-Reliant Act of the state can provide necessary frame to this effect by detecting the provisions which mitigate against the democratic character and autonomy of Cooperatives. People need to be motivated to join the Cooperatives under the new act. This conception is held mainly by male officials in rural as well as in urban areas and female officials in urban areas. Cooperatives under previous acts have enjoyed little public confidence due to political conduct of office bearers and domination by a selected group of individuals.

However, majority of officials in rural areas stress on Cooperative Education to general masses, in order to establish new Cooperatives in Kashmir. The majority of Members of rural Cooperatives are uneducated and cannot properly understand the role they are expected to play in the management of their Cooperatives. Cooperative Member's Education Programme is the only answer to overcome this problem. Without Cooperative Education, the existence of vast and enlightened membership is not possible. In order to implement Cooperative Education, all Cooperatives should make provision for education of their Members, employees and of the general public.

For the revival of Cooperatives, amalgamation is considered a favourable step by majority of male officials in urban areas, followed by female officials in the same area. Financial assistance should also be provided to poor Cooperatives in order to improve their economic status and thereby convert them into viable Cooperative. Such view is held by an equal per centage of female officials in rural and urban areas; but the highest per centage of rural male officials stress on the exposition of new technology to Members of Cooperatives. The educational modules should be so designed to provide basic skills to Members in taking business decisions not only for themselves but for the Cooperatives. However, Cooperatives should also be ensured continuous and qualitative supply of inputs and services. Urban male and rural female officials mainly stress that activities or services for Cooperatives should be chosen on sound socio-economic reasons. Cooperatives should be provided qualitative supply of services and inputs so as to gain the public confidence.

5

# SCOPE FOR WOMEN COOPERATIVES

Women, through the participation in co-operatives, have been able to contribute to the economy of the household and improve their social situation within their communities. At grassroots levels, women have reported that participation in co-operatives have increased their self-esteem, assisted in earning the respect of their spouses, provided a degree of independence, provided access to education (functional literacy, health and nutrition, etc.) and training and has helped them to develop their leadership skills. In addition, co-operatives through access to income-generating activities and solidarity among members, have contributed to reducing violence against women. Participation of women in co-operatives has sensitized women in the importance of education and preventive health measures for their children.

The Cooperative Development Foundation (CDF) founded in 1982 promotes women's credit and thrift societies to empower women economically, socially and politically. In Andhra Pradesh the process is illustrated by the Mulukanoor and Narsampet cooperatives. CDF helped with group formation and enhancement of management skills. Preparation of bylaws, conduct of meetings, accounting and monitoring of loan repayments is done by the members themselves. External financing is discouraged. From 1991 to 1995, membership, savings and loans grew rapidly. New businesses were begun and old ones expanded. Membership of cooperatives enhanced credit-worthiness with other financial institutions. Because of cooperative membership, women now enjoy greater self-confidence, security and independence both within and outside the household. They have a sense of solidarity; caste divisions have weakened. Women now advise their husbands on crop decisions and their advice is sought on community matters such as sanitation. Greater political awareness has led to more participation in local elections.

There are numerous examples of how co-operatives have provided women access to income-generating activities which in turn have contributed to their economic and social development. The Self-Employed Women's Association (SEWA) in Gujarat, India, has organised women's co-operatives in artisan, land-based, live stock, trading and service sectors. These co-operatives are providing opportunities to unemployed women to obtain sustainable work and income. However, there are also examples of efforts undertaken by co-operatives to achieve equality, access to education, the respect of women's human rights and peace in terms of racial, religious, and cultural tolerance. For example, in India, co-operatives have provided women the possibility of coming together outside of their households, exchanging views and going to markets etc. Co-operative activities in addition to providing women an income of their own, have diminished the incidence of violence against women within the family by the factthat women are contributing this income to the family economy. Thrift and credit co-operatives have provided women a network of solidarity for protecting women against violence within the family. The same co-operatives have also contributed to the community by financing libraries for children and community centres, organizing recreational activities such as excursions for women. Women only co-operatives have made a difference in the lives of women in all these areas, but mixed co-operatives have also made substantial contributions. Thus, women's co-operatives should be encouraged.

Organising workers into co-operatives is a viable alternative given the reality of the self-employed. Within a co-operative, the worker is herself the owner, she owns means of production, and she directly links with the buyer or consumer eliminating the middleman and stands to gain or lose from her own work. Workers' co-operatives can counter the exploitation of middlemen, contractors, merchants and employers. Co-operatives are important source and means of alternative employment for workers.

Special programmes like 'Women in Agriculture' were launched in 1993 to train women farmers having small and marginal holdings in agriculture and its allied programmes like animal husbandry, dairying, horticulture, fisheries, bee-keeping etc. Since inception of the scheme, 210 Farm Women's Groups were constituted and training was provided to 4200 Farm Women in 7 selected States. Another programme called Training of Women in Agriculture with DANIDA and DUTCH assistance imparted training to 1.89 lakh women. To assist women in agro-based industries, 6866 Women's Cooperatives were formed with 100 per cent financial assistance from the Government. Under the programme of Operation Flood, rural women involved in dairy development on cooperative lines were given training in various activities relating to milk production, preservation and co-operative group formation. By the end of the Eighth Five Year Plan, 74,300 Dairy Co-operative Societies were organised. The percentage of women members has risen from about 14 per cent, a decade ago, to about 20 per cent in 1997 (approx. (19 lakh women members). By the end of 1996, there were 8,171 exclusive Women Cooperative Societies (non-credit) with a total membership of 6.93 lakh women. Women Milk Co-operatives were leading in many States especially in Haryana, Punjab, Uttar Pradesh, Rajasthan and Karnataka.

The Co-operative Sector in India has emerged as one of the largest in the world with 5.3 lakh societies of various types with a membership of 229 million. The scheme of Assistance to Women's Co-operatives, initiated during 1993-94, aims exclusively at the economic betterment of women, by focusing special attention on their needs and providing assistance in the form of assured work and income by organising co-operative societies for taking up economic activities in agro-based commercial/industrial sectors. Under the scheme, a total number of 850 women's co-operatives were benefited during the Ninth Plan. The Women Dairy Co-operative Leadership Programme nurtures leadership amongst women dairy farmers for economic and social empowerment besides ensuring their say in the governance of dairy cooperatives. Presently, the programme is being implemented by 39 milk unions and each milk union covers 25 to 30 village dairy co-operatives every year.

## Scope for Women cooperatives

This includes hold of women in economic activities, reasons of favour or un-favour for the organisation of independent Women Cooperatives, ways to provide encouragement to Kashmir women for joining the Cooperative Movement and the extent of voluntary participation by Cooperative officials/ officers, in an intervention programme which has been conducted under the present thesis.

### Women in Cooperatives (Table 5.1)

An equal percentage of male Cooperative officials in rural as well as in urban areas (50 per cents respectively) feel that women of Kashmir have a good hold on agricultural and consumer activities. While 68.75 per cent urban female officials and 31.25 per cent rural female officials also feel the same. But 76.92 per cent urban male and 23.08 per cent rural male officials hold the view that women of Kashmir are not the good participants in economic activities. Same view is held by 60 per cent urban female and 40 per cent rural female officials of Cooperative Department. Nevertheless, 75 per cent rural male, followed by 73.33 per cent urban female officials, 26.67 per cent rural females and 25 per cent urban male officials have found Kashmir women's good hold on consumer activities.

Nevertheless, 55 per cent urban male officials of Cooperative Department favour the organisation of independent

**Table 5.1**
**Women in Cooperatives**

*(n = 100)*

| *Variables* | *Male* | | | *Female* | | *p-Value* |
|---|---|---|---|---|---|---|
| | *Urban* | *Rural* | *p-Value* | *Urban* | *Rural* | |
| ***Hold of Women in Economic Activities*** | | | | | | |
| Consumer Activities | 4 (25.00) | 12 (75.00) | | 11 (73.33) | 4 (26.67) | |
| Agriculture Activities | 1 (100.00) | - | | - | 14 (100.00) | |
| Both | 10 (50.00) | 10 (50.00) | <0.05 | 11 (68.75) | 5 (31.25) | <0.01 |
| None | 10 (76.92) | 3 (23.08) | | 3 (60.00) | 2 (40.00) | |
| Total | 25 (50.00) | 25 (50.00) | | 25 (50.00) | 25 (50.00) | |
| ***Independent Women Cooperatives*** | | | | | | |
| Favouring | 22 (55.00) | 18 (45.00) | | 19 (48.72) | 20 (51.28) | |
| Not-Favouring | 3 (30.00) | 7 (70.00) | >0.05 | 6 (54.55) | 5 (45.45) | >0.05 |
| Total | 25 (50.00) | 25 (50.00) | | 25 (50.00) | 25 (50.00) | |
| ***Reason for Favour*** | | | | | | |
| Women Empowerment | 10 (47.62) | 11 (52.38) | | 7 (50.00) | 7 (50.00) | |
| Capable Cooperators | 10 (62.50) | 6 (37.50) | >0.05 | 12 (52.17) | 11 (47.83) | >0.05 |
| Other Reasons | 2 (66.67) | 1 (33.33) | | - | 2 (100.00) | |
| Total | 22 (55.00) | 18 (45.00) | | 19 (48.72) | 20 (51.28) | |
| ***Reason for Un-Favour*** | | | | | | |
| Incapability/ Bickering | - | 4 (100.00) | | 2 (50.00) | 2 (50.00) | |
| Inability Without Men's Assistance | 3 (50.00) | 3 (50.00) | >0.05 | 4 (57.14) | 3 (42.85) | >0.05 |
| Total | 3 (30.00) | 7 (70.00) | | 6 (54.54) | 5 (45.45) | |
| ***Encouragement to Women for Joining Cooperatives*** | | | | | | |
| Cooperative Education | 11 (57.89) | 8 (42.11) | | 4 (28.57) | 10 (71.43) | |
| Tours | 8 (47.06) | 9 (52.94) | >0.05 | 11 (64.71) | 6 (35.29) | >0.05 |
| Easier and Less Formalities | 6 (42.86) | 8 (57.14) | | 10 (52.63) | 9 (47.37) | |
| Total | 25 (50.00) | 25 (50.00) | | 25 (50.00) | 25 (50.00) | |
| ***Voluntary Participation in Intervention Programme to Women*** | | | | | | |
| Agreed | 25 (62.50) | 15 (37.50) | | 15 (60.00) | 10 (40.00) | |
| Disagreed | - | 10 (100.00) | <0.01 | 10 (40.00) | 15 (60.00) | >0.05 |
| Total | 25 (50.00) | 25 (50.00) | | 25 (50.00) | 25 (50.00) | |

Row percentage in parentheses.

Cooperatives for women, followed by 51.28 per cent rural females, 48.72 per cent urban females and 45 per cent rural male officials. Whereas, 70 per cent rural male officials, followed by 54.55 per cent urban female officials, 45.45 per cent rural female officials and 30 per cent urban male officials, are not in favour of independent Cooperatives for women.

Among the officials who favour Women Cooperatives, 52.38 per cent rural male and 47.62 per cent urban male officials consider Cooperatives as a best movement for women empowerment. In case of female officials, an equal per centage of them in rural and urban areas (50 per cents respectively) regard Cooperatives as best means for women empowerment. Most of the urban officials (62.50 per cent male and 52.17 per cent female officials) have found women Members of Cooperatives as capable Cooperators. About 47.83 per cent rural female officials and 37.50 per cent rural male officials also consider the same. While maximum per centage of rural female officials, followed by 66.67 per cent urban male and 33.33 per cent rural male officials favour establishment of Women Cooperatives for other reasons including economic uplift of Kashmir women, family welfare, social benefits, etc.

Among the officials who do not favour the exclusive establishment of Women Cooperatives, an equal percentage of female officials in rural and urban areas (50 per cents respectively) think that women are not capable to carry any economic activity. Similarly, an equal percentage of male officials of Cooperative Department in rural and urban areas (50 per cents respectively) think that women are unable to initiate any economic activity without men's assistance. The same views are also expressed by 57.14 per cent urban female officials and 42.85 per cent rural female officials.

Cooperative Education should be imparted particularly to women folk of Kashmir according to 71.43 per cent rural female officials and 57.89 per cent urban male officials. About 42.11 per cent male officials and 28.57 per cent urban female officials also favour Cooperative Education to women. Women Members of Kashmir should be taken on tours to those places where Women Cooperatives are running successfully, as per 64.71 per cent and 35.39 per cent female officials in rural and urban areas respectively. Men officials in rural and urban areas by 47.06 per cent and 52.94 per cent respectively have also recommended such tours for women. About 52.63 per cent urban female officials and 47.39 per cent rural female officials recommend easier and less formalities on part of the Cooperative Department, for the establishment of Women Cooperatives. About 57.14 per cent rural male officials, followed by 42.86 per cent urban male officials, have also suggested easier and less formalities for Women Cooperatives.

More than half i.e. 60 per cent female officials in urban areas and 40 per cent female officials in rural areas have agreed to join the proposed intervention programme under the present study. Moreover, 62.50 per cent urban male officials and 37.50 per cent rural male officials have also agreed to join the proposed intervention programme for the establishment of Women Cooperatives in Kashmir.

A highly significant difference is observed between urban and rural female officials ($p<0.01$) regarding their views towards the hold of women in economic activities of Kashmir. Similar highly significant difference is found between male officials in rural and urban areas regarding their voluntary participation in an intervention programme for the welfare of women in Kashmir. But insignificant differences are observed ($p>0.05$) between male officials residing in rural as well as urban areas regarding their views about the hold of women in economic activities in Kashmir, establishment of independent Women Cooperatives, reasons for favour or un-favour of Women Cooperatives and encouragement of women to join Cooperative Movement in Kashmir. Similar insignificant difference are observed between rural and urban female officials in respect of establishment of Women Cooperatives, reasons for favour or un-favour for establishment of such Women Cooperatives, encouragement to women for joining Cooperative Movement and the voluntary participation of female officials in an intervention programme for the organisation of Women Cooperatives in Kashmir.

## Existing Women Cooperatives (Table 5.2)

The existing percentage of Women Cooperatives is considered very meagre according to 61 per cent urban female officials and 38.71 per cent rural female officials. In case of male officials in urban and rural areas, 58.33 per cent and 41.67 per cent respectively have expressed their dissatisfaction for the less number of Women Cooperatives in Kashmir. Nevertheless,

**Table 5.2**
**Existing Women Cooperatives**

*(n = 100)*

| *Variables* | *Male* | | | *Female* | | *p-Value* |
|---|---|---|---|---|---|---|
| | *Urban* | *Rural* | *p-Value* | *Urban* | *Rural* | |
| ***Number of Women Cooperative*** | | | | | | |
| Satisfactory | 4 (28.57) | 10 (71.43) | | 6 (31.58) | 13 (68.42) | |
| Dissatisfactory | 21 (58.33) | 15 (41.67) | <0.05 | 19 (61.29) | 12 (38.71) | <0.05 |
| Total | 25 (50.00) | 25 (50.00) | | 25 (50.00) | 25 (50.00) | |
| ***Reason for Meagre Number*** | | | | | | |
| Poor Leadership | 1 (33.33) | 2 (66.67) | | 2 (100.00) | | |
| Lack of Efforts | 7 (70.00) | 3 (30.00) | | 8 (53.33) | 7 (46.67) | |
| Lack of Cooperative Awareness | 13 (56.52) | 10 (43.48) | >0.05 | 9 (64.29) | 5 (35.71) | >0.05 |
| Total | 21 (58.33) | 15 (41.67) | | 19 (61.29) | 12 (38.71) | |
| ***Performance of Women Cooperatives*** | | | | | | |
| Satisfactory | 11 (55.00) | 9 (45.00) | | 12 (50.00) | 12 (50.00) | |
| Dissatisfactory | 14 (46.67) | 16 (53.33) | >0.05 | 13 (50.00) | 13 (50.00) | >0.05 |
| Total | 25 (50.00) | 25 (50.00) | | 25 (50.00) | 25 (50.00) | |
| ***Reason for Poor Performance*** | | | | | | |
| Inactive membership | 2 (18.18) | 9 (81.82) | | 5 (55.56) | 4 (44.44) | |
| Lack of Knowledge | 18 (54.55) | 15 (45.45) | <0.05 | 13 (44.83) | 16 (55.17) | >0.05 |
| Lack of Financial Resources | 5 (83.33) | 1 (16.67) | | 7 (58.33) | 5 (41.67) | |
| Total | 25 (50.00) | 25 (50.00) | | 25 (50.00) | 25 (50.00) | |
| ***Avoidance of Training to Women Members*** | | | | | | |
| Poor Financial Position | 15 (65.22) | 8 (34.78) | | 8 (53.33) | 7 (46.67) | |
| No Cooperation | 3 (25.00) | 9 (75.00) | >0.05 | 11 (57.89) | 8 (42.11) | >0.05 |
| Lack of Efforts | 7 (46.67) | 8 (53.33) | | 6 (37.50) | 10 (62.50) | |
| Total | 25 (50.00) | 25 (50.00) | | 25 (50.00) | 25 (50.00) | |

Row percentage in parentheses.

71.43 per cent rural male, followed by 68.42 per cent rural female; and urban male and female Officials by 61.58 per cent and 28.57 per cent respectively, consider the present number of Women Cooperatives satisfactory for the Cooperative Movement in Kashmir.

The reason for such meagre participation of women in Cooperatives is the poor leadership qualities among women, according to 66.67 per cent rural male officials and 33.33 per cent urban male officials. But as per 70 per cent urban male officials and 30 per cent rural male officials, lack of efforts by Cooperative Department is the main cause of having meagre number of Women Cooperatives. Same view is held by 53.33 per cent urban females and 46.67 per cent rural female officials of Cooperative Department. Moreover, 64.29 per cent urban female officials consider the lack of Cooperative awareness among women, as a main cause of having less number of Women Cooperatives. Same concept is followed by 56.52 per cent urban males, 43.48 per cent rural males and 35.71 per cent rural female officials.

The functioning of existing Women Cooperatives is considered dissatisfactory as per female officials in urban and rural areas (50 per cents respectively). In case of male officials; 53.33 per cent in rural areas and 46.67 per cent in urban areas, are also dissatisfied by the performance of existing Women Cooperatives. On the contrary, the functioning of existing Cooperatives in Kashmir satisfies 55 per cent male officials in urban areas and 45 per cent male officials in rural areas. An equal percentage of female officials in rural and urban areas by 50 per cents respectively, are also satisfied by the performance of Women Cooperatives in Kashmir.

Among the officials, who are dissatisfied with Women Cooperatives, majority of rural male officials (81.82 per cent) blame inactive Membership of women for their poor performance in Cooperatives. About 55.56 per cent urban female officials and 44.44 per cent rural female officials hold same view. Moreover, 18.18 per cent urban male officials also consider inactive Membership of women as a main hurdle for the promotion of Women Cooperatives. Lack of knowledge is blamed by almost equal percentage of urban male and rural female officials by 54.55 per cent and 55.17 per cent respectively. About 45.45 per cent rural male and 44.83 per cent urban female officials have also found lack of knowledge about the functioning of Cooperatives among women Members. However, majority of urban male officials (83.33 per cent) have found lack of financial resources in Women Cooperatives. About 16.67 per cent male officials in rural areas also observe the problem of financial resources in Women Cooperatives. In case of officials, 58.33 per cent in urban areas and 41.67 per cent in rural areas consider poor financial resources in Women Cooperatives as their main cause of failure.

It is noteworthy to mention that there is only Women Cooperative in the Valley with two Members only that has been provided training regarding functioning of Cooperatives. Majority of male officials in urban areas (65.22 per cent) explain that due to poor financial position of the Cooperative Department, women Members are not being provided any training regarding their Cooperatives. Similarly, 53.33 per cent urban females and 46.67 per cent rural females also give the same explanation, followed by 34.78 per cent rural male officials. Non-cooperation on part of women Members is expressed by 75 per cent rural and 25 per cent urban male officials. Non-cooperation by women Members is also complained by urban and rural female officials (53.33 per cent and 46.67 per cent respectively). But 53.33 per cent rural male officials and 46.67 per cent urban male officials admit that very few efforts have been made by the Cooperative Department to conduct training programmes for women Members. Female officials in urban and rural areas (37.50 per cent and 62.50 per cent respectively) also assume the same view.

However, a significant difference is seen ($p<0.05$) among urban and rural male as well as female officials of Cooperative Department regarding their satisfaction for number of Women Cooperatives in Kashmir. Similar significant difference is also found among male officials in rural and urban areas regarding reasons for poor performance of Women Cooperatives. But insignificant differences ($p>0.05$) are observed between male and female officials in urban and rural areas regarding reasons for meagre number of Women Cooperatives, performance of Women Cooperatives and avoidance of training to women Members. Similar insignificant difference is also observed among female officials in urban and rural areas, for their reasons of poor performance by Women Cooperatives.

**Empowerment of Women Cooperatives (Table 5.3)**

An equal percentage of male Cooperative officials in urban and rural areas (50 per cents respectively) suggest less interference of Government in Women Cooperatives. About 58.33 per cent rural female officials and 41.67 per cent urban female officials also emphasise less interference of Government in Women Cooperatives. Exposition of new technology to Women Cooperatives is suggested by 60 per cent female officials in urban areas and 40 per cent female officials in rural areas. Similar suggestion is also given by 61.76 per cent urban male officials and 38.24 per cent rural male officials. But few officials also stress on adequate financial assistance to Women Cooperatives. About 83.33 per cent rural male officials and 16.67 per cent urban male officials think that financial assistance by Government is the best measure to improve their functioning. Same views are also expressed by 61.54 per cent rural female officials, followed by 38.45 per cent urban female officials.

Majority of male and female officials in urban areas (63.89 per cent and 52.94 per cent respectively) suggest the decentralisation of powers in Women Cooperatives. This is also favoured by 47.06 per cent rural female officials followed by 36.11 per cent rural male officials of Cooperative Department. But male officials in urban and rural areas by 14.29 per cent and 85.71 per cent respectively, do not favour decentralisation of powers in Women Cooperatives. Similar disfavour is also expressed by female officials in urban and rural areas by 43.75 per cent and 56.25 per cent respectively.

Reservation for women Members in managing committees is favoured by all urban male officials of the department. In case of female officials, 52.78 per cent in urban areas and 47.22

per cent in rural areas also favour reservation for Women Cooperatives. About 41.86 per cent male officials also favour the same. But 57.14 per cent rural female officials and 42.86 per cent urban female officials do not favour any reservation for women Members in the board or managing committees of their Cooperatives.

Insignificant differences are observed ($p>0.05$) among female officials in urban and rural areas regarding measures to be taken for improvement of Women Cooperatives, decentralisation of powers in Women Cooperatives and reservation for women Members in boards/managing committees. But a significant difference is found ($p<0.05$) between the male officials of urban and rural areas regarding the measures which should be taken to improve the conditions of existing Women Cooperatives. Moreover, highly significant differences ($p<0.01$) are also found between male officials in urban and rural areas, as per their views about decentralisation of powers in Women Cooperatives and reservation for women Members in boards/managing committees of Cooperatives.

**Table 5.3**
**Empowerment of Women Cooperatives**

*(n = 100)*

| *Variables* | *Male* | | | *Female* | | *p-Value* |
|---|---|---|---|---|---|---|
| | *Urban* | *Rural* | *p-Value* | *Urban* | *Rural* | |
| ***Measures to Improve Women Cooperatives*** | | | | | | |
| Less Interference | 2 (50.00) | 2 (50.00) | | 5 (41.67) | 7 (58.33) | |
| New Technology | 21 (61.76) | 13 (38.24) | | 15 (60.00) | 10 (40.00) | |
| Financial Assistance | 2 (16.67) | 10 (83.33) | <0.05 | 5 (38.45) | 8 (61.54) | >0.05 |
| Total | 25 (50.00) | 25 (50.00) | | 25 (50.00) | 25 (50.00) | |
| ***Decentralisation of Powers in Women Cooperatives*** | | | | | | |
| Favouring | 23 (63.89) | 13 (36.11) | | 18 (52.94) | 16 (47.06) | |
| Not-Favouring | 2 (14.29) | 12 (85.71) | <0.01 | 7 (43.75) | 9 (56.25) | >0.05 |
| Total | 25 (50.00) | 25 (50.00) | | 25 (50.00) | 25 (50.00) | |
| ***Reservation for Women in Managing Committees*** | | | | | | |
| Favouring | 25 (58.14) | 18 (41.86) | | 19 (52.78) | 17 (47.22) | |
| Not-Favouring | - | 7 (100.00) | <0.01 | 6 (42.86) | 8 (57.14) | >0.05 |
| Total | 25 (50.00) | 25 (50.00) | | 25 (50.00) | 25 (50.00) | |

Row percentage in parentheses.

## Scope for Women Cooperatives

There is a considerable scope for involvement of women in Cooperative activities. Women have a large say in consumer, milk-supply, weavers, fisheries and most of the agricultural activities. Their involvement in Cooperatives can be increased by promoting self-help groups exclusively of women and providing representation to them in boards/committees of Cooperatives.

Equal percentage of male officials in rural and urban areas feels that women of Kashmir have a good hold on agricultural as well as consumer activities. Majority of female officials in urban areas also feel the same. But some officials feel that women of Kashmir are not good participants in economic activities. It is noteworthy to mention here that the views hold by Cooperative officials do not necessarily represent the views of general Kashmir masses.

Almost all officials, be it male or female, in rural or urban areas, equally favour the organisation of independent Cooperatives for women. Very few officials are against the establishment of independent Cooperatives for women. Among those officials who favour independent Women Cooperatives, most of them considered it good for women empowerment in Kashmir. Women should be given equal opportunity for their self-development, control and access over resources and they in turn should take advantage of these opportunities and equip themselves to come into the main stream of development. This, in turn, will make them truly empowered, because a women empowered is a family empowered and families empowered is a country empowered.

Most of the urban officials have found women Members of Cooperatives as capable Cooperators. All rural female officials favour Women Cooperatives for their economic uplift, family welfare, social benefits etc. Among the officials, who do not favour the exclusive organisation of Women Cooperatives; an equal percentage of female officials in rural and urban areas and all rural male officials think that women alone are not capable to carry any economic activity. After a dramatic start, Women Cooperatives often become lifeless and paralysed with the passage of time. Bickering take place between women over petty issues, lack of unity and cohesion paves the way for the doom for Cooperative. Similarly, an equal percentage of male officials in urban and rural areas and majority of urban female officials think that women are unable to initiate any economic activity without men's assistance.

However, the officials who do not favour on independent establishment of Women Cooperatives do not mean that they do not recommend women's active participation in Cooperatives. Rather, such officials feel that women should work with shoulder to shoulder with men and the Cooperatives of Kashmir should have the combination of men's and women's active participation. In order to encourage women to join Cooperative sector, Cooperative Department should be imparted particularly to women folk of Kashmir. This view is expressed mainly by rural female and urban male officials.

Only Cooperative Education can prepare the Members to run their Cooperatives as service institutions on democratic lines. But unfortunately *Cooperative Education Programme* in Kashmir has not yet received the support which it deserves either from Government or from the movement itself. Responsibility of movement in this behalf is much more. The movement cannot and should not look the other way. Exclusive women education programmes should be initiated by Jammu and Kashmir Cooperative Union, in this regard. Women Members of Kashmir should be taken on tours to those places where Women Cooperatives are running successfully. This is recommended mainly by urban female and rural male officials. They recommend tours for women so that they can see and believe about the adoption of modern management practices in action in Cooperatives.

Moreover, women of Kashmir do not have an easy access to the formation of Cooperatives. This does not allow them to take up independent economic ventures through Cooperatives. They are unable to reach higher authority, particularly in rural areas. Rural women are reluctant to approach Registrar of Cooperatives, because they are unfamiliar with policies and cumbersome procedures of Cooperative Department. That is why almost half of the male and female officials in rural and urban areas stress on easier and less formalities, on part of Cooperative Department, for the establishment of Women Cooperatives.

For the encouragement of women to join Cooperatives, majority of officials have expressed their desire for voluntary participation in an intervention programme regarding involvement of Kashmir women in Cooperative Movement of the state. Such intervention has been supposed to be conducted under present thesis. In this connection, more than half of the officials in urban areas have mainly agreed to join the proposed intervention programme. All such officials have been noted for their participation in the programme and also invited through proper channel in the intervention programme mentioned in the later chapter of the present thesis. Majority of them, male officials in particular, are reported to be present in the intervention programme and convey their opinions, views and suggestions for the promotion of Women Cooperatives.

The existing number of Women Cooperatives in Kashmir is regarded satisfactory by some officials of Cooperatives, but majority of them consider this percentage very meagre. The reason for such meagre participation of women in Cooperatives has been their poor leadership quality. Urban female officials have mainly identified poor leadership qualities among women. *Prakash* (2000) also found that Cooperative standards and procedures restrict women's opportunities to be in leadership in Cooperatives. Some Cooperatives require that a Member must have served a certain number of years in an elected position before he/she can get into the board. Her practice discriminates against Members who have no or have limited prior experience in an elected position. Between women and men, in general, more women will be able to meet their requirement.

It is no secret in Kashmir that many persons with a will to serve the people and the community do not feel encouraged accepting the leadership of Cooperatives because of the bureaucratic interference and high-handedness of officials. If we have to make good use of leadership qualities of the Kashmir valley, it is necessary that the stifling atmosphere in which the women Cooperators are expected to work should be changed forthwith. For this, leadership development programmes should be conducted by Jammu and Kashmir Cooperative Union. Through such programmes, women should be prepared to assume leadership in Cooperatives. Seminars and group discussions should be organised so that women may grasp problems and prospects of Cooperative development. The women Members of Cooperatives should be convinced that they are the real owners of the Cooperatives. They belong to the Cooperatives and Cooperatives belong to them. In this connection, Cooperative Department has made very less efforts. According to most of the urban officials, lack of efforts by Cooperative Department is the main cause of having meagre number of Women Cooperatives. They also consider lack of Cooperative awareness as another cause of less participation of women in Cooperatives.

The functioning of existing Women Cooperatives is dissatisfactory according to an equal percentage of female officials in urban and rural areas. Rural officials mainly blame inactive membership of women as a main hurdle for the promotion of Women Cooperatives. The reason for vast inactive membership of women is their poverty. They have no land or no other productive assets. They have almost no security to offer. Thus, individually they are unable to avail the benefits of Cooperatives. But it would be better to organise self-help groups of inactive Members in Cooperative.

Lack of knowledge is another reason for poor performance of Women Cooperatives in Kashmir. This reason is given by almost equal percentage of male officials in urban areas and female officials in rural areas. Most of the male officials in urban areas also consider poor financial resources in Women Cooperatives as their main cause of failure.

The greatest challenge before Women Cooperatives is how to accrue economic benefits. Financial resources of Women Cooperatives should be increased by Government's intervention by way of investing its capital in women Cooperatives, in addition to providing them easy access to credit facilities, specialised loans and managerial and other subsidies. Increase in finance, by this way, will lead to increase in productivity of Women Cooperatives and thereby increase in the income of women. The increase in income will lead to increase in standard of living, housing and development of social and cultural values. The increase in income will also improve literacy level, health standards and family welfare activities. It is noteworthy to mention, that only one Women Cooperative, in this study, has two Members who have been provided training regarding efficient functioning in Cooperatives.

Majority of male officials in urban areas explain that due to poor financial position of the Cooperative Department, women Members are not being provided any training regarding Cooperatives. But rural male officials also feel that non-cooperation sought by women Members of Cooperatives is the hurdle in providing training to them; whereas, majority of female officials in rural areas admit that very few efforts have been made by the Cooperative Department to conduct training programmes for Women Cooperatives.

In order to improve the condition of existing Women Cooperatives, an equal percentage of male officials in urban and rural areas suggest less interference by Government in Cooperatives. Another measure suggested mainly by urban officials for improving the functioning of Women Cooperatives in Kashmir, is the exposition of new technology to Women Cooperatives. But most of the male officials in rural areas also stress on adequate financial assistance to Women Cooperatives. The officials also favour the decentralization of powers in Women Cooperatives under the Jammu and Kashmir Self-Reliant Cooperatives Act, 1999.

6

# COOPERATIVE SECTOR FOR ENTREPRENEURSHIP DEVELOPMENT

It is important to emphasize the need to challenge the current perception of women and men having equal access to opportunities, resources and leadership positions. However, the general lack of data on gender disparities makes it difficult to challenge this perception. The perceptions of these issues are different among women and men in the Cooperative Promotion Department and agricultural cooperatives. While women are aware of the prevalent gender bias in the attitudes of institutions, they do not articulate it publicly. It is important to have continuing discussion on gender issues related to education, health and vocational training so that positive changes can be brought about. Women's leadership in cooperatives must be supported by greater networking among women.

Women can bring new perspectives to co-operative management control systems and corporate governance. Research supports the fact that women have skills to offer in view of the changing challenges in working life. If women are given the opportunity to break the glass ceiling and advance to committees, boards and professional leadership positions, they can prove that strong, innovative and effective leaders do not come from the male mould alone. They can demonstrate that the command-and-control or top-to-bottom systems often associated with large, traditional co-operatives, can be replaced by a non-traditional leadership style which allows people to participate and contribute. This can increase co-operative chances to improve efficiency and success in the changing world. Diversity of leadership styles and a combination of the strengths and talents of women and men can change systems and routines within organisations and bring new competitiveness into the co-operative form of enterprise. The importance of gender equality should be recognised at Board level and gender issues should be on Board meeting agendas. It is important that resources, including management time, are made available to examine and progress the issue. As women are the ones who are disadvantaged mostly in gender issues, each co-operative should set itself targets for increasing opportunities for women. In a co-operative, the targets should cover both membership, with the intention of improving female representation on committees and at Board level, and employees; the latter to improve opportunities in the workplace including increasing the proportion of senior female managers. The targets should be achievable within a fixed period of time and should be made public to members and employees. Development programmes to achieve these targets need to be organised and progress has to be monitored and reported.

## Attitude Towards Cooperative Movement

The administration of scale regarding *'Attitudes of Cooperative Personnel towards Cooperative Movement'* (ACPCM) has brought forward the extent of positive attitudes of Cooperative officials towards the Cooperative Movement. Such positive attitudes of the officials/officers have been categorised under low, average and high attitudes. Officials possessing 25-50 per cent positive responses have been classified under *'Low'* attitudes; while positive responses with 50-70 per cent are put under *'Average'* attitudes and 75-1000 per cent positive attitudes are classified as *'High'* attitudes.

## Attitudes of Cooperative Personnel towards Cooperative Movement (Table 6.1)

The observation of table reveals that no male official in urban areas has low attitude towards Cooperative Movement in Kashmir. Only 25 per cent urban female officials have low attitudes towards Cooperatives but majority of rural female officials i.e. 75 per cent also have low attitudes regarding Cooperative Movement. An equal percentage of male officials in rural and urban areas (50 per cents respectively) have average attitudes towards Cooperatives. While 60.61 per cent rural females and 39.39 per cent females in urban areas, also possess average attitudes for the movement. As far as high attitudes are concerned, the highest percentage is represented by 84.62 per cent urban female officials, followed by 60 per cent urban male officials, 40 per cent rural males and 15.38 per cent rural female officials of Cooperative Department. A significant difference ($p<0.05$) is seen between rural and urban male officials regarding their attitudes towards Cooperative Movement. A highly significant difference is also found ($p<0.01$) between rural and urban female officials of Cooperative Department regarding their positive attitudes towards Cooperative Movement in Kashmir.

**Table 6.1**
**Attitude of Cooperative Personnel Towards Cooperative Movement**

*(n = 100)*

| | *Male* | | | *Female* | | |
|---|---|---|---|---|---|---|
| *Variables* | *Urban* | *Rural* | *p-Value* | *Urban* | *Rural* | *p-Value* |
| Low | - | 5 (100.00) | | 1 (25.00) | 3 (75.00) | |
| Average | 10 (50.00) | 10 (50.00) | | 13 (39.39) | 20 (60.61) | |
| High | 15 (60.00) | 10 (40.00) | <0.05 | 11 (84.62) | 2 (15.38) | <0.01 |
| Total | 25 (50.00) | 25 (50.00) | | 25 (50.00) | 25 (50.00) | |

Row percentage in parentheses.

## Attitude of Cooperative Personnel as per their Personal Characteristics (Table 6.2)

The table reveals that about 57.89 per cent early aged officials have average attitudes, followed by 26.32 per cent with high attitudes and 15.79 per cent with low attitudes for the movement. Middle aged officials have average attitudes by only 55.26 per cent, high attitudes by 39.47 per cent and low attitudes by 5.26 per cent. As far as late aged officials of Department are concerned; 60 per cent of them achieve high attitudes and 40 per cent achieve low attitudes. While no official under this group possess average attitudes towards Cooperatives. Overall, only 9 per cent officials have low attitudes, followed by 38 per cent achieving high attitudes and 53 per cent achieving average attitudes.

About 70.37 per cent low qualified officials obtain average attitudes, followed by 22.22 per cent high attitudes and 7.41 per cent with low attitudes. Same trend is true in case of medium qualified officials by 55.81 per cent average attitudes, 37.21 per cent high attitudes and 6.98 per cent low attitudes. In case of highly qualified officials, 53.33 per cent have high attitudes, followed by 33.33 per cent average attitudes and 13.33 per cent with low attitudes towards the movement.

As per the designation of Cooperative officials in Kashmir, 73.08 per cent have average attitudes, 15.38 per cent are with high attitudes and 11.54 per cent have low attitudes. About 62.16 per cent officials with medium designations are representing with average attitudes, 27.03 per cent with high attitudes and 10.81 per cent with low attitudes. In case of highly designated Cooperative officials; majority of them i.e. 64.86 per cent possess high attitudes towards Cooperatives, followed by 29.73 per cent with average attitudes and only 5.41 per cent with low attitudes. Officials with low salary have attitudes by 15.79 per cent, average attitudes by 73.69 per cent and high attitudes by 10.53 per cent. Average attitudes are also held by 61.90 per cent officials receiving medium salary, 30.95 per cent officials possessing high attitudes and 7.14 per cent with low attitudes at same level of salary. Officials receiving high amount of salary, represent 58.97 per cent high attitudes, followed by 33.33 per cent with average attitudes and only 7.69 per cent with low attitudes.

Officials, who have been working in the Department since 5 years, have achieved very high attitudes towards the movement by 53.33 per cent, followed by 40 per cent with average attitudes and 6.67 per cent with low attitudes. An almost equal percentage of officials have average attitudes in their service career between 5-10; and 10-15 years; by 73.33 per cent and 71.43 per cent respectively. Similarly, an almost equal percentage of officials have low and high attitudes in

**Table 6.2**

**Attitude of Cooperative Personnel as per their Personal Characteristics**

*(n = 100)*

| *Variables* | *Attitude* | | | *p-value* |
|---|---|---|---|---|
| | *Low* | *Average* | *High* | |
| ***Age*** | | | | |
| Early | 3 (15.79) | 11 (57.89) | 5 (26.32) | |
| Middle | 4 (5.26) | 42 (55.26) | 30 (39.47) | <0.05 |
| Late | 2 (40.00) | - | 3 (60.00) | |
| Total | 9 (9.00) | 53 (53.00) | 38 (38.00) | |
| ***Educational Status*** | | | | Less |
| 2(7.14) | 19 (70.37) | 6 (22.22) | | |
| Medium | 3 (6.98) | 24 (55.81) | 16 (37.21) | >0.05 |
| High | 4 (13.33) | 10 (33.33) | 16 (53.33) | |
| Total | 9 (9.00) | 53 (53.00) | 38 (38.00) | |
| ***Designation*** | | | | |
| Low | 3 (11.54) | 19 (73.08) | 4 (15.38) | |
| Medium | 4 (10.81) | 23 (62.16) | 10 (27.03) | <0.01 |
| High | 2 (5.41) | 11 (29.73) | 24 (64.86) | |
| Total | 9 (9.00) | 53 (53.00) | 38 (38.00) | |
| Salary | | | | |
| Low | 3 (15.79) | 14 (73.68) | 2 (10.53) | |
| Medium | 3 (7.14) | 26 (61.90) | 13 (30.95) | <0.01 |
| High | 3 (7.69) | 13 (33.33) | 23 (58.97) | |
| Total | 9 (9.00) | 53 (53.00) | 38 (38.00) | |
| ***Service Duration (Years)*** | | | | |
| Up to 5 | 2 (6.67) | 12 (40.00) | 16 (53.33) | |
| 5-10 | 3 (20.00) | 11 (73.33) | 1 (6.67) | |
| 10-15 | 1 (7.14) | 10 (71.43) | 3 (21.43) | >0.05 |
| 15-20 | 1 (5.56) | 10 (55.56) | 7 (38.89) | |
| More than 20 | 2 (8.70) | 10 (43.48) | 11 (47.83) | |
| Total | 9 (9.00) | 53 (53.00) | 38 (38.00) | |
| ***Job Satisfaction*** | | | | |
| Positive | 4 (8.00) | 21 (42.00) | 25 (50.00) | |
| Negative | 5 (10.00) | 32 (64.00) | 13 (26.00) | <0.05 |
| Total | 9 (9.00) | 53 (53.00) | 38 (38.00) | |

Row percentage in parentheses.

the cohorts of 5-10 years; and 10-15 years respectively; by 20 per cent and 21.43 per cent respectively. While only 6.67 per cent and 7.14 per cent officials in the cohort of 5-10 years; and 10-15 years respectively achieve high and low attitudes respectively. Among the officials with considerable service duration of 15-20 years; 55.56 per cent have average attitudes, followed by 38.89 per cent with high attitudes and only 5.56 per cent with low attitudes. Whereas, among those officials who are about to retire, achieving the service career of more than 20 years, have high and average attitudes by 47.83 per cent and 43.48 per cent respectively. But 8.70 per cent of them also possess low attitudes towards the Cooperative Movement in Kashmir.

About 50 per cent officials having adequate job satisfaction in Cooperative Department, achieve high attitudes. Moreover, 42 per cent and only 8 per cent of them also possess average and low attitudes respectively. Among the officials being dissatisfied with their jobs; 64 per cent have average attitudes, followed by 26 per cent with high attitudes and 10 per cent with low attitudes towards the Cooperative Movement.

Insignificant differences ($p>0.05$) are observed between the attitudes of officials as per their qualification and service duration. But significant differences are found ($p<0.05$) between the attitudes of officials; and their age and job satisfaction. Whereas, very high ($p<0.01$) significant differences are seen among the attitudes of officials as per their designation and salary.

### Chi-Square Analysis of the Scale Regarding Attitudes of Cooperative Personnel towards Cooperative Movement—ACPCM (Table 6.3)

The chi- square analysis of the scale according to *age*, *qualification, designation* and *salary* of the officials are studied at the degree of freedom at 2; while *service duration* of officials has 4 degrees of freedom; and *job satisfaction* of officials has 1 degree of freedom. The analysis has shown that the age of the Cooperative officials has an insignificant difference ($p>0.05$) with all the 22 items of the scale. The qualification of the officials is seen significant ($p<0.05$) with

**Table 6.3**
**Chi-Square Analysis of Scale Regarding 'Attitude of Cooperative Personnel Towards Cooperative Movement' (ACPCM)**

*(n = 100)*

| | Chi-Square Analysis ($\chi^2$) | | | | | |
|---|---|---|---|---|---|---|
| *Parameters of ACPCM* | *Age* | *Educational Status* | *Designation* | *Salary* | *Service Duration* | *Job Satisfaction* |
| Degree of Freedom (d.f) | 2 | 2 | 2 | 2 | 4 | 1 |
| Cooperative Movement for the Uplift of Poor People | 3.92 | 0.10 | 1.40 | 0.42 | 5.71 | 3.34 |
| Promotion of Mutual Cooperation and Community Development through Cooperatives | 4.91 | 2.53 | 1.87 | 0.12 | 8.36 | 0.05 |
| Self Reliance among People through Cooperatives | 2.61 | 3.32 | 4.27 | 6.89* | 12.69** | 0.43 |
| Self-Employment Opportunities through Cooperatives | 2.27 | 0.29 | 3.57 | 2.42 | 5.23 | 1.77 |
| Easy Formation of Cooperatives | 3.03 | 3.51 | 6.61* | 4.75 | 3.45 | 0.36 |
| PACS being Beneficial for Rural People | 1.53 | 2.84 | 3.21 | 2.74 | 11.56* | 0.05 |
| Dissemination of Cooperative Education through National Cooperative Union of India and State Cooperative Union | 0.78 | 0.19 | 1.30 | 2.72 | 6.54 | 0.05 |
| Women Participation in Cooperatives to be Increased | 0.87 | 3.08 | 1.85 | 2.32 | 10.95* | 0.33 |
| Organisation of Self-Help Groups of Inactive Members | 1.58 | 2.19 | 4.05 | 3.71 | 7.06 | 0.06 |
| Continuous and Qualitative Supply of Inputs through Cooperatives | 1.66 | 2.16 | 2.24 | 3.41 | 2.02 | 3.50 |
| Dissemination of Cooperative Education to Masses | 1.08 | 1.46 | 2.15 | 1.60 | 3.00 | 2.83 |
| Financial Assistance to Cooperatives | 1.55 | 0.07 | 0.24 | 0.09 | 2.43 | 2.15 |

*Contd...*

(n = 100)

| Parameters of ACPCM | Chi-Square Analysis ($\chi^2$) | | | | | |
|---|---|---|---|---|---|---|
| | Age | Educational Status | Designation | Salary | Service Duration | Job Satisfaction |
| Winding up of Non-Functional Cooperatives | 0.40 | 6.77* | 6.61* | 5.60 | 7.49 | 4.90* |
| Amalgamation of Cooperatives Proven Unsuccessful for Cooperatives | 1.16 | 0.34 | 3.95 | 1.80 | 1.41 | 0.40 |
| Elimination of Government Control on Cooperatives | 0.71 | 0.10 | 5.35 | 5.96* | 1.46 | 2.06 |
| Members Taken to Study Tours and Exposed to New Technology | 2.37 | 1.32 | 8.07** | 2.78 | 7.60 | 3.84* |
| Incompetent Management being the Cause of Failure for Cooperatives | 2.06 | 6.73* | 12.54** | 16.54** | 7.14 | 1.41 |
| Elimination of One-Member from One-Family for Cooperatives | 1.55 | 4.72 | 5.90* | 0.98 | 1.31 | 3.25 |
| Mutual Rivalries Making Cooperatives Lifeless and Paralysed | 4.23 | 4.22 | 7.62* | 2.84 | 2.02 | 0.36 |
| People being Less Motivated to Join Cooperative Movement | 0.15 | 1.15 | 5.56 | 0.08 | 4.52 | 0.06 |
| Misappropriation of Funds Weakening the Cooperative Movement | 0.79 | 1.77 | 2.06 | 3.01 | 6.04 | 0.87 |
| Full disclosure of affairs Preventing the Secrecy of Cooperatives | 3.11 | 1.76 | 0.63 | 2.19 | 2.14 | 0.36 |

*Significant at 0.05 level.
**Significant at 0.01 level.

only 2 items of the scale namely the winding up of the poor Cooperatives in Kashmir and incompetent management being responsible for the weak functioning of Cooperatives in Kashmir. Similar significant differences are seen as per the designation of officials regarding their attitudes towards winding up of poor Cooperatives, the principle of one-family one-Member in Cooperatives, and mutual rivalries being responsible for the slow functioning of Cooperatives. Very highly significant differences ($p<0.01$) are seen among the designation of officials with their recommendations for study tour for Members, along with their exposition to new technology and incompetent management of Cooperatives weakening the Cooperative Movement in Kashmir. The incompetent management in Cooperatives has also shown similar highly significant difference between the salaries of officials. Moreover, significant difference is seen ($p<0.05$) between the salary of officials and self reliance of Members through Cooperatives along the elimination of Government control on Cooperatives. As far as service duration of the officials are concerned; it has highly significant difference ($p<0.01$) with self reliance promoted through Cooperatives, and a significant difference ($p<0.05$) with Primary Agricultural Cooperative Societies being beneficial for rural people and increasing participation of women in Cooperatives. Nevertheless, job satisfaction of Cooperative personnel is found significant in its difference with winding up of poor Cooperatives, and Members exposed to new technology, along with Study tours. All other items of the scale have been found insignificant in its differences ($p>0.05$) with qualification, designation, salary, service duration and job satisfaction of Cooperative officials in Kashmir.

**Difference between Positive Attitudes towards Cooperative Movement with Various Factors (Table 6.4)**

The analysis of table reveals that the average of high attitudes is more among urban officials and male officials as compared to rural officials and female officials. These differences are also found statistically significant at 0.01 level. The mean score of attitudes is 16 among male officials and urban officials; whereas it is 14 among female officials and rural officials in the department. The percentage of these scores comprise of 72.72 per cent and 63.63 per cent respectively. This means that the officials of both sexes in rural and urban areas have average level of attitudes towards the Cooperative Movement in Kashmir. As far as the levels of attitudes are concerned, the mean score of low attitudes is 9; while average has scored

13 and high attitudes constitute 18. Thus, the average percentage of these levels constitutes 40.90 per cent at low level, 63.63 per cent at average level and 86.36 per cent at high level. But such difference between the levels of attitudes is not found significant (p>0.05).

**Table 6.4**
**Difference between Attitudes Towards Cooperative Movement and Various Factors (ANOVA)**

| *Positive Attitude Towards Cooperative Movement* | *Mean* | *S.E* | *F-Value* |
|---|---|---|---|
| ***Sex*** | | | |
| Male | 16.08 (50) | ± 0.48 | 6.04** |
| Female | 14.48 (50) | ± 0.43 | |
| Residence | | | |
| Urban | 16.34 (50) | ± 0.40 | 11.12** |
| Rural | 14.22 (50) | ± 0.48 | |
| ***Level of Attitude*** | | | |
| Low | 9.33 (9) | ± 0.23 | |
| Average | 13.92 (53) | ± 0.23 | 147.33 |
| High | 18.57 (38) | ± 0.28 | |

S.E denotes Standard Error of Mean
Sample in parentheses
** Significant at 0.01 level

## Attitudes of Male and Female Personal towards Cooperative Movement as per their Residence (Figure 6.1.1 to 6.1.22)

The diagrammatic representation of various statements regarding the attitudes of Cooperative personnel towards the Cooperative Movement in Kashmir reveals the average level of attitudes among male and female Cooperative personnel. Majority of rural male and urban female officials consider Cooperatives as sole organisation truly working for the uplift of poor people, best way to promote mutual cooperation among people and means of community development and self employment. They also realise that full disclosure of affairs has weakened the Cooperative Movement in Kashmir. An equal percentage of male and female officials, in rural and urban areas, stress on increased participation of women in Cooperatives and dissemination of Cooperative Education to masses. While the highest percentage of urban male and rural female officials feel that Cooperatives are helping people to become self reliant, Primary Agricultural Cooperative Societies are beneficial for rural people and National Cooperative Union of India; and Jammu and Kashmir Cooperative union are appropriate agencies to undertake the responsibility of dissemination of Cooperative Education. They explain that a Cooperative can be easily formed because of its easier formalities. They further suggest the organisation of self help groups of inactive Members in Cooperatives, continuous and qualitative supply of inputs to Cooperatives, financial assistance to Cooperatives, elimination of Government control on Cooperatives and exposition of Members to study tours and new technology. They also admit that the amalgamation has not proved beneficial for the success of Cooperatives, lack of competent management being the main cause of failure of most of the Cooperatives, mutual rivalries and misappropriation of funds weakening the Cooperatives and people being less motivated to join Cooperatives. They further suggest that non-functional Cooperatives in the State should be winded up and the law of one Cooperative Member from one family should be eliminated.

The study put forward that no male official in urban area has low attitude towards Cooperative Movement in Kashmir; while rural male officials with low attitudes towards Cooperative Movement comprise a considerable percentage. The average level of attitudes towards Cooperative Movement is equally contributed by male officials in rural and urban areas. But high level of attitudes for same are mainly held by urban male officials.

In case of female officials, low and average levels of attitudes are mainly held in rural areas; while urban female officials have mainly high level of attitudes towards Cooperative Movement in Kashmir. Officials with early and middle age have average level of attitudes towards Cooperatives; but later aged officials have very high attitudes towards the movement. Similarly, low and medium qualified

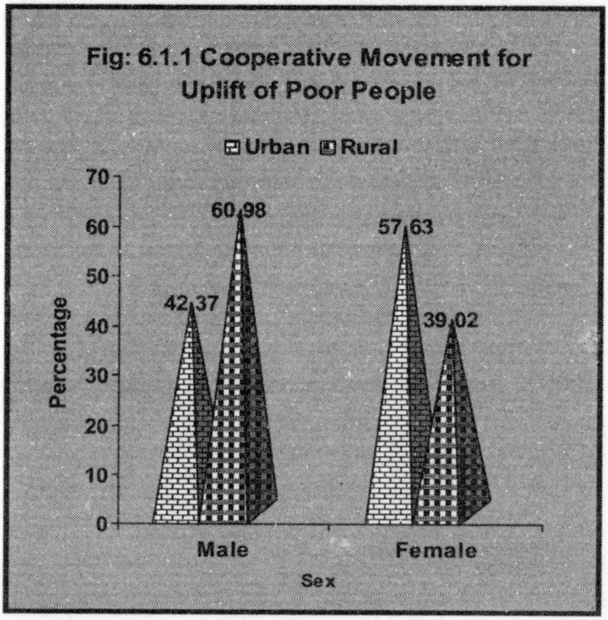


Fig: 6.1.1 Cooperative Movement for Uplift of Poor People

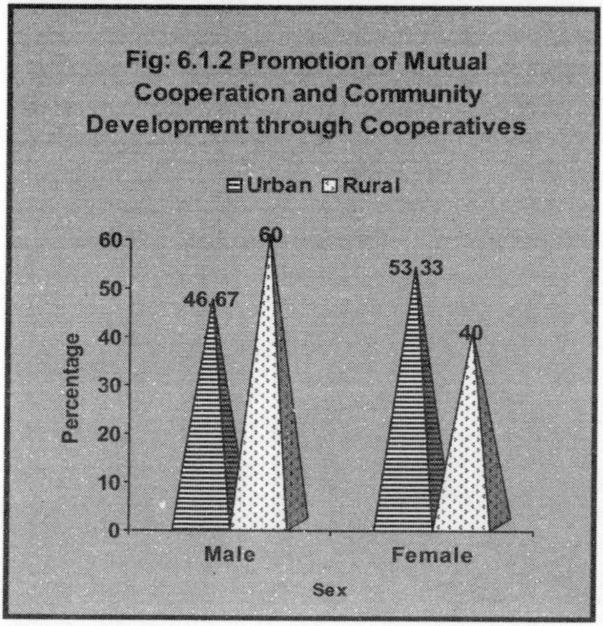


Fig: 6.1.2 Promotion of Mutual Cooperation and Community Development through Cooperatives

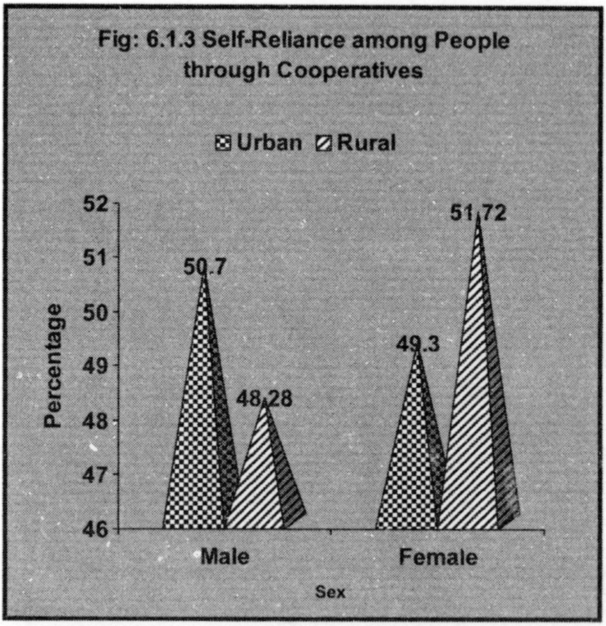
Fig: 6.1.3 Self-Reliance among People through Cooperatives
Urban
Rural
52
51
50
49
48
47
46
Percentage
50.7
48.28
49.3
51.72
Male
Female
Sex

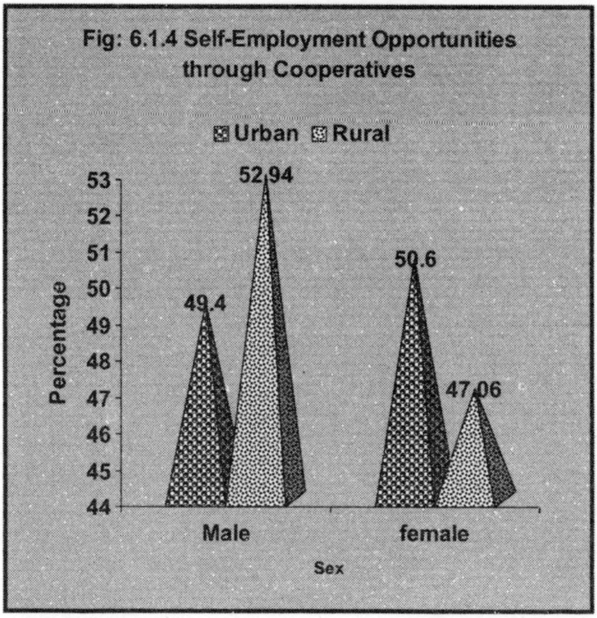
Fig: 6.1.4 Self-Employment Opportunities through Cooperatives
Urban
Rural
53
52
51
50
49
48
47
46
45
44
Percentage
49.4
52.94
50.6
47.06
Male
female
Sex

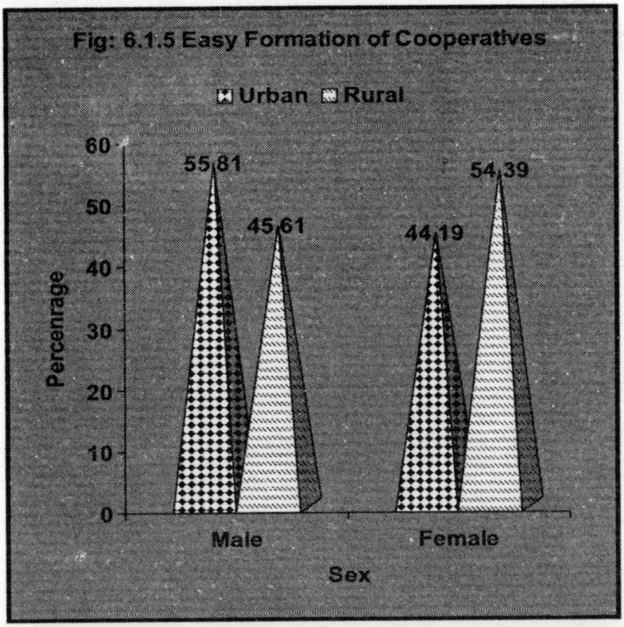
Fig: 6.1.5 Easy Formation of Cooperatives
Urban
Rural
60
50
40
30
20
10
0
Percenrage
55.81
45.61
44.19
54.39
Male
Female
Sex

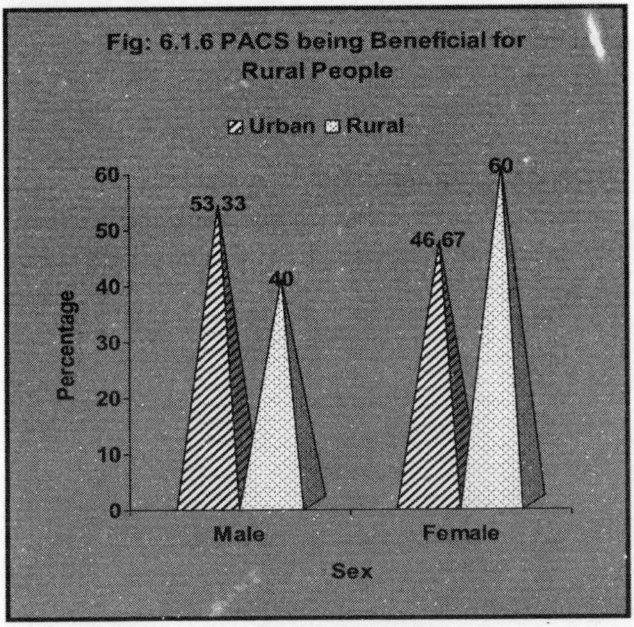
Fig: 6.1.6 PACS being Beneficial for Rural People
Urban
Rural
60
50
40
30
20
10
0
Percentage
53.33
40
46.67
60
Male
Female
Sex

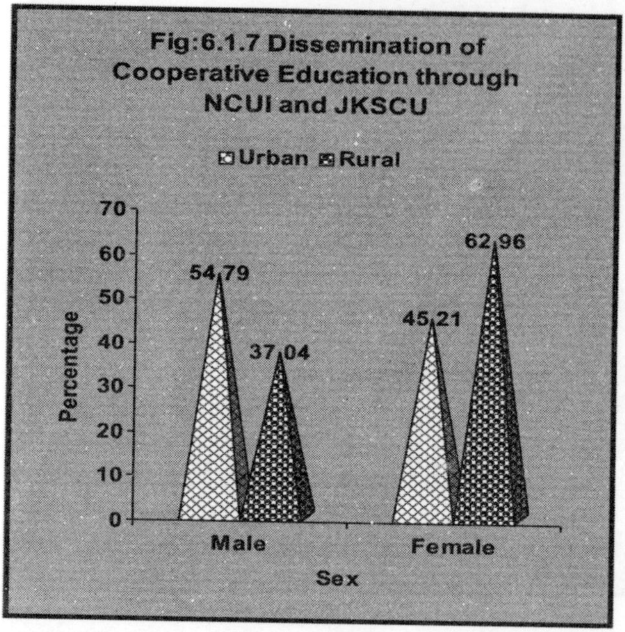
Fig:6.1.7 Dissemination of Cooperative Education through NCUI and JKSCU
Urban
Rural
70
60
50
40
30
20
10
0
Percentage
54.79
37.04
45.21
62.96
Male
Female
Sex

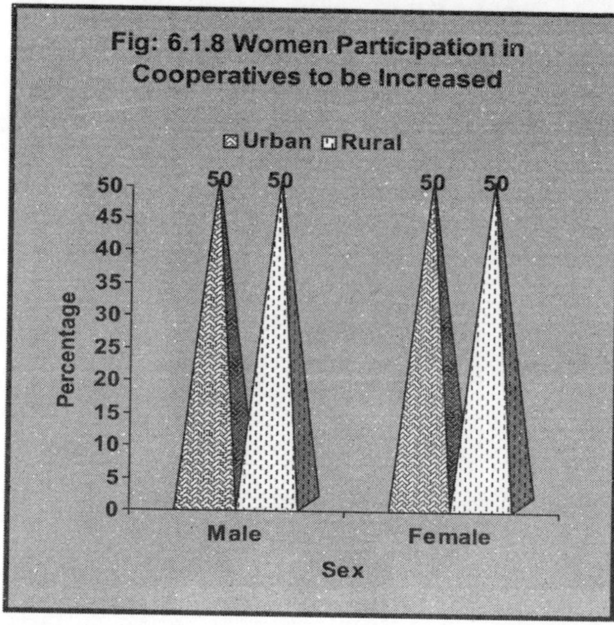
Fig: 6.1.8 Women Participation in Cooperatives to be Increased
Urban
Rural
50
45
40
35
30
25
20
15
10
5
0
Percentage
50
50
50
50
Male
Female
Sex

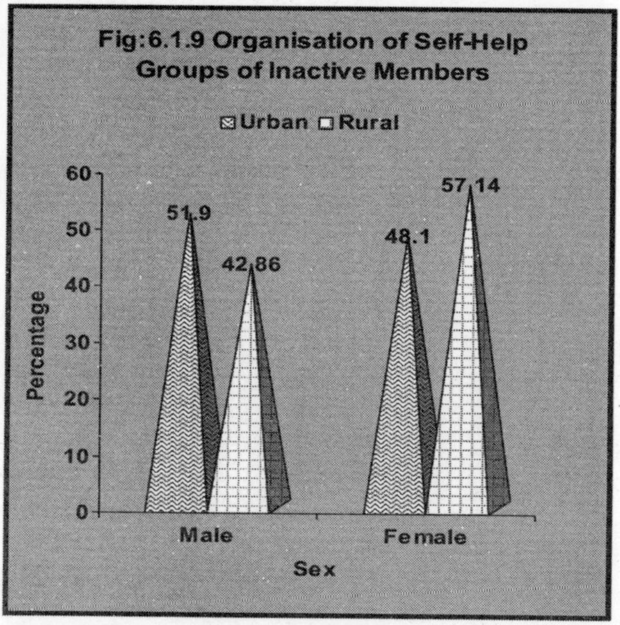
Fig:6.1.9 Organisation of Self-Help Groups of Inactive Members
Urban
Rural
60
50
40
30
20
10
0
Percentage
51.9
42.86
48.1
57.14
Male
Female
Sex

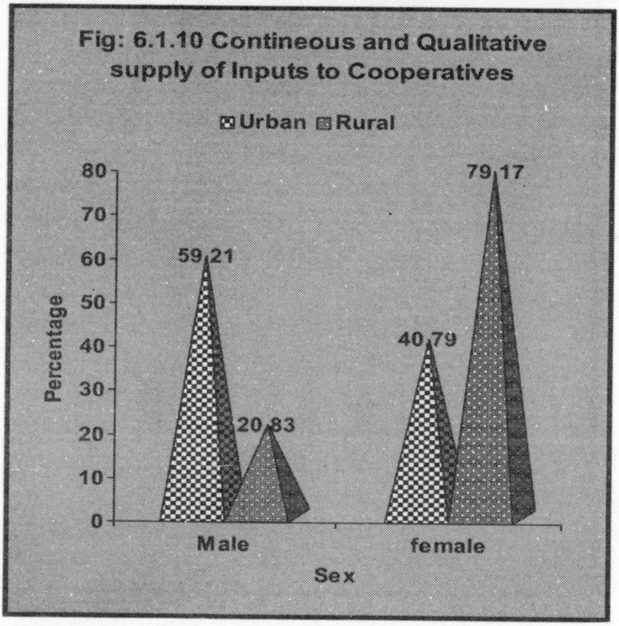
Fig: 6.1.10 Contineous and Qualitative supply of Inputs to Cooperatives
Urban
Rural
80
70
60
50
40
30
20
10
0
Percentage
59.21
20.83
40.79
79.17
Male
female
Sex

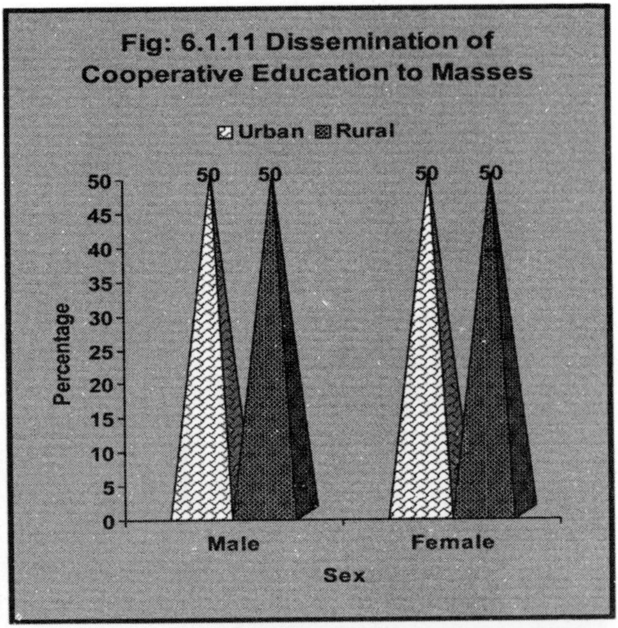
Fig: 6.1.11 Dissemination of Cooperative Education to Masses
Urban
Rural
50
50
50
50
Percentage
0
5
10
15
20
25
30
35
40
45
50
Male
Female
Sex

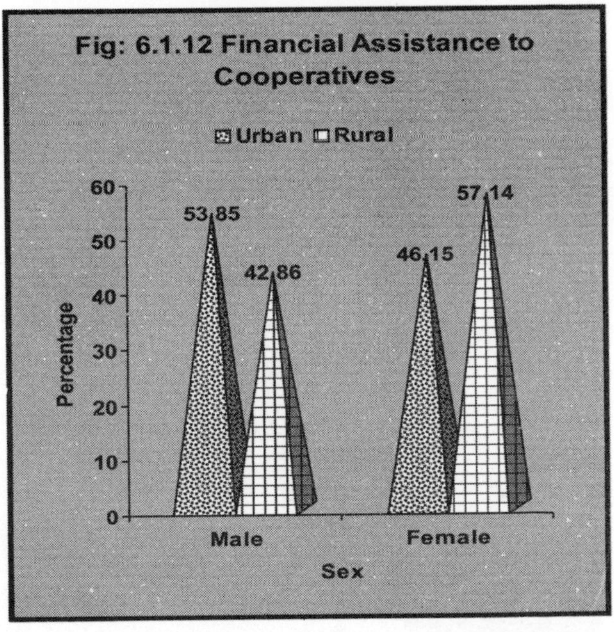
Fig: 6.1.12 Financial Assistance to Cooperatives
Urban
Rural
53.85
42.86
46.15
57.14
Percentage
0
10
20
30
40
50
60
Male
Female
Sex

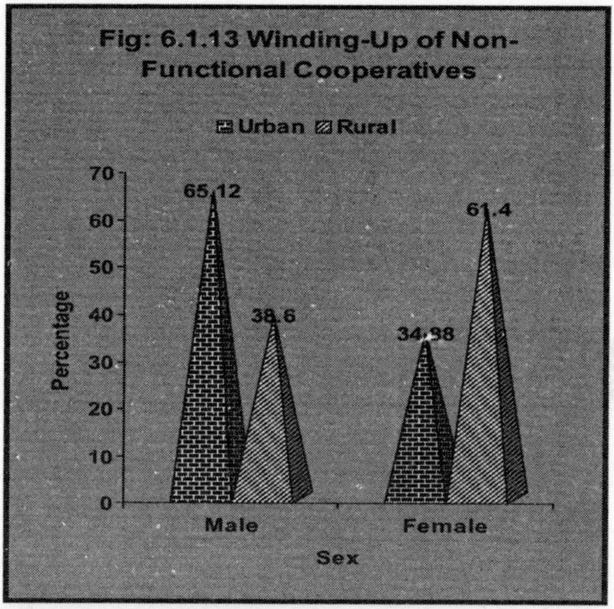
Fig: 6.1.13 Winding-Up of Non-Functional Cooperatives
Urban
Rural
Percentage
70
60
50
40
30
20
10
0
65.12
38.6
34.88
61.4
Male
Female
Sex

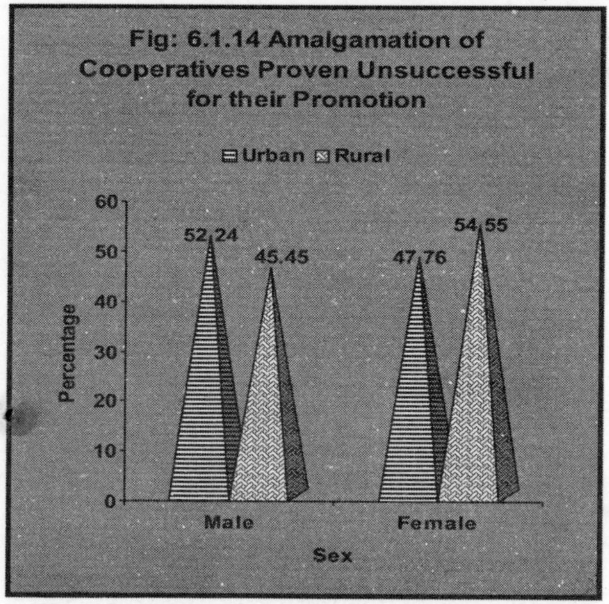
Fig: 6.1.14 Amalgamation of Cooperatives Proven Unsuccessful for their Promotion
Urban
Rural
Percentage
60
50
40
30
20
10
0
52.24
45.45
47.76
54.55
Male
Female
Sex

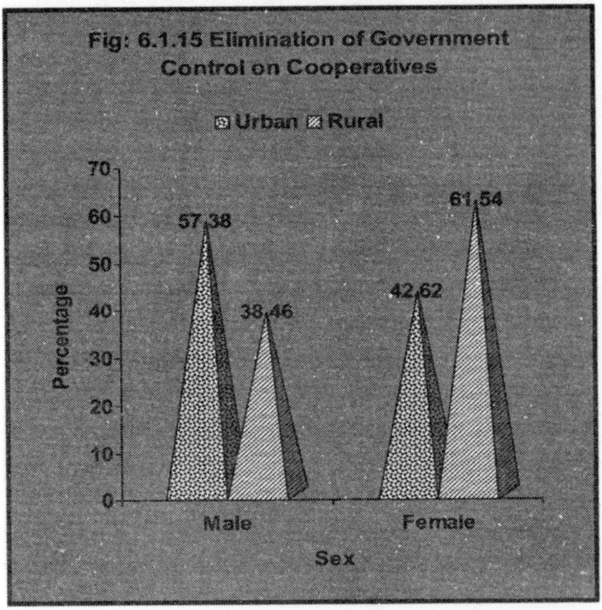
Fig: 6.1.15 Elimination of Government Control on Cooperatives
Urban Rural
70
60
50
40
30
20
10
0
Percentage
57.38
38.46
42.62
61.54
Male
Female
Sex

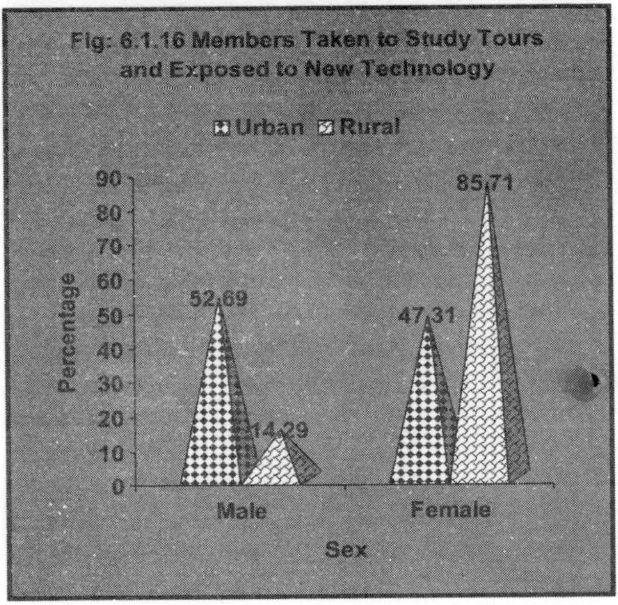
Fig: 6.1.16 Members Taken to Study Tours and Exposed to New Technology
Urban Rural
90
80
70
60
50
40
30
20
10
0
Percentage
52.69
14.29
47.31
85.71
Male
Female
Sex

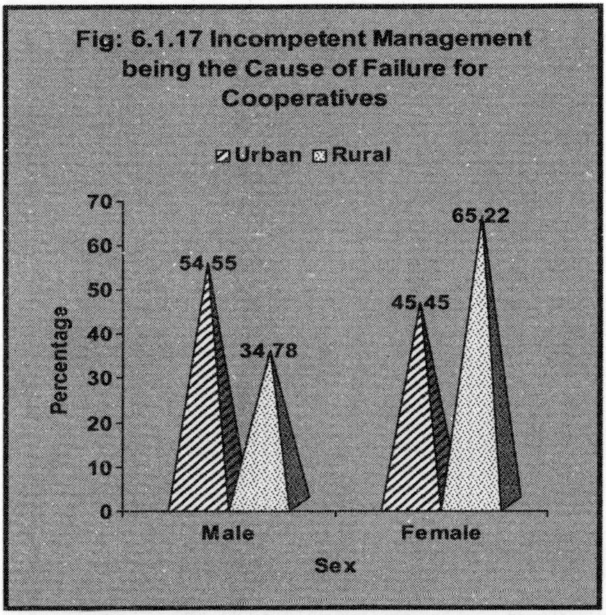
Fig: 6.1.17 Incompetent Management being the Cause of Failure for Cooperatives
Urban
Rural
70
60
50
40
30
20
10
0
Percentage
54.55
34.78
45.45
65.22
Male
Female
Sex

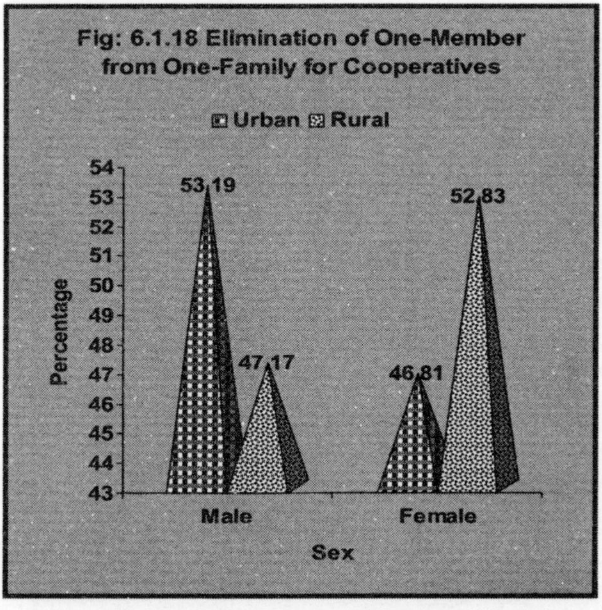
Fig: 6.1.18 Elimination of One-Member from One-Family for Cooperatives
Urban
Rural
54
53
52
51
50
49
48
47
46
45
44
43
Percentage
53.19
47.17
46.81
52.83
Male
Female
Sex

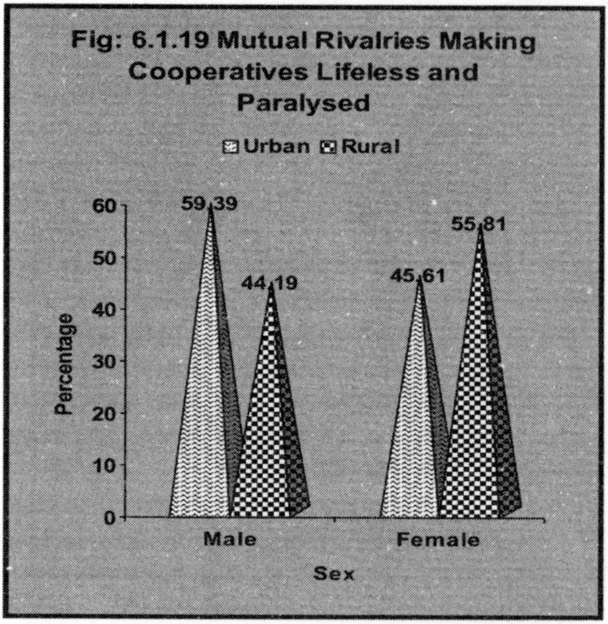
Fig: 6.1.19 Mutual Rivalries Making Cooperatives Lifeless and Paralysed
Urban
Rural
60
50
40
30
20
10
0
Percentage
59.39
44.19
45.61
55.81
Male
Female
Sex

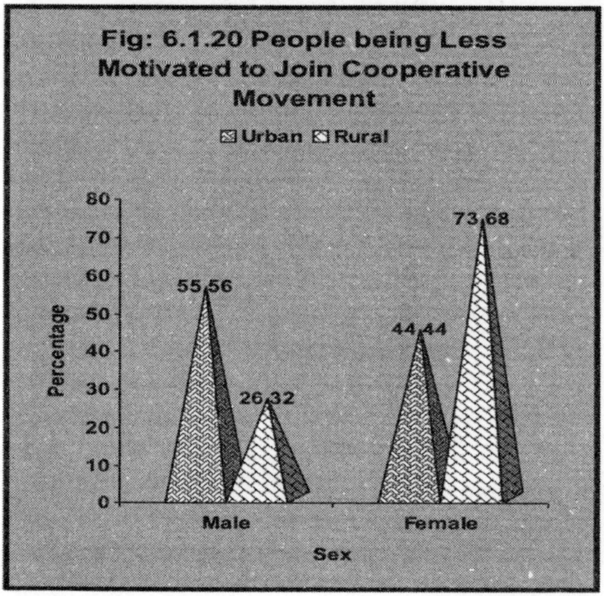
Fig: 6.1.20 People being Less Motivated to Join Cooperative Movement
Urban
Rural
80
70
60
50
40
30
20
10
0
Percentage
55.56
26.32
44.44
73.68
Male
Female
Sex

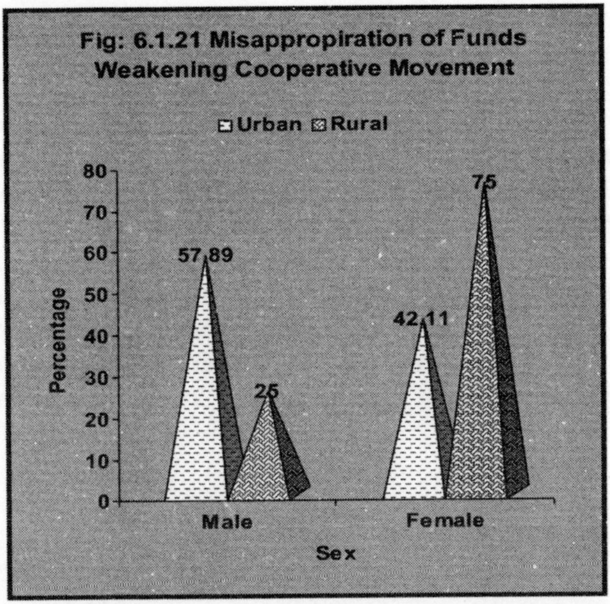


Fig: 6.1.21 Misappropiration of Funds Weakening Cooperative Movement

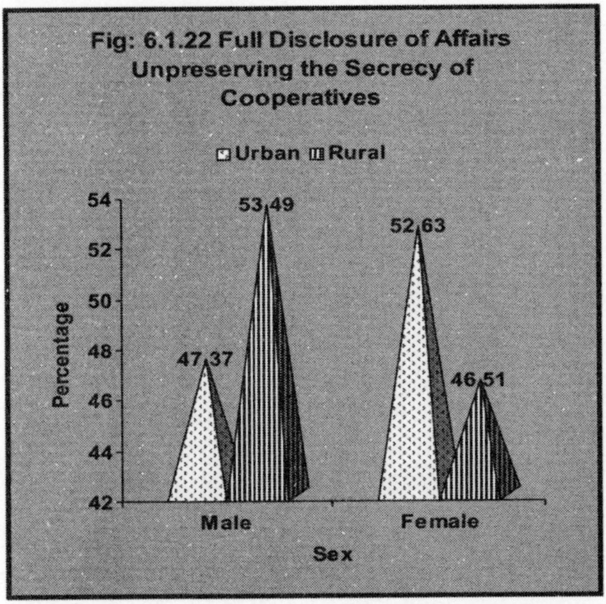


Fig: 6.1.22 Full Disclosure of Affairs Unpreserving the Secrecy of Cooperatives

officials have average positive attitudes towards Cooperatives; while highly qualified officials possess high attitudes. Same is true with regard to designation and salary of the officials.

As far as service duration of the officials is concerned, those who have less experience mainly possess high attitudes towards the movement. Job satisfaction of the officials has also influenced their attitudes towards the movement. Overall, the maximum percentage of officials has average positive attitudes towards the Cooperative Movement in Kashmir. Urban officials as well as male officials of the department have high attitudes towards the Cooperative Movement than rural officials and the female officials in the department.

7

# ENHANCEMENT OF THE QUALITY OF COOPERATIVE EDUCATION

Education is meaningless for the learners if it does not provide them with the intellectual and behavioural equipment of putting their creative potential to use. Higher education has to be relevant both to the individual and to the society. Higher education requires linkage of education with socio-economic activities and enhanced resources for the implementation of the new form and content of education. Awareness and insight can come from proper books and courses, accompanied by discussions among students and with teachers in tutorials and seminars, but it can come strongly when students are put in experimental situations. Vocationalisation with due attention on the links between what is taught and what society needs and on the creation of technical jobs will make higher education meaningful and remove uncertainties from the minds of the young. There is a need for job-degree delinking. The university should not be looked upon only as a means for earning a degree or diploma as a passport into the employment market. Many graduates and post graduates in our country work as bus conductors or handymen or book-keepers in small shops, cursing their fate. This has given rise to a need for communication and mobility. Such a need is today universally felt. Cooperative education performs a good role in eradication of unemployment. Thus cooperative education has a great scope of inclusion in higher education under the all streams i.e. social science, agriculture, industry, business management, science and technology. Cooperative education must be included in the formal system of higher education. The development of cooperative education in universities can play an important role in cooperative movement as well as national development. Apart from preparing a young queue to take over the duties of cooperative members and leaders in the country, students can contribute their brain and brawn directly to national development through cooperative movement efforts. There is an urgent need of intervention of universities for cooperative education. The separate faculty of cooperation is recommended in Kashmir University to educate students in cooperation as a distinctive discipline, along-with allied and relative subjects. Cooperative education is also recommended in the curriculum of all post-graduate departments of Kashmir University preferably as an independent discipline of study.

### Quality Enhancement of Higher Education

Human beings must be understood as cultural creatures whose characteristics and development are profoundly influenced by their institutional experiences. The process of formal education is an important part of the social process by which the human personality is moulded. Education is meaningless for the learner if it does not provide them with the intellectual and behavioural equipment of putting their creative potential to use. It will be of no value for industry and agriculture if the necessary technologies are not posted to them as and when required. There has to be a proper mix of both utility and value, the conscious and deliberate purpose being the self-actualisation of each individual as part of an all round social advancement on a global scale. The good citizen who is not useful is a drone, taking everything from society without giving anything to it in return.

Without education, social and cultural development cannot be achieved; inadequate education, the period of economic disabilities, regional imbalances and social injustice will be prolonged, leading to the possible build-up of disintegrative tensions. Through proper education, the achievement of economic and social development can be facilitated and expedited. The human resource would have a multiplier effect on the utilisation of all other resources. That is why the concept of education as an investment in development has been increasingly accepted.

**Excellence in Higher Education**

It was once generally accepted that school education, conceived of as the necessary and sufficient basis for higher education, had as its goal, if not to realise the full development of the pupil's personality, at least to foster the openness of mind, sound judgement, a capacity for moral and intellectual enrichment, a readiness to assume civic responsibilities and a general aptitude for further education and more specialised studies. However, over the last quarter of the century the 'threshold' for specialisation or the selection of options has been progressively introduced, for various resources, into the secondary school course. The growing need for scientific and professional specialisation, the increasing diversification and complexity of the basic sciences, the completion for places by an ever increasing number of students and the first attempts at implementing the concept of lifelong education are among the most cogent reasons for earlier specialisation. At the same time, the need has been felt in higher education to continue and even deepen liberal education for the individual and thus to strengthen the foundations of his personal culture.

Higher education has to be relevant both to the individual and to the society. Higher education requires linkage of education with socio-economic activities and enhanced resources for the implementation of the new form and content of education. But in such a case, education would enhance productivity in the widest sense and prepare manpower for new activities, promote technological development and solve problems of application, thus generating new resources.

Education of either a professional or a generalist cannot remains confined to mere knowledge of the subject and practices of related skills. It must include in its scope an awareness of our history, culture and tradition, together with knowledge of the problems we face in the socio-economic plan and what efforts we are making and should be making to carry our society forward. Awareness and insight can come from proper books and courses, accompanied by discussions among students and with teachers in tutorials and seminars, but it can come strongly when students are put in experimental situations. Interaction with the community in a variety of forms and participation in developmental activities would be most valuable in this respect.

### Enhancing the Quality of Higher Education

The criterion of relevance necessarily brings us to a consideration of the irrelevance of some knowledge. The size of knowledge is growing at a very fast pace. It is now said to double itself every five years. This brings us to a knotty problem, what was good and useful teaching twenty years ago may be outdated and practically useless today. The teacher has to make some critical and effective choices, the deadwood of knowledge has to be chopped off and modern, up-to-date and relevant and innovation in the knowledge field, thus, emerge as an important value. A good teacher can never rest on his oars; mentally he has continuously to be on the move. Cooperation between students, scholars, professors and researchers has never ceased to occur, although its progress has failed to match that of science and technology. By contrast, the great systems of education, have tended to become enclosed in a rigid framework, no matter how widespread have been or has become their sphere of influence, generally linked to a cultural hegemony arising from territorial conquest. Vocationalisation with due attention on the links between what is taught and what society needs and on the creation of technical jobs will make higher education meaningful and remove uncertainties from the minds of the young. Our present system makes students crammers even at the lower levels and they continue this undesirable practice at the college or university level. There is, therefore, an urgent need to redesign higher education with stress on information that can be put to good practical use for the benefit of the students and of society in general. The success of the new economic policies will depend greatly on the streamlining of higher education and thereby empowering the future generations of young men and women leading to 'production by the masses' instead of mass production that can throw many more into the sea of idleness.

## Higher Education and Employment

Higher education must take into account the actual employment potential in each state and in the country as a whole. Education should be viewed in relation to socio-economic needs and national priorities. It should train the body and discipline the mind. It should aim at a scientific cultivation of the mental and physical faculties of the pupil. There is a need for job-degree delinking. Post graduates compete with graduates and undergraduates for positions requiring only high school education—this phenomenon should disappear from the job market, especially because the overqualified persons entering lower level jobs are frustrated after the first flush of enthusiasm. The number of unemployed youth has already exceeded the 30 million mark. What is particularly disturbing is the fact that 20 per cent of these are educated unemployed with graduate and postgraduate qualifications. Yet the number of institutions of higher education is increasing constantly, as if the problem of narrowing the gap between the nature of supply and of demand for higher education did not exist. Experiments have been undertaken in some universities during the recent past to re-structure the course spectrum of their first degree programmes. As a consequence, the content of education today—particularly at the lower tertiary level—is not the same as it was a generation ago. We have recorded a substantial progress in several sectors during the last quarter of this century. Agriculture, mass media, electronics, pre-clinical and para-clinical sciences are some of the areas wherein significant advances have been made. The university should not be looked upon only as a means for earning a degree or diploma as a passport into the employment market. It should instead, be considered to be a centre for cultivating the mind and for the building up of the community of learning capable of reasoning the truth and distinguishing the right from the wrong. There should be planned exposure to skill-oriented programmes, as educational bridges to the employment market. Such a policy would produce an appropriate kind of manpower, a work force of useful as well as good citizens required by the developmental needs of the country.

## Introducing of Cooperative Education in Higher Education

In India because other openings or opportunities are non-existent, every one wants to join a college or university for not having anything better to do. It is a kind of status symbol or to seek white collar jobs. Gone are the days when a youngster just blindly followed in his father's footsteps and pursued whatever profession his forefather had practiced, be it with or without success. The youngsters completing senior secondary education must ask themselves questions like— Do they really have a purpose in going to college, or do they want to go simply because it is the 'thing to do', or because it will give them social prestige? What chances have they to expect if they do graduate? Unfortunately, high school boys and girls do not give as much careful thought to this important problem as it deserves. They are unwilling to face the realities of vocational life. Many drift through graduate without making any vocational decision and enter life without training of any kind by which they can make living. Academic education of today does not prepare the youth in colleges and universities; for the employment, keeping in view their aptitude or motivate them for undertaking any job after completing their educational career and when they really enter into life they feel themselves quite ineligible or incompetent to adjust themselves anywhere and they remain dependent on their parents even after completing the education. This in due course of time leads such young boys and girls to discontentment, destruction and frustration which also adversely affect the nation as a whole.

The mad rush to colleges and the consequent wastage of man-hours, material and money can be avoided. Almost sixty per cent of those who earn degrees find it difficult to utilise what they gained from college because it does not match the requirements of the job they apply for. Finally they end up doing something that is much below their expectations, something that is even remotely related to what they have learnt in three to five years. Many graduates and post graduates in our country work as bus conductors or handymen or book-keepers in small shops, cursing their fate. This has given rise to a need for communication and mobility. Such a need is today universally felt. Not only must higher education facilitates the requirements of different occupations, but must also study the abilities of pupils, if they are to make wise choice of occupations. Such abilities can be identified and bring under common fold through higher education by the introduction of cooperative education in it. Cooperative Education performs a good role in eradication of unemployment. Cooperative's many fold activities and self-employment schemes could go a long way to help unemployed young people to run their own ventures instead of running after the white collar jobs. Cooperatives can wipe out the unemployment to a certain extent, if implemented in honest and earnest way.

**Cooperative Education in Academic Stream (Table 7.1)**

Almost equal percentage of urban male and female (57.50 per cent and 58.33 per cent respectively) suggest Cooperative Education in academic stream. Similarly, about 42.50 per cent rural male and 41.67 per cent rural female officials also suggest the same. But majority of rural male officials (80 per cent) are not favouring Cooperative Education in formal system of education. Similar views are held by 71.43 per cent rural female, 28.57 per cent urban female and 20 per cent urban male officials.

Cooperative Education can increase the participation of youth in Cooperatives as per the officials comprising 64.29 per cent urban male, followed by 57.14 per cent rural female, 42.86 per cent urban female and 35.71 per cent rural male officials. About 69.23 per cent urban female and 62.50 per cent urban male officials perceive Cooperative Education as best means for the irradiation of unemployment in the State. Same view is also perceived by 37.50 per cent rural male and 30.77 per cent rural female officials of the Cooperative Department in Kashmir. An equal percentage of rural and urban male officials (50 per cents respectively) of Cooperative Department ensure the success of Cooperatives through the dissemination of its education. Moreover, 66.67 per cent urban females and 33.33 per cent rural female officials also believe the same.

Female officials of Cooperatives (50 per cent in rural areas and 50 per cent in urban areas), encourage Cooperative Education at school level. About 63.64 per cent male officials in rural areas and 36.36 per cent male officials in urban areas also favour Cooperative Education at school level. Whereas, 55.64 per cent rural male and 55 per cent urban female officials, followed by 45 per cent rural female and 44.44 per cent urban male officials, have recommended Cooperative Education at college level. Majority of urban male officials i.e. 80 per cent suggest intervention of universities for Cooperative Education, followed by 66.67 per cent urban female officials, 33.33 per cent rural female officials and 20 per cent rural male officials of Cooperative Department. Most of the officials i.e. 80 per cent urban females and 73.33 per cent urban males recommend Cooperative Education at all levels of academics, followed by 26.67 per cent rural male and 20 per cent rural female officials of the Cooperative Department.

About 66.67 per cent urban female officials and 57.14 per cent urban male officials recommend Cooperative Education as an optional subject. Same is also recommended by 42.86 per cent rural male and 33.33 per cent rural female officials. But almost equal percentage of urban male and rural female officials (57.89 per cent and 58.33 per cent respectively) recommends Cooperative education as a compulsory subject in school, colleges or universities. This is also recommended by 42.11 per cent rural male and 41.67 per cent urban female officials of Cooperative Department in Kashmir. There is found significant difference at 0.05 level between male and female officials in rural and urban areas regarding their view for inclusion of Cooperative Education in academic stream. But no significant difference is observed between male and female officials in rural and urban areas (p>0.05) regarding their favour for Cooperative Education in formal system of education, level of education to be included and type of subject to be offered.

**Table 7.1**
**Cooperative Education in Academic Stream**

*(n = 100)*

| | *Male* | | | *Female* | | |
|---|---|---|---|---|---|---|
| *Variables* | *Urban* | *Rural* | *p-Value* | *Urban* | *Rural* | *p-Value* |
| ***Cooperative Education in Academic Stream*** | | | | | | |
| Favouring | 23 (57.50) | 17 (42.50) | | 21 (58.33) | 15 (41.67) | |
| Not-Favouring | 2 (20.00) | 8 (80.00) | <0.05 | 4 (28.57) | 10 (71.43) | <0.05 |
| Total | 25 (50.00) | 25 (50.00) | | 25 (50.00) | 25 (50.00) | |
| ***Reason for Favour*** | | | | | | |
| Participation or Youth | 9 (64.29) | 5 (35.71) | | 6 (42.86) | 8 (57.14) | |
| Eradication of Unemployment | 5 (62.50) | 3 (37.50) | >0.05 | 9 (69.23) | 4 (30.77) | >0.05 |
| Ensure Success | 9 (50.00) | 9 (50.00) | | 6 (66.67) | 3 (33.33) | |
| Total | 23 (57.50) | 17 (42.50) | | 21 (58.33) | 15 (41.67) | |
| ***Level of Education*** | | | | | | |
| School | 4 (36.36) | 7 (63.64) | | 4 (50.00) | 4 (50.00) | |
| College | 4 (44.44) | 5 (55.64) | | 11 (55.00) | 9 (45.00) | |
| University | 4 (80.00) | 1 (20.00) | >0.05 | 2 (66.67) | 1 (33.33) | >0.05 |
| All | 11 (73.33) | 4 (26.67) | | 4 (80.00) | 1 (20.00) | |
| Total | 23 (57.50) | 17 (42.50) | | 21 (58.33) | 15 (41.67) | |
| ***Type of Subject*** | | | | | | |
| Optional | 12 (57.14) | 9 (42.86) | | 16 (66.67) | 8 (33.33) | |
| Compulsory | 11 (57.89) | 8 (42.11) | >0.05 | 5 (41.67) | 7 (58.33) | >0.05 |
| Total | 23 (57.50) | 17 (42.50) | | 21 (58.33) | 15 (41.67) | |

Row percentage in parentheses

## Cooperative Education in Academic Stream

Education is one of the principles of Cooperatives. Cooperative Education is a life-long process and all persons engaged in Cooperation need to participate to this process of education and re-education. The people who are potentially, rather than actually Cooperators, i.e. the greater public outside the movements, should be trained in interest of Cooperative Movement. That is why majority of Cooperative officials in Kashmir are favouring the inclusion of Cooperative Education in formal system of education. But majority of rural male officials do not favour Cooperative Education in formal system of education; because according to them, such strategy would not work. In spite of this, the importance of Cooperative Education can not be ignored. The analysis of *Veerakumaran* (2002) reveals the importance of cooperation as an academic discipline, organisational framework for Cooperative Education and training in India, the recent trends in education and the need for separate specialised university for cooperation. Such education can increase the participation of youth in Cooperatives, as per majority of urban male and rural female officials. Opportunity should be provided to youth by their involvement in the actual working of various types of Cooperative institutions at various levels. They should be appointed, nominated and associated on the management committees of the Cooperatives. They should be sponsored by Cooperatives to various programmes of training and education in cooperation as management trainees, as prospective employees, as young leaders in Cooperatives and in various other capacities. Bigger and stronger Cooperative institutions can provide scholarships and give financial assistance at attractive scales to promising young men to conduct studies, research and experiments in cooperation.

The *National Debating Competition* on youth organised by the *National Council for Cooperative Training* in Delhi, in 2001, with participation from various universities was also a clear indication that the youth are aware of the latest trends in Cooperatives and feel the need to discuss and debate these issues with fresh perspectives. Now, there is need for more practical action from the youth to involve themselves in large numbers. Thus, Cooperative Education performs a good role in eradication of unemployment. More than half of the urban officials in Cooperative Department hold this view.

Academic education of today does not prepare the youth in schools, colleges and universities; for the employment, keeping in view their aptitude or motivate them for undertaking any job after completing their educational career and when they really enter into life they feel themselves quite ineligible or incompetent to adjust themselves anywhere and they remain dependent on their parents even after completing the education. This in due course of time leads such young boys and girls to discontentment, destruction and frustration which also adversely affect the nation as a whole.

Cooperative's many fold activities and self-employment schemes could go a long way to help unemployed young people to run their own ventures instead of running after the white collar jobs. Cooperatives can wipe out the unemployment to a certain extent, if implemented in honest and earnest way. Organising Cooperative activities in schools, colleges and universities by way of Cooperative stationery shops, Cooperative consumer stores, Cooperative canteens, Cooperative study forum etc. Some of these activities are already in practice since long but the approach is half hearted and the impact is negligible. This needs to be taken up more vigorously and special cells need to be set up exclusively for this purpose in the Cooperative Department and Cooperative Union. Apart from thrift and credit Cooperatives, consumer stores, bakeries, stationery, book shops, libraries, book banks and even processing units can be considered for the campus life of educational institutions.

*Gupta* (1982) pointed out that employment potential of the Cooperatives has not been assessed, identified and tapped systematically and with determination. Each institution in each sector like consumers, marketing, processing, banking, industries, transportation, fisheries, handicrafts, dairying and schools etc. can provide indefinite range of employment opportunities. There is always and there will always remain the dearth of right type of skilled and educated workers in the ever expanding and ever diversifying Cooperative Movement, provided these Cooperatives themselves are promoted and run on proper lines and their activities are protected and supported by suitable Government policies and the people themselves are involved in running them. Thus, the proper implementation of Cooperative Education can ensure the success of Cooperatives in Kashmir.

An equal percentage of rural and urban male officials of Cooperative Department ensure the success of Cooperatives through the dissemination of its education. Most of the female officials in urban areas also ensure success of Cooperatives through its education. Male officials in rural areas mainly encourage Cooperative Education at school and college level. *Khan* (2001) recommended the development of school Cooperatives which can play an important role in Cooperative Movement as well as national development. Apart from preparing a young queue to take over the duties of Cooperative Members and leaders in the country, students can contribute their brain and brawn directly to national development through Cooperative Movement efforts while being members of school Cooperatives. Secondary schools can also implement Cooperative Education in their curriculum.

*Sharma* (1982) also recommended cooperation in the curriculum at the levels right from primary classes to post-graduate preferably as an independent discipline of study. *Anshuma, Singh, et al* (2002) put forth the need of cooperation to be introduced as a compulsory subject at $10^{th}$ and $12^{th}$ standard. The picture of the Cooperative sector at this level should be high lightened in a simple and effective language for advantage of the young minds. More and more universities should offer B.A and M.A courses in cooperation, not only few universities in this regard.

Majority of urban male officials, in the present study, suggest intervention of universities for Cooperative Education. But the fact is that Cooperative Education should be introduced at all levels of education; be it school, college or university level. That is why urban female officials recommend Cooperative Education at all levels of academics. Nevertheless, one should not forget that university education is the base on which future leadership development is to be founded and that a university is not an end itself but a means to an end. The Cooperative sector of Kashmir should utilise to the maximum extent, the Kashmir University as well as Sheri-

Kashmir Agricultural University and Science Technology (SKAUST), for the development of its leadership in its proper perspective. Such universities through their faculties of arts, science, agriculture, commerce, law, engineering and technology etc, provide for imparting of basic knowledge in the concerned areas to meet the needs of the organisations functioning in our economic, social, political, cultural and other lives and in that regard, the role of universities in Kashmir can be regarded as accredited and note-worthy and to that extent, the Cooperative sector should take the advantage of such specialists in the concerned areas of their operations. The Department of Management and Business administration of Kashmir University can play a pivotal role in this regard. Cooperation has been inter-disciplinary subject, falling within the jurisdiction of the faculties of arts, home-science, commerce and agriculture. One or all these faculties may decide to include one or more compulsory and/or optional papers of Cooperation in their syllabi at one or more levels—undergraduate, post graduate, doctoral and post doctoral—and the university departments and the colleges and/or the constituent and/or the affiliated colleges of the university may start actual teaching of the subject. The Maharaja Sayajirao University of Baroda had, since long, instituted two full-time diploma courses i.e. under-graduate diploma in cooperation and post-graduate diploma in cooperation. It has also introduced cooperation as one of the optional groups, comprising three papers—one at the second B.com level and two at the third B.com level, in addition to the introduction of one paper at M.com stage, in the faculty of commerce. It has set up an independent full-fledged department, headed by a professor, for teaching all these papers at different levels and for guiding doctoral researches in Cooperative. *Joshi* (1981) also recommended a separate faculty of cooperation in universities to educate students in cooperation as a distinctive discipline, along-with allied and relative subjects.

Moreover, 'Vaikunth Mehta National Institute of Cooperative Management', Pune (VAMNICOM) is the only university in India, which provides exclusive Cooperative education to subjects, training to foreign scholars; research both academic and problem oriented and consultancy services to Cooperative institutions. Nevertheless, 'Cooperative Training College' of Chandigarh also needs mention for its dissemination of Cooperative Education. In addition 'Institute of Cooperative Management' functions in different states of India. The state of Jammu and Kashmir also has separate 'Institute of Cooperative Management'—each in Jammu and Kashmir—which provides diploma course in cooperation. Cooperative Education can be introduced as an optional subject or as a compulsory discipline. More than half of the urban officials recommend Cooperative Education as an optional subject. While rural female officials, followed by urban male officials, suggest inclusion of cooperation as a compulsory subject.

8

# DEVELOPMENT OF WOMEN COOPERATIVES

The highest percentage of population in Kashmir valley is comprised by Srinagar, Anantnag and Baramulla; followed by Pulwama, Kupwara and Badgam. As per the Census 2001, 47 per cent of Kashmir population are female. The highest percentage of Cooperatives have been organised in district Srinagar; whereas the least Cooperatives have been organised in district Kupwara. Though Anantnag and Baramulla have more population than Pulwama, but the number of Cooperatives established in these districts is almost same. Srinagar district comprising the highest number of Cooperatives has the least number of Members enrolled in Cooperatives, proceeding by district Kupwara. Baramulla has the highest number of Members in Cooperatives and also covers the highest number of population per Cooperative; whereas district Badgam covers least number of populations per Cooperative. However, this does not mean that Cooperative net work is more wide spread in Badgam district than in other districts. Rather, this difference is due to less population in Badgam district. Kupwara district which has least number of Cooperatives, comprise higher number of Members per Cooperatives. Anantnag and Pulwama have almost same number of Cooperatives, also comprising almost same Members per Cooperative. Pulwama district has enrolled more

Cooperative Members than Srinagar district. Overall, Kashmir valley comprise 54,41,341 number of persons, with 520 Agricultural and Consumer Cooperatives, having 3,03,317 Members. The valley has one Cooperative for 9,716 persons; with an average of 541 Members per Cooperative and one Cooperative Member among almost 18 persons.

The highest number of PACS has been established in Baramulla district and the least number in Kupwara district. The highest number of Consumer Cooperatives and Women Cooperatives has been established by district Srinagar. However, district Kupwara does not have even a single Consumer Cooperative. Sale and Service Cooperatives are headed by Anantnag and Kupwara districts. Marketing Cooperatives are leaded by Badgam and Pulwama districts. Srinagar district also comprise the highest number of other Cooperatives including Credit Cooperatives, Transport Cooperatives, Milk/Dairy Cooperatives, Meat Cooperative etc. Among all types of Cooperatives in Kashmir, the highest number Comprise of PACS, followed by Consumer Coopera tives, Marketing Cooperatives and others; including Sale and Service and Women Cooperatives.

## Overview of Women Cooperatives

Up to 1970, Cooperative Movement in Kashmir was in its peak. In the decade of 70's the movement got a down fall; but again rose in the decade of 80's. During1980-90, Cooperative Movement gained popularity and most of the Cooperatives were established in the same decade. Unfortunately, in the present decade, no encouraging boost has been given to this movement till date. Majority of PACS, Sale and Service, Women Cooperatives and others have been registered by Deputy Registrars Cooperatives in their concerned districts. Consumer Cooperatives and Marketing Cooperatives have mostly been registered by Registrar of Cooperatives.

### Status of Women Cooperatives

Majority of Cooperatives in Kashmir (94.36 per cent) are Men Cooperatives Women Cooperatives being few in number (5.63

per cent). Over the past century, very few efforts have been made to enrol Women under Cooperative Movement. Most of the Women Cooperatives have been established in the post-independence period. In the decade of 90's a tremendous change has been found in the Cooperative Movement when a shift from men Cooperatives to Women Cooperatives has been observed by 60 per cent. But the same trend has not been observed in the present decade. In urban Kashmir, only 8.05 per cent Cooperatives belong to Women; whereas only 91.95 per cent are Men Cooperatives. Similarly only 4.47 per cent Women Cooperatives have been established in rural Kashmir and 95.53 per cent have been established exclusively by men. The areas of operation of all Women Cooperatives are within the limits of district where these have been established. Most of the Women Cooperatives operate only within the institutional limits, be it school, colleges and/or orphanages, whereas few are spread over block or tehsil levels. No Women Cooperative is working at divisional or state level.

**Physical Condition**

The physical condition of Men and Women Cooperatives is more or less same. None of the Women Cooperative is under *'very good'* condition. No Women Cooperative has its branch within the area of operation, which means the functioning of Women Cooperatives have been limited to its headquarter only. With the increase in the branches of Cooperatives, its employees including trained employees also increase. The mean hired and own number of godowns is more in Men Cooperatives than in Women Cooperatives. In case of hired godown capacity, the mean of Women Cooperatives is, again, less than Men Coopera-tives. But in context of own godowns, the mean of Women Cooperatives is more than Men Cooperatives. As the number of godowns in Cooperatives increases, the employment opportunity in such Cooperatives also increase; and the more the intake capacity of godowns, the more employees are needed.

### Membership

There is a wide difference in the membership between Women Cooperatives and Men Cooperatives. The average membership in Men Cooperatives is more than Women Cooperatives. Inactive women membership is also high lightened in their own Cooperatives. The percentage of Men Cooperatives holding state government as its Members is greater than Women Cooperatives. No Women Cooperative is holding any other organisation or Cooperative as its Member. The study shows that with the increase in active women membership in Cooperatives, men membership decreases. Individual share capital, sales and assets of the Cooperative increases with the increase in membership including men as well as women membership. Managerial subsidy provided to Cooperatives decreases with the increase in membership. Bank borrowings provided to Cooperatives decrease with the increase in inactive women membership. Moreover, the increase in membership leads increase in branches of Cooperatives, number of employees, trained employees and number of godowns.

### Capital Investment

The Capital investment in Women Cooperatives is in the form of individual and government share capital, managerial assistance, interest-free loan, special assistance, bank borrowing and other types of assistances. There is a wide difference between the government share in Men and Women Cooperatives. But, in case of managerial subsidy, the difference is reversed by Women Cooperatives. This means that state government has provided managerial subsidy more to Women Cooperatives than to Men Cooperatives. No Women Cooperatives has been provided interest free loan. Moreover, no Women Cooperative has any bank borrowing. All Women Cooperatives have been exempted from taxes, fees and other duties pertaining to their functioning under 'Jammu and Kashmir Cooperative Societies Act 1960' and 'Jammu and Kashmir Cooperative Societies Act 1989'. With the increase in government and individual share capital, the own number of godowns as well as their intake capacity increases and prove the valuable assets for Cooperatives. Managerial subsidy provided to Cooperatives increases the employment opportunities in Cooperatives as well as facilitate the training of employees.

**Employment opportunities**

The number of employees in Cooperatives is positively influenced by the training provided to them. Unfortunately, no emphasis has been given on the training of employees in Cooperatives. The condition, in this context, is same among Men and Women Cooperatives. But the number of employees in Women Cooperatives is less than Men Cooperatives.

**Amalgamation and Amendment**

Majority of Women Cooperatives have not been amalgamated. Only one Woman Cooperative under study has been voluntarily amalgamated before 1990, in order to raise its share capital. The same Cooperative has also amended its By-Laws after amalgamation. The other Women Cooperatives have not amended their By-Laws for any reason.

**Credit Facilities**

All Cooperatives have provision of loaning to their Members as per their By-Laws. Among the Cooperatives which do not provide loan to its Members; most of them face poor financial position, others have no confidence on their Members due to non availability of security furnished by them and the other Members have felt no need based desire to undertake loan from their Cooperatives. There is huge outstanding of prior debts against Members of Men Cooperatives. No such condition is observed in Women Cooperatives. Thus, there is more misappropriation of funds in Men Cooperatives than in Women Cooperatives.

**Financial Position**

Almost 33.33 per cent Women Cooperatives have updated audit position. About 26.66 per cent Women Cooperatives have been audited either between the years 1998-2001 or before 1998. Moreover, 13.33 per cent Women Cooperatives are un-audited since their establishment. Among such un-audited Women Cooperatives, half have incomplete records which are creating hurdles in the processing of their audit; while one Woman Cooperative under study has dispute with Cooperative Department which is preventing to ascertain the latest financial position of same Cooperative. Almost half of the Cooperatives in Kashmir are functioning on profit. Badgam district has the highest percentage of profitable Cooperatives, followed by Srinagar and Anantnag districts. An equal percentage of Cooperatives in Baramulla and Kupwara districts are in profit. In case of viable Cooperatives, Badgam and Srinagar districts are at the top; while Baramulla and Kupwara districts have least viable Cooperatives, preceded by Pulwama and Anantnag districts. Among profitable Cooperatives, almost all of them are viable. The mean business turnover of Men Cooperatives is more than Women Cooperatives. The average profit or loss is also more in Men Cooperatives than in Women Cooperatives. The same difference is found in case of assets of Men and Women Cooperatives. The percentage of Women Cooperatives being in profit is more than the Men Cooperatives. Overall, 73.33 percent Women Cooperatives are viable i.e. they ensure more sound socio-economic activities than Men Cooperatives which are viable only by 49 per cent. Thus Kashmir women have been proved better Cooperators than men. With the increase in government share capital; the business turnover, profit and assets of the Cooperatives also increase. Increase in individual share capital lead Cooperatives towards their profitability. The lesser the number of trained employees, the more Cooperatives have chances to be in loss. Assets of the Cooperatives increase with the raise in branches, number of godowns and their intake capacity. Moreover, with the increase in profit and business turnover of Cooperatives, their assets also increase.

## Organisation of Intervention Programme for the Establishment of Women Cooperatives

The Cooperative Department is headed by *Registrar,* followed by *Additional Registrar, Joint Registrars, Deputy Registrars,*

*Assistant Registrars* and Others. The approach for intervention programme covered all these officers/officials. In order to make intervention programme successful, it became very necessary to establish adequate rapport with the concerned authority. The following inferences helped to understand the scope for women in Cooperatives and supported to develop an intervention programme for involvement of women in Cooperatives.

**Cooperative Officials/Officers**

The young male and female officials are mainly in urban areas than in rural areas. Middle aged male and female officials are more in rural areas than in urban areas. Late aged Cooperative personnel are equally distributed in rural as well as in urban areas. No urban female personnel belong to late age. The mean age, salary and distance covered from residential to posted area, are more among male officials than the female officials. The average age of urban and rural officials is almost equal. But the mean of monthly salary received by urban officials is more than rural official. Urban officials have to cover less distance than rural officials, from their residential to posted area. With the increase in the age of officials, their salary also raises high. Rise in salary has led to the favourable attitudes of officials towards the Cooperative Movement.

**Perceptions**

Majority of Cooperative officials have found application of cooperation in the economic uplift of people. Such perception is more common among urban officials than rural officials. Majority of male and female officials in rural areas perceive mutual cooperation as an aim of Cooperatives. But there are few officials who think Cooperatives have lost its importance in the present century and their establishment has now become only a formality to expand the Cooperative Movement in Kashmir. Majority of rural females perceive that social uplift of people can be achieved through Cooperatives. The highest percentage of officials is satisfied with the functioning of Cooperatives. But majority of rural male and urban female has opposite perception of it. The officials of Cooperative Department in Kashmir also think that community development programmes can be held through Cooperatives. An equal percentage of urban male and female officials regard Cooperatives as a measure for holding the price line. The community development through Cooperatives can also be ensured by mutual cooperation among Members of Cooperatives. The highest percentages of rural male and female officials are satisfied by the coordination between Cooperative administration and Cooperative management. But urban male officials also feel communication gap between the two levels, lack of confidence on management of Cooperatives and/or Cooperative administration. Cooperatives in Kashmir have not been provided any financial assistance during 1995-2000, due to financial crunch in the state. But female officials also blame huge outstanding against the Members of Cooperatives. Lack of coordination between administration and management of Cooperatives is also responsible for the avoidance of financial assistance.

**Government Administration**

The highest percentage of rural male officials and urban female officials favour the government control on Cooperatives. But majority of urban male officials and rural female officials are against such favour. Among the officials favouring the control of government on Cooperatives, an equal percentage of rural male and urban female consider government as a good guide for Cooperatives. Urban female officials also perceive that government financial assistance to Cooperatives make it necessary to have its control on them. An equal percentage of rural male and female officials realise that government membership in Cooperatives make it important to have an overlook on them. While the officials who un-favour the control of government on Cooperatives think that it weakens the self-reliance of Cooperatives. Undue hindrance in the affairs of Cooperatives and lack of secrecy are another factors for un-favour of government control on Cooperatives. Over administered interference reduces the flexibility of day-to-day operations of Cooperatives. Majority of rural male officials consider incompetent management as the main cause of failure of Cooperatives. Lack of supervision is another cause of failure of most of the Cooperatives. Majority of urban male officials consider limited financial resources of Cooperatives, being responsible for its failure.

**Strategies**

Most of the rural male officials suggest the organisation of new Cooperatives in Kashmir. Urban female officials think that the existing poor Cooperatives should be revived. But the Cooperative Movement can be promoted by the organisation of new Cooperatives as well as by revival of existing Cooperatives. For the organisation of new Cooperatives, most of the urban male officials and rural female officials stress on the enforcement of Jammu and Kashmir Self-Reliant Cooperatives Act, 1999. People also need to be motivated to join the Cooperatives under this act. This conception is held by equal percentage of rural and urban male officials. Cooperative Education to people is favoured by most of the rural male and female officials. In order to implement Cooperative Education, all Cooperatives should make provision for education of their Members, employees and of the general public. For the revival of Cooperatives, amalgamation is considered a favourable step by urban male and female officials. Financial assistance should also been provided to poor Cooperatives in order to improve their economic status and thereby convert them into viable Cooperatives. Such view is held by an equal percentage of urban and rural female officials. The highest rural male officials stress on the exposition of new technology to Members of Cooperatives. Cooperatives should also ensure continuous and qualitative supply of inputs and service so as to gain the public confidence.

**Cooperative Education**

Majority of Cooperative officials in Kashmir favour the inclusion of Cooperative Education in formal system of education. An equal percentage of urban male and female officials suggest Cooperative Education in a main academic stream. Such education can increase the participation of youth as per majority of urban male officials; followed by rural female, urban female and rural male officials. Opportunity should be provided to youth by their involvement in the actual working of various types of Cooperative institutions at various levels. Thus, Cooperative Education performs a good role in eradication of unemployment. An equal percentage of rural and urban male officials ensure the success of Cooperatives through the dissemination of its education. Female officials encourage Cooperative Education at school level. Secondary schools should implement Cooperative Education in their curriculum. Majority of rural male and urban female officials recommend Cooperative Education at college level; while majority of urban male officials suggest intervention of universities for Cooperative Education. Urban male and female officials recommend Cooperative Education as an optional subject, but others recommend it as a compulsory subject in schools, colleges or universities.

**Women Cooperatives**

Women of Kashmir have a good hold on agricultural as well as consumer activities. Therefore, majority of urban male and rural female officials favour independent Cooperatives for women. Urban male officials consider Cooperatives as a best movement for women empowerment. Women should be given equal opportunity of their self-development, control and access over resources and they in turn should take advantage of these opportunities and equip themselves to come into main stream of development. Most of the urban officials have found women Members of Cooperatives as capable Cooperators. The maximum number of rural female and urban male officials favours Women Cooperatives for their economic uplift, family welfare and social benefits. Among the officials who do not favour independent establishment of Women Cooperatives, does not necessarily mean that they do not recommend women's active participation in Cooperatives. Rather, such officials feel that women should work shoulder to shoulder with men and Cooperatives of Kashmir should have the combined membership of men and women.

In order to join Cooperative Movement, most of the officials encourage Cooperative Education to women. Women should be taken on tours so that they can see and believe about the adoption of modern management practices in action in Cooperatives. Mostly, rural women are reluctant to approach Cooperative administration. That is why; most of the officials recommend easier and less formalities for the Women Cooperatives. The officials are not satisfied with the present number of Cooperatives and regard poor leadership qualities of women responsible for it.

Cooperative Department has also made fewer efforts in this direction and lack of Cooperative awareness among women is also responsible for it. The functioning of existing Women Cooperatives is considered dissatisfactory by an equal percentage of female officials in urban and rural areas. The reasons for poor functioning of Women Cooperatives are their inactive membership, lack of knowledge and lack of financial resources. Most of the women Members are untrained due to poor financial position of *Cooperative Department,* non-cooperation of women and lack of efforts by the department. Most of the officials suggest less interference of government in Women Cooperatives, women exposed to new technology and adequate financial assistance to Women Cooperatives. The officials also favour decentralization of powers in Women Cooperatives and reservation for women in managing committees of Cooperatives.

For the encouragement of women to join Cooperatives, majority of officials have expressed their desire for voluntary participation in an intervention programme regarding involvement of Kashmir women in Cooperative Movement; which has been held under the present thesis and majority of them are reported to be present in the same intervention programme.

### Attitudinal Orientation

No male official in urban areas has low attitude towards Cooperative Movement in Kashmir; while rural male officials with low attitudes towards Cooperative Movement comprise a considerable percentage. Urban officials as well as male officials of the department have high attitudes towards the Cooperative Movement than the rural officials and female officials in the department. Overall, the officials of both sexes in rural and urban areas have average level of attitudes towards the Cooperative Movement in Kashmir.

# ANNEXURE-1.1

**Table 1.1**
**Random Number**

| | | | | | | | | | |
|---|---|---|---|---|---|---|---|---|---|
| 20 17 | 42 28 | 23 17 | 59 66 | 38 61 | 02 10 | 86 10 | 51 55 | 92 52 | 44 25 |
| 74 49 | 04 49 | 04 49 | 10 33 | 53 70 | 11 54 | 48 63 | 94 60 | 94 49 | 57 38 |
| 94 70 | 49 31 | 38 67 | 23 42 | 29 65 | 40 88 | 78 71 | 37 18 | 48 64 | 06 57 |
| 22 15 | 78 15 | 69 84 | 32 52 | 32 54 | 15 12 | 54 02 | 01 37 | 38 37 | 12 93 |
| 93 29 | 12 18 | 27 30 | 30 55 | 91 87 | 50 57 | 58 51 | 49 36 | 12 53 | 96 40 |
| 45 04 | 77 97 | 36 14 | 99 45 | 52 95 | 69 85 | 03 83 | 51 87 | 85 56 | 22 37 |
| 44 91 | 99 49 | 89 39 | 94 60 | 48 49 | 06 77 | 64 72 | 59 26 | 08 51 | 25 57 |
| 16 23 | 91 02 | 19 96 | 47 59 | 89 65 | 27 84 | 30 92 | 63 37 | 26 24 | 23 66 |
| 04 50 | 65 04 | 65 65 | 82 42 | 70 51 | 55 04 | 61 47 | 88 83 | 99 34 | 82 37 |
| 32 70 | 17 72 | 03 61 | 66 26 | 24 71 | 22 77 | 88 33 | 17 78 | 08 92 | 73 49 |
| 03 64 | 59 07 | 42 95 | 81 39 | 06 41 | 20 81 | 92 34 | 51 90 | 39 08 | 21 42 |
| 62 49 | 00 90 | 67 86 | 93 48 | 31 82 | 19 07 | 67 68 | 49 03 | 27 47 | 52 03 |
| 61 00 | 95 86 | 98 36 | 14 03 | 48 88 | 51 07 | 33 40 | 06 86 | 33 76 | 68 57 |
| 89 03 | 90 49 | 28 74 | 21 04 | 09 96 | 60 45 | 22 03 | 52 80 | 01 79 | 33 81 |
| 01 72 | 33 85 | 52 40 | 60 07 | 06 71 | 89 27 | 14 29 | 55 24 | 85 79 | 31 96 |
| 27 56 | 49 79 | 34 34 | 32 22 | 60 53 | 91 17 | 33 26 | 44 70 | 93 14 | 99 70 |
| 49 05 | 74 48 | 10 55 | 35 25 | 24 28 | 20 22 | 35 66 | 66 34 | 26 35 | 91 23 |
| 49 74 | 37 25 | 97 26 | 33 94 | 42 23 | 01 28 | 59 58 | 92 69 | 03 66 | 73 82 |
| 20 26 | 22 43 | 88 08 | 19 85 | 08 12 | 47 65 | 65 63 | 56 07 | 97 85 | 56 79 |
| 48 87 | 77 96 | 43 39 | 76 93 | 08 79 | 22 18 | 54 55 | 93 75 | 97 26 | 90 77 |
| 08 72 | 87 46 | 75 73 | 00 11 | 27 07 | 05 20 | 30 85 | 22 21 | 04 67 | 19 13 |
| 95 97 | 98 62 | 17 27 | 31 42 | 64 71 | 46 22 | 32 75 | 19 32 | 20 99 | 94 85 |
| 37 99 | 57 31 | 70 40 | 46 55 | 46 12 | 24 32 | 36 74 | 69 20 | 72 10 | 95 93 |
| 05 79 | 58 37 | 85 33 | 75 18 | 88 71 | 23 44 | 54 28 | 00 48 | 96 23 | 66 45 |
| 55 85 | 63 42 | 00 79 | 91 22 | 29 01 | 41 39 | 51 40 | 36 65 | 26 11 | 78 32 |
| 67 28 | 96 25 | 68 36 | 24 72 | 03 85 | 49 24 | 05 69 | 64 86 | 08 19 | 91 21 |
| 85 86 | 94 78 | 32 59 | 51 82 | 86 43 | 73 84 | 45 60 | 89 57 | 06 87 | 08 15 |
| 40 10 | 60 09 | 05 88 | 78 44 | 63 13 | 58 25 | 37 11 | 18 47 | 75 62 | 52 21 |
| 94 55 | 89 48 | 90 80 | 77 80 | 26 89 | 87 44 | 23 74 | 66 20 | 20 19 | 26 52 |
| 11 63 | 77 77 | 23 20 | 33 62 | 62 19 | 29 03 | 94 15 | 56 37 | 14 09 | 47 16 |

*Contd...*

| 64 00 | 26 04 | 54 55 | 38 57 | 94 62 | 68 40 | 26 04 | 24 25 | 03 61 | 01 20 |
|---|---|---|---|---|---|---|---|---|---|
| 50 94 | 13 23 | 78 41 | 60 58 | 10 60 | 88 46 | 30 21 | 45 98 | 70 96 | 36 89 |
| 66 98 | 37 96 | 44 13 | 45 05 | 34 59 | 75 85 | 48 97 | 27 19 | 17 85 | 48 51 |
| 66 91 | 42 83 | 60 77 | 90 91 | 60 90 | 79 62 | 57 66 | 72 28 | 08 70 | 96 03 |
| 42 58 | 12 18 | 02 07 | 19 40 | 21 29 | 39 45 | 90 42 | 58 84 | 85 43 | 95 67 |
| 52 49 | 40 16 | 72 40 | 73 05 | 50 90 | 02 04 | 98 24 | 05 30 | 27 25 | 20 88 |
| 74 98 | 93 99 | 78 30 | 79 47 | 96 92 | 45 58 | 40 37 | 89 76 | 84 41 | 74 68 |
| 50 26 | 54 30 | 01 88 | 69 57 | 54 45 | 69 88 | 23 21 | 05 69 | 93 44 | 05 32 |
| 49 46 | 61 89 | 33 79 | 96 84 | 28 34 | 19 35 | 28 73 | 39 59 | 56 34 | 97 07 |
| 19 65 | 13 44 | 78 39 | 73 88 | 62 03 | 36 00 | 25 96 | 86 76 | 67 90 | 21 68 |
| 64 17 | 47 67 | 87 59 | 81 40 | 72 61 | 14 00 | 28 28 | 55 86 | 23 38 | 16 15 |
| 18 43 | 97 37 | 68 97 | 56 56 | 57 95 | 01 88 | 11 89 | 48 07 | 42 60 | 11 92 |
| 65 58 | 60 87 | 51 09 | 96 61 | 15 53 | 66 81 | 66 88 | 44 75 | 37 01 | 28 88 |
| 79 90 | 31 00 | 91 14 | 85 65 | 31 75 | 43 15 | 45 93 | 64 78 | 34 53 | 88 02 |
| 07 23 | 00 15 | 59 05 | 16 09 | 94 42 | 20 40 | 63 76 | 65 67 | 34 11 | 94 10 |
| 90 08 | 14 24 | 01 51 | 95 46 | 30 32 | 33 19 | 00 14 | 19 28 | 40 51 | 92 69 |
| 53 82 | 62 02 | 21 82 | 34 13 | 41 03 | 12 85 | 65 30 | 00 97 | 56 30 | 15 48 |
| 98 17 | 26 15 | 04 50 | 76 25 | 20 33 | 54 84 | 39 31 | 23 33 | 59 64 | 96 27 |
| 08 91 | 12 44 | 82 40 | 30 62 | 45 50 | 64 54 | 65 17 | 89 25 | 59 44 | 99 95 |
| 37 21 | 46 77 | 84 87 | 67 39 | 85 54 | 96 37 | 33 41 | 11 74 | 90 50 | 29 62 |

Each digit is an independent sample from a population in which the digits 0 to 9 are likely, that is each has a probability of 1/10.

# ANNEXURE-1.2

**Table 1.2**
**Random Number**

| 16 16 | 57 04 | 81 71 | 17 46 | 53 29 | 73 46 | 42 73 | 77 63 | 62 58 | 60 59 |
|---|---|---|---|---|---|---|---|---|---|
| 98 63 | 89 52 | 77 23 | 61 08 | 63 90 | 80 38 | 42 71 | 85 70 | 04 81 | 05 50 |
| 01 03 | 09 35 | 02 54 | 51 96 | 92 75 | 58 29 | 24 23 | 25 19 | 89 97 | 91 29 |
| 29 07 | 16 34 | 49 22 | 52 96 | 89 34 | 17 11 | 06 91 | 24 38 | 55 06 | 83 59 |
| 72 61 | 80 54 | 70 99 | 24 64 | 11 38 | 83 65 | 27 23 | 40 37 | 84 58 | 48 53 |
| 71 11 | 41 82 | 79 37 | 00 45 | 98 54 | 52 89 | 26 34 | 40 13 | 60 38 | 08 86 |
| 61 05 | 66 18 | 76 37 | 11 18 | 61 90 | 90 63 | 78 57 | 32 06 | 39 95 | 75 94 |
| 81 89 | 42 34 | 00 49 | 97 53 | 33 16 | 26 91 | 57 58 | 42 48 | 51 05 | 48 27 |
| 10 24 | 90 84 | 22 16 | 26 96 | 54 11 | 01 96 | 58 81 | 37 97 | 80 98 | 72 81 |
| 14 28 | 33 43 | 01 32 | 58 39 | 19 54 | 56 57 | 23 58 | 24 87 | 77 36 | 20 97 |
| 35 41 | 17 89 | 87 04 | 28 32 | 13 45 | 59 03 | 91 08 | 69 24 | 84 44 | 42 83 |
| 07 89 | 36 87 | 98 73 | 77 64 | 75 19 | 05 61 | 11 64 | 31 75 | 49 38 | 96 60 |
| 27 59 | 15 58 | 19 68 | 95 47 | 25 69 | 11 90 | 26 19 | 07 40 | 83 59 | 90 95 |
| 95 98 | 45 52 | 27 35 | 86 81 | 16 29 | 37 60 | 39 35 | 05 24 | 49 00 | 29 07 |
| 12 95 | 72 72 | 81 84 | 36 58 | 05 10 | 70 50 | 31 04 | 12 67 | 74 01 | 72 90 |
| 35 23 | 06 68 | 52 50 | 39 55 | 92 28 | 28 89 | 64 87 | 80 00 | 84 53 | 97 97 |
| 86 33 | 95 73 | 80 92 | 26 49 | 54 50 | 41 21 | 06 62 | 73 91 | 35 05 | 21 37 |
| 02 82 | 96 23 | 16 46 | 15 51 | 60 31 | 55 27 | 84 14 | 71 58 | 94 71 | 48 35 |
| 44 46 | 34 96 | 32 69 | 48 22 | 40 17 | 43 25 | 33 31 | 26 26 | 59 34 | 99 00 |
| 08 77 | 07 19 | 94 46 | 17 51 | 03 73 | 99 89 | 28 44 | 16 87 | 56 16 | 56 09 |
| 61 59 | 37 08 | 08 46 | 56 76 | 29 48 | 33 87 | 70 79 | 03 80 | 96 81 | 79 68 |
| 67 70 | 18 01 | 67 19 | 29 49 | 58 67 | 08 56 | 27 24 | 20 70 | 46 31 | 04 32 |
| 23 09 | 08 79 | 18 78 | 00 32 | 86 74 | 78 55 | 55 72 | 58 54 | 76 07 | 53 73 |
| 89 40 | 26 39 | 74 58 | 59 55 | 87 11 | 74 06 | 49 46 | 31 94 | 86 66 | 66 97 |
| 84 95 | 66 42 | 74 90 | 13 71 | 00 71 | 24 41 | 67 62 | 38 92 | 39 26 | 30 29 |
| 52 14 | 49 02 | 19 31 | 28 15 | 51 01 | 19 09 | 97 94 | 52 43 | 22 21 | 17 66 |
| 89 56 | 31 41 | 37 87 | 28 16 | 62 48 | 01 84 | 46 06 | 04 39 | 94 10 | 76 21 |
| 65 94 | 05 93 | 06 68 | 34 72 | 73 17 | 65 34 | 00 65 | 75 78 | 23 97 | 13 04 |
| 13 08 | 15 75 | 02 83 | 48 26 | 53 77 | 62 96 | 56 52 | 28 26 | 12 15 | 75 53 |
| 03 18 | 33 57 | 16 71 | 60 27 | 15 18 | 39 32 | 37 01 | 05 86 | 25 14 | 35 41 |

*Contd...*

| 10 04 | 00 95 | 85 04 | 32 80 | 19 01 | 85 03 | 29 29 | 80 04 | 21 52 | 14 76 |
|---|---|---|---|---|---|---|---|---|---|
| 23 94 | 97 28 | 60 43 | 42 25 | 26 48 | 48 13 | 34 68 | 39 22 | 74 85 | 03 25 |
| 35 63 | 42 90 | 90 74 | 33 17 | 73 17 | 83 36 | 76 22 | 00 89 | 61 55 | 13 17 |
| 42 86 | 03 36 | 45 33 | 60 77 | 53 77 | 10 76 | 22 55 | 11 00 | 37 60 | 47 73 |
| 67 26 | 92 87 | 09 96 | 85 37 | 15 18 | 39 01 | 70 05 | 12 66 | 17 39 | 99 34 |
| 91 93 | 88 56 | 35 76 | 97 35 | 19 37 | 14 66 | 07 57 | 24 41 | 06 90 | 07 72 |
| 37 14 | 73 35 | 32 01 | 07 94 | 78 28 | 90 33 | 71 56 | 63 77 | 89 24 | 24 28 |
| 07 46 | 50 58 | 08 73 | 42 97 | 20 42 | 64 68 | 48 35 | 04 38 | 28 28 | 36 94 |
| 92 18 | 09 46 | 94 99 | 17 41 | 28 60 | 67 94 | 26 54 | 63 70 | 84 73 | 76 61 |
| 00 49 | 98 43 | 39 67 | 68 40 | 41 31 | 92 28 | 49 57 | 15 55 | 11 81 | 41 89 |
| 08 59 | 41 41 | 33 59 | 43 28 | 14 51 | 02 71 | 24 45 | 41 57 | 22 11 | 79 79 |
| 67 05 | 19 54 | 32 33 | 34 68 | 27 93 | 39 35 | 62 51 | 35 55 | 40 99 | 46 19 |
| 24 99 | 48 06 | 96 41 | 21 25 | 29 03 | 57 71 | 96 49 | 94 74 | 98 90 | 21 52 |
| 65 86 | 27 46 | 70 93 | 27 39 | 64 37 | 01 63 | 21 03 | 43 78 | 18 74 | 77 07 |
| 52 70 | 03 20 | 84 96 | 14 37 | 51 05 | 63 99 | 81 02 | 84 56 | 17 78 | 48 45 |
| 32 88 | 29 93 | 58 21 | 71 05 | 68 58 | 79 08 | 86 37 | 98 76 | 70 45 | 66 23 |
| 54 16 | 39 40 | 98 57 | 02 05 | 65 15 | 73 23 | 51 51 | 75 06 | 38 13 | 51 68 |
| 95 22 | 18 59 | 54 57 | 44 22 | 72 35 | 81 24 | 14 94 | 24 04 | 42 26 | 92 14 |
| 93 10 | 27 94 | 90 45 | 39 33 | 50 26 | 88 46 | 90 57 | 40 47 | 71 63 | 62 59 |
| 19 20 | 85 20 | 15 67 | 78 03 | 32 23 | 50 59 | 24 83 | 64 99 | 18 00 | 78 50 |

Each digit is an independent sample from a population in which the digits 0 to 9 are likely, that is each has a probability of 1/10.

*Source:* Miller. J, (1996), Statistics for Advanced Level, Second Edition, New York, Cambridge University Press.

# ANNEXURE-2

## CHECK LIST AND ANECDOTAL RECORDS AS PER EXAMINATION OF RECORDS AND OBSERVATION OF COOPERATIVE SOCIETIES [GROUP-1]

*(n = 266)*

### General Information

i. Name of the District:______________________________

ii. Name of the Block:________________________________

iii. Total Population of District: _______ (a) Male____________ (b) Female__________

iv. Number of Cooperatives (Agricultural and Consumer) under the jurisdiction of each District:____________________

v. Number of Cooperatives (Agricultural and Consumer) under the jurisdiction of each Block:___________________________

vi. Number of Members in the Agricultural and Consumer Cooperatives in the District:_________________________

vii. Number of Members in the Agricultural and Consumer Cooperatives in the Block: ___________________________

### Specific Information

1. General Condition of the Cooperative:
   (a) Very Good (b) Good (c) Average (d) Poor (e) Very Poor:
   ________________________________________________
2. Name of the Cooperative : ___________________________
3. (a) Type of Cooperative : ______________________________
   (b) Category of Cooperative: (i) Women Cooperative (ii) Men Cooperative: __________________________________

4 Address: ____________________
5. Urban/Rural Cooperative: ____________________
6. Registration Number: ____________________
7. Date of Establishment/Registration: ____________________
8. Registration Authority: ____________________
09. Act under which the Cooperative is registered:____________________
10. Area of operation: ____________________
11. Number of branches/depots: ____________________
12. Individual Membership: Total: ____________________
    (a) Male: ________ (i) Active: ________ (ii) Inactive: ________
    (b) Female: ________ (i) Active: ________ (ii) Inactive: ________
13. Is Government Member of the Cooperative:
    (a) Yes (b) No ____________________
14. If Yes; Level of Government being the Member of Cooperative:
    (a) State Government
    (b) Central Government ____________________
15. Is any other organisation of Cooperative the Member of the Cooperative?
    (a) Yes
    (b) No ____________________
16. If yes; name of the organisation or Cooperative being the Member of the Cooperative ____________________
17. Individual share capital (in Rupees): ____________________
18. Has Government share capital provided to the Cooperative:
    (a) Yes
    (b) No ____________________
19. If yes; amount of share capital provided by Government to the Cooperative (in Rupees): ____________________
20 Is the Cooperative provided any other financial assistance by the Government?
    (a) Yes
    (b) No ____________________
21. If yes; type of financial assistance provided by the Government:
    (a) Managerial subsidy (b) Special assistance (c) Interest free loan (d) Any Other____________________
22. Amount provided under such financial assistances (in Rupees):
    ____________________

23. Year(s) during which such financial assistances have been provided: ____________________
24. Has Cooperative borrowed any loan from bank:

    (a) Yes (b) No ____________________
25. If yes; amount of bank borrowing (in Rupees): ____________
26. Name of the bank from which the loan is borrowed: ________
27. Major marketing channels:

    (a) Private traders (b) Hostel/School/College (c) Cooperative Organisations (d) Local market (e) All ____________
28. Total number of employees in the Cooperative:____________
29. Number of trained employees/Members given training by Cooperative Department: ____________________
30. Number of employees/Members taken on tours at successful Cooperative enterprises outside the State by the Cooperative Department: ____________________
31. Whether employees are working on: (a) Salary basis (b) Commission basis ____________________
32. In case of salary; the amount ((in Rupees) of salary per month: ____________________
33. In case of commission; the percentage of profit distributed per employee per annum: ____________________
34. If Cooperative is having:

    (a) Own Office (b) Rented Office ____________________
35. Number of Godowns pertaining to the Cooperative:

    Total: ____________ (a) Hired: ____________ (b) Own: ____________
36. Capacity in Godowns pertaining to the Cooperative (in quintals):

    Total: ____________ (a) Hired: ____________ (b) Own: ____________
37. Who conducts the audit of the Cooperative: ____________
38. Last audit held on: ____________________

    (a) Reason for Un-audit of Cooperative:____________
39. Whether Cooperative is exempted from certain taxes, fees and/ or duties:

    (a) Yes (b) No ____________________
40. (a) Is Cooperative amalgamated with any other Cooperative

    (i) Yes (ii) No ____________________

(b) If By-Laws are amended due to amalgamation:
(i) Yes (ii) No ____________________

41. In case of yes; year of amalgamation: ____________
42. Reason for amalgamation:
    (a) Raise share capital
    (b) Increase area of Operation
    (c) Any other; ____________________
43. Have By-Laws ever been amended since its establishment:
    (a) Yes (b) No ____________________
44. In case of Yes; reasons for amendment of By-Laws: ________
45. Year of amendment of By-Laws: ____________
46. As per By-Laws; if Cooperative shall provide loan to its Members:
    (a) Yes (b) No ____________________
47. Type of loan which Cooperative shall provide; (a) Long-Term Loan (b) Medium-Term Loan (c) Short-Term Loan (d) All ____________________
48. Is Cooperative providing loan to its Members
    (a) Yes (b) No ____________________
49. If yes; type of loan provided to Members:
    (a) Long-Term Loan (b) Medium-Term Loan (c) Short-Term Loan (d) All ____________________
50. If no; reason for not providing loan to Members:
    (a) Poor financial Position
    (b) Lack of confidence on Members
    (c) No desire by Members
    (d) Any other ____________________
51. Economy of Cooperative
    (a) Profit (b) Loss ____________________
52. Business Turnover/ Sales during 2001-2002 (in Rupees): ________
53. (a) Assets (in Rupees) as per latest audit note: ____________
    (b) Liabilities (in Rupees) as per latest audit note: ________
54. (a) Net Profit (in Rupees ) as per latest audit note: ________
    (b) Net Loss (in Rupees) as per latest audit note: ________
55. Whether the Cooperative is:
    (a) Viable (b) Non-Viable ____________________

# ANNEXURE-3

## QUESTIONNAIRE FOR OFFICERS/OFFICIALS OF COOPERATIVE DEPARTMENT [GROUP II]

*(n = 100)*

**General Information**

i. Name ____________________

ii. Sex: ____________________

iii. Age: ____________________

iv. Qualification: ____________________

v. Designation: ____________________

vi. Monthly Salary: ____________________

vii. Posted at: ____________________

viii. Whether posted area is rural or urban: ____________________

ix. Residential area: ____________________

x. Whether residential area is rural or urban : ____________________

xi. Approximate distance covered from residential to posted area (Kms): ____________________

**Specifiec Information**

1. Since how long you are working in Cooperative Department?
   (a) Up to 5 years
   (b) 5-10 years
   (c) 10-15 years
   (d) 15-20 years
   (e) 20-25 years

(f) 25-30 years

(g) More than 30 years

2. (a) Being an Official/Officer of the Cooperative Department, are you:
   - i. Satisfied
   - ii. Dissatisfied

   (b) If Satisfied; reasons:
   - i. Achieve economic independence
   - ii. Feel like serving the nation
   - iii. Has improved/increased the status

   (c) If Dissatisfied; reasons:
   - i. Less salary
   - ii. Less chances of promotion
   - iii. No encouragement for good performance
   - iv. Heavy load of work
   - v. Bad treatment by employer
   - vi. Distance

3. What is the main idea behind establishing Agricultural and Consumer Cooperatives in the State?

   (a) Economic uplift of poor people

   (b) Promoting mutual cooperation among people

   (c) Just to expend a Cooperative Movement

4. Do you think Cooperative Department is fulfilling its basic aim?

   (a) Yes

   (b) No

5. Are you satisfied with the functioning of existing Cooperatives in the State?

   (a) Yes

   (b) No

6. (a) Is there appropriate coordination between the Members of Cooperatives and the department?

   (a) Yes

   (b) No

   (b) If no; reasons:
   - i. Communication gap
   - ii Lack of confidence on Cooperatives by department
   - iii. Lack of confidence on department by Cooperatives

7. At present, why not financial assistance is provided to Agricultural and Consumer Cooperative Societies by the Cooperative Department?
   (a) Due to financial crunch
   (b) Huge outstanding of loans in existing Cooperative Societies
   (c) Lack of coordination between Members of Cooperative Societies and administration
8. (a) Do you favour the control of Cooperative Department on Cooperative Societies?
   (a) Yes
   (b) No
   (b) If yes; reasons:
   i. Keeps the Society on right path
   ii. Ensures the financial assistance
   iii. Government being the Member of Cooperative Societies
   (c) If no; reasons:
   i. Weakens self reliance of Cooperative Members
   ii. Undue hindrance in functioning of Cooperative Societies
   iii. Control of Cooperative Department lacks secrecy of Cooperative business
9. How can Cooperatives contribute for community development?
   (a) By providing self employment to people
   (b) By holding the price line
   (c) By promoting mutual cooperation among people
10. What are the reasons of failure of most of the Cooperative Societies in the State?
   (a) Incompetent Management
   (b) Lack of supervision
   (c) Limited financial resources
11. (a) Which of the following is the urgent need of Cooperative Department:
   i. Organise new Cooperatives
   ii. Revive the existing Cooperative Societies
   iv. Both
   (b) What strategies should be adopted to organise new Cooperatives?

i. Enforcement of new act
ii. Motivation to people
iii. Cooperative education to people

(c) What strategy should be adopted for the revival of Cooperative Societies in the State?

i. Amalgamation of Cooperative Societies
ii. Financial assistance to the Cooperative Societies
iv. Members should be exposed to new technology
v. Continuous and qualitative supply of inputs to Cooperative Societies

(d) What strategy should be adopted for the revival of Cooperative Societies in the State?

12. (a) Should there be independent Cooperatives for women?

i. Yes
ii. No

(b) If yes; why?

i. For women empowerment
ii. Women can prove good co-operators than men
iii. Any other reason

(c) If no; why?

i. Incapability of women
ii. Bickering take place among women over petty issues
iii. Women cannot do anything without men's assistance
iv. Any other reason

13. (a) Is the present number of Women Cooperative Societies satisfactory?

i. Yes
ii. No

(b) In case of no; what is the reason for having such meagre number of Women Cooperative Societies in the State?

i. Poor leadership qualities in women
ii. Lack of efforts by Cooperative Department
iii. Lack of Cooperative awareness among women

14. Are the existing Women Cooperative Societies efficiently running their business?

i. Yes
ii. No

15. What is the reason for slow development of Women Cooperatives?
    (a) Most of women Members are inactive
    (b) Lack of knowledge
    (c) Lack of financial resources
16. Do you favour more decentralisation of powers for Women Cooperative Societies?
    i. Yes
    ii. No
17. Should there be reservation for women Members in managing committees/boards?
    i. Yes
    ii. No
18. What steps should be taken to improve the status of existing Women Cooperatives?
    (a) Less interference by Cooperative Department
    (b) Exposing women to new technology and Cooperative Education
    (c) Adequate financial assistance to Women Cooperatives
19. How can be women of the State encouraged joining the Cooperative Movement?
    (a) By disseminating Cooperative Education among women
    (b) By taking women to tours at places where Women Cooperatives are highly successful
    (c) By making avenues for establishment of Women Cooperatives easier for them
20. In your opinion, have women of the State:
    (a) More say in Consumer activities only
    (b) More say in Agricultural activities only
    (c) In both activities
    (d) None
21. Why is not Cooperative Department providing training programmes to women Members of Cooperatives?
    (a) Poor financial position of Cooperative Department
    (b) Non-cooperation on part of women Members
    (c) Lack of efforts by the field staff
22. (a) Should Cooperative Education be included in formal system of education?

i. Yes

ii. No

(b) If yes; why?

i. Increase participation of youth in Cooperatives

ii. Eradicate unemployment

iii. Ensure the success of Cooperatives

(c) At which level such education should be included?

i. School level

ii. College level

iii. University

iv. All

(d) Should Cooperative Education be imparted as:

i. An optional Subject

ii. Compulsory subject

23. Would you to join voluntarily any intervention programme in order to motivate women of the state to establish their own Cooperative?

a. Yes

b. No

# ANNEXURE-4

**SCALE REGARDING ATTITUDES OF COOPERATIVE PERSONNEL TOWARDS COOPERATIVE MOVEMENT (ACPCM) [GROUP II]**

*(n = 100)*

| *Sl. No.* | *Statements* | *Pasitive* | *Negative* |
|---|---|---|---|
| 1. | Cooperative is a sole organisation truly helping for the upliftment of poor people. | ❑ | ❑ |
| 2. | Cooperatives promote mutual cooperation among people and serve as a means of community development. | ❑ | ❑ |
| 3. | Cooperatives are helping people to become self reliant. | ❑ | ❑ |
| 4. | Cooperative Movement is best to make people self employed. | ❑ | ❑ |
| 5. | A Cooperative can be easily formed because the formalities required for its establishment are less. | ❑ | ❑ |
| 6. | Primary Agricultural Cooperative Societies are really benefiting rural people. | ❑ | ❑ |
| 7. | National Cooperative Union of India and Jammu and Kashmir Cooperative Union are appropriate agencies to undertake the responsibility of disseminating Cooperative Education. | ❑ | ❑ |

*Contd...*

| Sl. No. | Statements | Pasitive | Negative |
|---|---|---|---|
| 8. | Women participation among Cooperatives should be increased. | ❑ | ❑ |
| 9. | It is best to organise self help groups of the inactive Members in Cooperatives. | ❑ | ❑ |
| 10. | Cooperative Department should ensure continuous and qualitative supply of inputs to Cooperatives. | ❑ | ❑ |
| 11. | Cooperative Education should be disseminated to general masses. | ❑ | ❑ |
| 12. | Government should continue to finance the Cooperative Societies. | ❑ | ❑ |
| 13. | The non-functional Cooperative Societies should be winded up. | ❑ | ❑ |
| 14. | Amalgamation of Cooperative Societies is not beneficial for the success of Cooperative Societies. | ❑ | ❑ |
| 15. | Excessive Government control on Cooperative Societies should be eliminated. | ❑ | ❑ |
| 16. | Cooperative Members should be taken to study tours and exposed to new technology. | ❑ | ❑ |
| 17. | Lack of competent management is the cause of failure of most of the Cooperatives. | ❑ | ❑ |
| 18. | The law of one-Cooperative Member from one-family should be eliminated. | ❑ | ❑ |
| 19. | After a dramatic start, a Cooperative often becomes lifeless and paralysed because of mutual rivalries. | ❑ | ❑ |
| 20. | People are less motivated to join Cooperatives. | ❑ | ❑ |
| 21. | Misappropriation of funds has weakened the Cooperative Movement. | ❑ | ❑ |
| 22. | Full disclosure of its affairs has made it difficult to preserve the secrecy of Cooperatives. | ❑ | ❑ |

## REFERENCE


Agarwal, K. (1988), *"Status and Role of Middle Class Educational Earning Women in the Indian Family"*, in Dak, T.M., (ed.), *'Women and Work in Indian Society'*, 1st Edition, Delhi, Discovery Publishing House.

Agha, S.A., Rao, P.C., and Singh, S.T. (1960), *"Cooperative: Economic and Social Background"*, Jammu, Jammu and Kashmir Cooperative Union Limited.

Ahanger, G.N. (1998), *"Cooperative Development in Jammu and Kashmir"*, Paper Presented at 3 days Workshop on Cooperatives, Jammu and Kashmir State, 16th-18th April, Organised by University of Jammu, Department of Management Studies.

Aharoni, Y. (1991), *"The Israeli Economy:Dreams and Realities"*, London/New York, Routledge.

Ahmad, R. and Haque, B. (1997), *"Ninth Plan and Challenges before Agriculture"*, Cooperator's Bulletin, XXXX (7-8), July-Aug., Jammu, Jammu and Kashmir Cooperative Union Limited.

Ahmad, S. M. and Bano, R. (1984), *"Historical Geography of Kashmir: Based on Arabic and Persian Sources from A.D. 800 to 1900"*, New Delhi, Ariana Publishing House.

Alva, M. (1998), *"Women in India"*, Manorama Year Book, Kottayam, Kerala, Malayala Manorama.

Amarchand, D., and Varadhara, J.B. (1979), *"An Introduction to Marketing"*, 1st Edition, New Delhi, Vikas Publishing House.

Anjaria, J.J. (1968), *"Development of Cooperative Marketing"*, Bombay, Reserve Bank of India.

*Annual Report* (1998), Jammu, Jammu and Kashmir Cooperative Union Limited.

Anshuman, Singh,Y., and Singh, U. (2002), *"Youth and Cooperatives: Some Vital Aspects", Cooperators Bulletin,* XXXXV (8), Aug., Jammu, Jammu and Kashmir Cooperative Union Limited.

Attallah, N. (1987), *"Women and Muslim Society",* London, Ouartlet Books.

Attwood, D.W., and Baviskar, B.S. (1987), *"Why do some Cooperatives Work but not others? A Comparative Analysis of Sugar Cooperative in India",* Economic and Political Weekly, XXII (26), June, ICSSR Journal of Abstracts and Reviews, Economics, XVII (2), April-June, New Delhi, Indian Council of Social Science and Research.

Awasty, I. (1982), *"Rural Women in India",* Delhi, B. R. Publishing Corporation.

Bachute, K.V. (2000), *"A Study of Human Resource Aspect of Non-Agricultural Cooperative Credit Societies in Wai Taluks: District Satara; Maharashtra",* The Maharashtra Cooperative Quarterly, LXXXIII (4), April-June, Pune, Maharashtra Rajya Sahakari Sangh.

Bakki, R. (1986), *"The Demographic Crisis of the Jewish People",* June, 1, Ha'aretz.

Bamzai, P.N.K. (1973), *"A History of Kashmir: Political, Social, Cultural; From Earliest Times to the Present Day",* 2nd Ed., N. Delhi, Metro-Politian Book Co. Pvt. Ltd.

Bamzai, P.N.K., (1994), *"Cultural and Political History of Kashmir",* Vol.1, (Ancient Kashmir), Vol. 2, (Medieval Kashmir), Vol. 3 (Modern Kashmir), New Delhi, M.D. Publications Pvt. Ltd.

Bandna (2000), *"A Case Profile of a Community Polytechnic, Jammu: Special Focus on Women's Programme",* An Unpublished Dissertation Submitted to the University of Jammu in Partial Fulfilment of the Requirement for the degree of Masters of Home Science, Jammu, P.G. Department of Home Science, Human Development, University of Jammu.

Bedi, R.D. (1984), *"Mudialy Fishermen's Cooperative Society Ltd.",* ICA Regional Bulletin, 24(3), July, New Delhi, International Cooperative Alliance.

Beena, S., and Sharma, D.N. (1997), *"Cooperative Movement among Neo-Literate Women of Durg District: A Case Study", Journal of Education and Social Change,* 10-11 (4-1), Jan-Mar/April-June, Suchan Quary Output, SISN 19750, Shreemati Nathibai Damodar

Thackersey, Women's University Library, Mumbai, National Information Centre.

Behara, M., and Dash, T.R. (2001), *"An Economic Analysis of the Growth and Performance of Cooperatives in Orrisa"*, The Maharashtra Cooperative Quarterly, LXXXV (1), July-Sept., Pune, Maharashtra Rajya Sahakari Sangh.

Beniwal, K. (1981), *"Women in the Indian Cooperative Movement"*, Cooperative News Digest, XXXII (8), Aug., Bombay, Reserve Bank of India.

Berthoin, A.A, and Izraeli, D.N. (1993), *"A Globe Comparison of Women in Management: Women Managers in their Homelands and as Expatriates"*, in Ellen, A.F., (ed.), *'Women in Management: Trends, Issues and Challenges in Managerial Diversity'*, Vol. 4, Newbury Park, Calif, Sage Publications.

Bharti, K.S. (1982), *"Role of Women in Consumer Cooperation"*, Cooperator's Bulletin, XXV (8), Aug., Jammu, Jammu and Kashmir Cooperative Union Limited.

Bharati, S. (1975), *"Role of Women in Cooperatives"*, The Cooperator, XIII (1), July, New Delhi, National Cooperative Union of India.

Bhasin, K. (1991), *"Women's Literacy for Domestication or Empowerment"*, in Anita, (ed.), *'Women's Quest for Equality: Land Relations and Women'*, Jaipur, Institute of Public Administration.

Bhatt, E. (1991), *"Women and Self Employment: Case Study of SEWA"*, in Kalbag, C., (ed.), *'Women and Development: Women, Employment and the Work Place'*, Vol. 1, New Delhi, Discovery Publishing House.

Bhatt, E. (1992), *"Cooperatives and Empowerment of Women"*, PLN Raju Memorial Lecture, Hyderabad, Samakhya.

Bhattacharya, S. (1985), *"On the Issue of Under Remuneration of Women's Work in the Indian Data Collection System"*, in Jain, D., Banerjee, N., (eds.), *'Women in Poverty: Tyranny of the Household—Investigative Essays on Women's Work'*, New Delhi, Vikas Publishing House Pvt. Ltd.

Bhatnagar, V.S. (1996), *"Women in Medieval India: A Study of Position and Images"*, in Jain, P., Mahan. R., (eds.), 'Women Images', New Delhi, Rawat Publications.

Bhave, G.P. (1982), *"Cooperative Education: Backbone of the Movement"*, Cooperative News Digest, XXXIII (2), April, Bombay, Reserve Bank of India.

Bird, E., David, M., Malas, E. *et al.* (1979), *"Half the Sky: An Introduction to Women Studies"*, London, VIRAGO Press.

Bisht, L.S. (2000), *"LDB vis-à-vis Farm Development; A Case Study of Long Term Cooperative Credit"*, The Maharashtra Cooperative Quarterly, LXXXIII (4), April-June, Pune, Maharashtra Rajya Sahakari Sangh.

Britt, S.H., and Boyd, H.W. (1968), *"Marketing Management and Administrative Action"*, New Delhi, McGraw-Hill Company.

Bryant, W. (1990), *"Child Care Options for Employers"*, Aug., Institute of Personal Management Journal.

Buddhapriya, S. (1999), *"Women in Management"*, New Delhi, Andhra Pradesh, H. Publishing Corporation.

Burkner, A. (1998), *"The Japanese Cooperatives"*, IRU Courier, Raiffeison, 1, April, Adenauralle, International Raiffeisen Union.

Census of India (2001), *"Provisional Population Totals"*, Series 2 & 3, Paper 2 & 3, Jammu and Kashmir, Director of Census Operations.

Central Statistical Organisation (2000), *"Women and Men in India"*, New Delhi, Ministry of Statistics and Programme Implementation, Government of India.

Chachal, S.S., and Gill, G.S. (1988), *"Milk Cooperatives for Rural Development in Punjab", Yojana*, XXXVI (5), Feb., ICSSR Journal of Abstracts and Review, Economics, XVIII (4), Jan-Dec., New Delhi, Indian Council of Social Science and Research.

Chadha, K. (1990), *"The Impact of Tourism on the Ecosystem in Kashmir", in* S.K. Chadha (ed.), *'Ecology of Kashmir'*, New Delhi, Ashish Publishing House.

Chan, A., and Lee, J. (1994), *"Women Executives in a Newly Industrialized Economy: The Singapore Scenario"*, in Adler, N.J., Izraeli, D.N., (eds.), *'Competitive Frontiers: Women Managers in a Global Economy'*, Cambridge (United States of America)/ Oxford (England), Black Well Publishers.

Chander, J. (2001), *"Performance of Primary Agricultural Credit Societies (PACS) in Himachal Pradesh: A Comparative Study"*, The Maharashtra Cooperative Quarterly, LXXXIV (4), April-June, Pune, Maharashtra Rajya Sahakari Sangh.

Chandra, S.K. (1996), *"Women's Development: Problems and Prospects", in* Aleem, S., (ed.), New Delhi, APH Publishing Corporation.

Chandra, S. K., and Lahshmirwaramma, M. (1991), *"Working Women and Infant Care"*, 1st Edition, New Delhi, Mittal Publications.

Chatt, Z.A. (1996), *"Management of Cooperative Institutions"*, 1st Edition, New Delhi, Dilpreet Publishing House.

Cheng, W. and Liao, L. (1994), *"Women Managers in Taiwan"*, in Adler, N.J., Izraeli, D.N., (eds.), *'Comparative Frontiers: Women Managers in a Global Economy'*, Cambridge (United States of America)/ Oxford (England), Black Well Publishers.

Chohan, A.S. (1998), *"Communications and Transport in the Princely State of Jammu and Kashmir"*, 1st Edition, Jammu, Radha Krishan Anand and Co.

Chuttervedi, R.K. (1978), *"Status of Women"*, Coimbatore, Oakla Publishers.

Cooperative Initiative Panel (1999), *"State of Cooperation in India: Statement on the Cooperative Identity"*, Based on ICA Contennial Congress of 23, Sept., 1995, Manchester, United Kingdom, Gujarat, Anand.

Country Paper (1985), *"Women in India"*, New Delhi, Ministry of Social and Women's Welfare, Government of India.

Dabir, N., and Bora, M. (1996), *"A Study of Women's Cooperatives in Mumbai"*, Shreemati Nathibai Damodar Thackersey Women's University, M. H. Sc. Dissertation, Suchi Query Output, SISN 101648, Shreemati Nathibai Damodar Thackersey Women's University Library, Mumbai, National Information Centre.

Dabla, B.A. (1991), *"Working Women in Kashmir"*, New Delhi, Rawat Publications.

Dash, D.K. (2001), *"Human Assets, the Factors of Turn Around: A Case-Study of Nav Nirman Cooperative Bank; Ahmedabad"*, The Maharashtra Cooperative Quarterly, LXXXIV (3), Jan-March, Pune, Maharashtra Rajya Sahakari Sangh.

Date, V. (1998), *"State Proposes 33 Percent Quota for Women in Cooperative Sector"*, The Times of India, July 22, ICVF 4629, Suchan Query Output, SISN 1311, Shreemati Nathibai Damodar Thackersey Women's University Library, Mumbai, National Information Centre.

Davar, R.S. (1977), *"Modern Marketing Management in the Indian Context"*, 4th Edition, Bombay Progressive Corporation Pvt. Ltd.

Desai, A.R. (1978), *"Village Cooperatives: An Analysis of their Failure"*, Rural Sociology in India, 5th Edition, Bombay, Popular Prakashan Pvt. Ltd.

Desai, J.C. (1978), *"A Unique Women's Cooperative: SEWA Bank"*, NCDC Bulletin, 4, Oct., New Delhi, National Cooperative Development Corporation.

Deshmukh, M. A. (1986), *"Scope and Limitations of Cooperative Law in Assisting Weaker Sections", The Cooperative Law Journal*, XXII (III), July, New Delhi, National Cooperative Union of India.

Dev, J.S. (1980), *"Women Industrial Cooperatives in Jammu and Kashmir"*, Cooperator's Bulletin, 23 (7), July, Jammu, Jammu and Kashmir Cooperative Union Limited.

Dev, J.S. (1982), *"Development of Cooperative Movement in Leh and Kargil"*, Cooperator's Bulletin, XXV (11), Nov., Jammu, Jammu and Kashmir Cooperative Union Limited.

Dev, J.S. (1983), *"Natural Calamities in Jammu and Kashmir"*, New Delhi, Ariana Publishing House.

Dev, J.S. (1988), *"Rural Women and Cooperatives"*, Cooperative Bulletin, XXXI (5), May, Jammu, Jammu and Kashmir Cooperative Union Limited.

Dev, J.S. (1992), *"Cooperatives and Development"*, Cooperator's Bulletin, XXXV (9), Septt., Jammu, Jammu and Kashmir Cooperative Union Limited.

Dev, J.S. (1998), *"Emerging Challenges to Cooperative Movement in Jammu and Kashmir State and Future Strategy", Cooperator's Bulletin*, XXXXI (4&5), April & May, Jammu, Jammu and Kashmir Cooperative Union Limited.

Dev, J.S. (2001), *"Cooperative Movement in Jammu and Kashmir", Cooperator's Bulletin*, XXXXIV (9-10), Oct.-Nov., Jammu, Jammu and Kashmir Cooperative Union Limited.

Devaraja, T.S. (2001), *"Performance Evaluation of Sarada Mahila Cooperative Bank Limited in Mygore City of Karnataka"*, The Maharashtra Cooperative Quarterly, LXXXIV (4), April-June, Pune, Maharashtra Rajya Sahakari Sangh.

Devi, U.L. (1982), *"Status and Employment of Women in India"*, New Delhi, B. R. Publishing Corporation.

Devi, U.S. (1994), *"Women, Development and Ecology"*, New Delhi, Har Anand Publications.

Devdas, R. P. (1983), *"Role of Women in Agricultural Development"*, Paper presented in the Seminar on *'Training for Agriculture and Rural Development'* Hisar, Haryana Agricultural University.

Dhar, S.N. (1998), *"Kashmiri Women"*, in Sharma, S.K., Sharma, U., (eds.), *'Kashmir through Ages: Society, Economy and Cultural'*, Vol. 3, New Delhi, Deep and Deep Publications.

Dharmarajan, S. (1999), *"Savings Linked Micro Credit to Women for Small Business: An Innovative Venture in Cooperation"*, The Maharashtra Cooperative Quarterly, 83 (2), Oct-Dec., Suchan Query Output, SISN 11742, Shreemati Nathibai Damodar Thackersey Women's University Library, Mumbai, National Information Centre.

Dharmarujan, S. (2001), *"Business Diversification of Kerala Dinesh Beedi: A Journey towards Strategic Management", The Maharashtra Cooperative Quarterly*, LXXXIV (4), April-June, Pune, Maharashtra Rajya Sahakari Sangh.

Dhingra, I.C. (1992), *"Business Economics"*, 1st Edition, New Delhi, Sultan Chand and Sons.

Directorate General of Information (1989), *"Jammu and Kashmir: The Changing Scenario"*, Srinagar, Kashmir, Public Relations and Tourism Publicity; Jammu and Kashmir Government.

Director of Tourism (1988), *"Kashmir: A-Z"*, Srinagar, Government of Jammu and Kashmir.

*Directory of Women Managers in South East Asia* (1990), Vol. (1, 2 & 3), Kuala Lumpur, WOW-Malaysia.

Doshi, S.L., and Jain, P. C. (1999), *"Rural Sociology"*, New Delhi, Rawat Publications.

D'Souza, V.S. (1980), *"Women in Contemporary Indian and South Asia"*, New Delhi, Manohar Publications.

Duggal, K. (2001), *"Cooperative Marketing in Uttar Pradesh", The Maharashtra Cooperative Quarterly*, LXXXIV (4), April-June, Pune, Maharashtra Rajya Sahakari Sangh.

Elayath, K.M.N. (1976), *"Bangalore Women's Successful Industrial Cooperative Enterprise"*, The Cooperator, IV (4-5), Aug-Sept., New Delhi, National Cooperative Union of India.

Elliot, M. A. and Marrill, F. (1961), *"Social Disorganisation"*, 4th Edition, New York, Harper and Raw Publishers.

Equal Opportunities Commission (1991), *"Women and Men in Britain"*, Manchester, Equal Opportunities Commission.

Erwee, R. (1988), *"Career Development Strategies in Organisation: Current Practices and Future Scenarios"*, Unpublished Research Report, University of Pretoria.

Erwee, R. (1994), *"South African Women: Changing Career Patterns"*, in Adler, N.J., Izraeli, D.N., (eds.), *'Competitive Frontiers: Women Managers in a Global Economy'*, Cambridge (United States of America)/Oxford (England), Blackwell Publishers.

Felder, A.C. (1980), *"The United States Cooperative Movement Today"*, Cooperative News Digest, XXXI (10), Oct., Bombay, Reserve Bank of India.

Fourteenth Indian Cooperative Congress (2001), *"Recommendations/ Resolutions"*, The Cooperator, XXXIX (4), Oct., New Delhi, National Cooperative Union of India.

Gandotra, S. (2001), *"Women's Desire for Social Freedom"*, An Unpublished Dissertation Submitted to University of Jammu in Partial Fulfilment of the Requirement for the Degree of Masters in Home Science (Human Development), Jammu, Post Graduate Department of Home Science, University of Jammu.

Ganesan, A.H. (1982), *"Mulukanoor Cooperative Rural Bank Limited"*, ICA Regional Bulletin, 22(1), Jan., New Delhi, International Cooperative Alliance.

Garg, R.B.L. (1978), *"Family Welfare through Cooperatives"*, NCDC Bulletin, XII (4), Oct., New Delhi, National Cooperative Development Corporation.

Gaur, V.P. and Narang, D.B. (1992), *"Income Tax, Law and Practice"*, 19th Edition, New Delhi, Kalyani Publishers.

General Studies Manual (2004), 'Five Year Plans', New Delhi, Competition Review Pvt., Limited.

Ghosh, G.N. (1998), *"Cooperative for the Other Fifty Percent"*, NAFED: Marketing Review, XXVIII (8-10), Aug-Oct., New Delhi, National Agricultural Cooperative Marketing Federation of India Limited.

Giriappa, S. (1988), *"The Role of Women in Rural Development"*, Delhi, Daya Publishing House.

Goel, B.B. (1983), *"Role of Cooperatives in Agricultural Development: Citizen's Perception"*, Indian Cooperative Review, XXI (2), Oct., New Delhi, National Cooperative Union of India.

Goel, B.B. (1991), *"Management of Marketing Cooperatives"*, New Delhi, Deep and Deep Publications.

Ghoel, S.K., and Pandey, R.N. (1987), *"An Analysis of Factors Affecting Over Dues of Primary Agricultural Cooperative Credit and Service Societies in Haryana"*, Indian Cooperative Review, XXV(1), July, ICSSR Journal of Abstracts and Review, Economics, XVII (3), July-Sept., New Delhi, Indian Council of Social Science and Research.

Gogoi, T. (1992), *"Sugar Industry and Cooperatives"*, NCDC Bulletin, XXV (6), Feb., New Delhi, National Cooperative Development Corporation.

Gopalakrishan, M.K. (1981), *"Development of Cooperative Leadership"*, Cooperator's Bullitin, XXIV (5), Oct., Jammu, Jammu and Kashmir Cooperative Union Limited.

Gopinath, C. and Kalra, A.H. (1985), *"India: Gujarat Medium Irrigation Project"*, in Overholt, C., Anderson, M., Cloud, K., Auston, J., (eds.), *'Gender Roles in Development Projects'*, West Hartfund, Kumarian Press.

Gopu, J.J. (1997), *"The Role of Cooperative Society in South Arkot District"*, Cooperator's Bulletin, XXXX (1), Jan., Jammu, Jammu and Kashmir Cooperative Union Limited.

Gosh, G.K. (1995), *"Women and Industry: Environment and Women Development"*, Lessons from Third World, New Delhi, Ashish Publishing House.

Gound, R.S. (1992), *"Rural Electric Cooperatives in Rural Development: A Case Study of CESS"*, in Sagar, G.V., Pani, K.C., Reddy, S.K., (eds.), *'Rural Development and Local Participation'*, New Delhi, Anmol Publications.

Government of Andhra Pradesh (1985), *"Handbook of Statistics on Cooperative Movement in Andhra Pradesh"*, Hyderabad, Registrar of Cooperative Societies.

Government of India (1987), *"Cooperative Movement in India: A Statistical Profile"*, Department of Agriculture and Cooperation, New Delhi, Ministry of Agriculture.

Government of Jammu and Kashmir (1988), *"Economic Review of Jammu and Kashmir"*, Planning and Development, Kashmir, Directorate of Economics and Statistics.

Government of Jammu and Kashmir (1994), *"Statistical Handbook: District Srinagar"*, Planning and Development Department, Kashmir, Directorate of Economics and Statistics.

Government of Maharashtra (1986), *"Cooperative Movement at a Glance in Maharashtra State"*, Pune, Commissioner of Cooperation.

Gowaikar, S. (1999), *"Bhagni Nivedita Cooperative Bank: A Women's Bank"*, Cooperator's Bulletin, XXXXII (5), Sept./Oct., Jammu, Jammu and Kashmir Cooperative Union Limited.

Grewal, S. (1978), *"Women's Employment and Fertility Control"*, Centre Calling September.

Gupta, C.B. (1993), *"Business Organisation and Management"*, 2nd Edition, New Delhi, Sultan Chand and Sons.

Gupta, R. D., Sharma, A.K., and Bhagat, G.R. (2003), "Self-Help Groups: Concept and Contribution of Women for their Maintenance", *Cooperator's Bulletin*, XXXXVI (2), Feb., Jammu, Jammu and Kashmir Cooperative Union Limited.

Gupta, S. (1982), *"Role of Cooperatives in Eradication of Unemployment"*, Cooperator's Bulletin, XXV (8), Aug., Jammu, Jammu and Kashmir Cooperative Union Limited.

Guttentag, M., and Secord, P.F. (1983), *"Too Many Women: The Sex Ratio Question"*, London, Sage Publications.

Hajela, T.N. (1982), *"Principles, Problems and Practice of Cooperation"*, Delhi, Shiva Lal Agarwala Company.

Hammond, V., and Holton, V. (1994), *"The Scenario for Women Managers in Britain in the 1990's"*, in Adler, N.J., Izraeli, D.N., (eds.), *'Competitive Frontiers: Women Managers in a Global Economy'*, Cambridge (United States of America)/Oxford (England), Blackwell Publishers.

Harper, M. and Roy, A.K. (2000), *"Cooperative Success: What makes Group Enterprise Succeed"*, *Journal of Rural Development*, 19 (3), July-Sept., Hyderabad, National Institute of Rural Development.

Heggadge, O. (1983), *"Women Participation in Cooperatives"*, Cooperator's Bulletin, XXVI (1), Jan., Jammu, Jammu and Kashmir Cooperative Union Limited.

Heggade, O.D., and Miranda, J.C. (1993), *"Industrial Cooperatives: Performance, Problems and Prospects"*, in Roa, M.G., Heggade, O.D., Yadapadithaya, P.S., (eds.), *'Industrial Economy: Trends, Problems and Prospects'*, Part-1, Industrial Development Series-IV, 1st Edition, Delhi, Kaniska Publishing House.

Heidrick and Struggles (1986), *"The Corporate Women Officer"*, Chicago, Heidrick and Struggles.

Himachalam, D. (2001), *"Consumer Cooperatives in India: Need for New Strategies"*, Cooperator's Bulletin, XXXXIV (8), Aug., Jammu, Jammu and Kashmir Cooperative Union Limited.

Hirsh, W., and Jackson, C. (1990), *"Women in Management: Issues Influencing the Entry of Women into Managerial Jobs"*, Brighton, U.K., Institute of Manpower Studies.

Hussain, M. (1987), *"Geography of Jammu and Kashmir"*, New Delhi, Rajesh Publishers.

IGNOU (1997), *"Cooperatives in Rural Development: Rural Development Administration"*, 3, RD.D.I, *'Rural Development: Indian Context'*, New Delhi, Indira Gandhi National Open University.

IGNOU (1997), *"Development of Rural Women: Rural Social Development"*, RD.D.4, I, New Delhi, Indira Gandhi National Open University.

Inamdar, P.P., Nawadkar, D.S., and Patle, P.K. (2001), *"Performance of Private Vis-à-Vis Cooperative Paddy Processing Mills in Bhandara District of Maharashtra State"*, The Maharashtra Cooperative Quarterly, LXXXIV (3), Jan-March, Pune, Maharashtra Rajya Sahakari Sangh.

Indiradevi, M. (1987), *"Women: Education, Employment and Family Living: A Study of Emerging Hindu Wives in Urban India"*, Delhi, Gian Publishing House.

Izareali, D.N. (1991), *"Women and Work: From Collective to Career"*, in Swirski, B., Safir, M.P., (eds.), *'Calling the Equality Bluff: Women in Israel'*, N. York, Pergamon Press.

Izraeli, D.N., and Adler, N.J. (1994), *"Competitive Frontiers: Women Managers in a Global Economy"*, in Adler, N.J., Izraeli, D.N., (eds.), *'Competitive Frontier: Women Managers in a Global Economy'*, Cambridge (United States of America)/Oxford (England), Blackwell Publishers.

Izraeli, D.N., and Zeira, Y. (1993), *"Women as Managers in International Business"*, A Research Review and Appraisal, Business and the Contemporary World, Cambridge (United States of America)/Oxford (England), Blackwell Publishers.

Jammu and Kashmir Cooperative Union (1981), *"Agricultural Cooperatives in Hungry: Cooperation Abroad"*, Cooperator's

Bulletin, XXIX (7), Dec., Jammu, Jammu and Kashmir Cooperative Union Limited.

Jammu and Kashmir State Level Cooperative Conference (1999), *"Background Material"*, 11th Oct., Banquet Hall, Srinagar, Jammu and Kashmir Cooperative Union Limited.

Jan, M. (1999), *"Agricultural and Consumer Cooperatives in Kashmir Division: With Special Reference to Srinagar District"*, A Study of Cooperative Enterprise, Unpublished M.Sc Dissertation, Department of Home Science, Kashmir, University of Kashmir.

Jan, M. (2004), "Role of Women in Agricultural and Consumer Cooperatives: Education and Intervention", Ph.D. Thesis submitted to Daprtment of Human Development, Home Science, University of Jammu.

Jena, S.K. (1993), *"Working Women and Modernization"*, New Delhi, Ashish Publishing House.

Joseph, K.M. (1989), *"Role of Women in Fisheries"*, Social Welfare, 36 (2), May, Suchi Query Output, SISN 11406, Shreemati Nathibai Damodar Thackersey Women's University Library, Mumbai, National Information Centre.

Joshi, S.S. (1995), *"Women Workers at Grass Root level: a Sociological Study"*, New Delhi, Ashish Publishing House.

Joshi, V.R. (1981), *"Role of Universities and Colleges in Cooperative Leadership Development Programme"*, Indian Cooperative Review, XIX (1), Oct., New Delhi, National Cooperative Union of India.

Joyce, T.A., and Thomas, N.W. (1985), *"Women of All Nations: A Record of their Characteristics, Habits, Manners, Customs and Influence"*, Vol. 1, Delhi, Gain Publishing House.

Junare, S.O. (2001), *Status of Women Cooperatives in Gujarat State"*, The Maharashtra Cooperative Quarterly, LXXXIV (4), April-June, Pune, Maharashtra Rajya Sahakari Sangh.

Kahol, Y. (2003), *"Kashmir: Return of Democracy"*, 1st Edition, New Delhi, Anmol Publications Pvt., Ltd.

Kakade, V.B., and Bagade, D.S. (2001), *"Profit and Loss of Dairy Industry: A Case Study of Malshiras Taluka"*,The Maharashtra Cooperative Quarterly, LXXXIV (4), April-June, Pune, Maharashtra Rajya Sahakari Sangh.

Kalamkar, S.S., Alshi, M.R., Shende, N.V., and Atkare, V.G. (2001), *"A Study of Credit Cooperative Movement in Vidarbha"*, The Maharashtra Cooperative Quarterly, LXXXIV (3), Jan-March, Pune, Maharashtra Rajya Sahakari Sangh.

Kalpagam, U. (1993), *"Women in the 21st Century"*, in Raj, S.l., (ed.), *'Quest for Gender Justice: A Critique of the Status of Women in India'*, New Delhi, T.R. Publications.

Kamat, G.S. (1974), *"Growth of Cooperatives within the Community Development Movement"*, in Inamdar, N.R., (ed.), *'Community Development and Democratic Growth'*, Bombay, Popular Prakashan Pvt., Ltd.

Kamat, G.S. (1978), *"New Dimensions of Cooperative Management"*, 1st Edition, Bombay, Himalaya Publishing House.

Kamli, S.A. (1982), *"Industrial Cooperatives in Jammu and Kashmir"*, Cooperator's Bulletin, XXV (5), May, Jammu, Jammu and Kashmir Cooperative Union Limited.

Kane, P. (1976), *"How Women Hold Up Half the Sky"*, Delhi, People.

Kanitkar, A. (1994), *"The Narmada Group Cooperative Fruit and Vegetable Society Limited, Panetha"*, Vikalpa, *The Journal of Decision Makers*, 19 (40, Oct-Dec., Ahmedabad, Indian Institute of Management.

Kapoor, A. (2000), *"Banking with Illiterate Women"*, Grassroots, 1 (4), April, ICVF 5888, Suchan Query Output, SISN 14647, Shreemati Nathibai Damodar Thackersey Women's University Library, Mumbai, National Information Centre.

Kapoor, D.R. (1988), *"Cooperative Movement in Rajouri District: An Appraisal"*, Cooperator's Bulletin, XXXI (5), May, Jammu, Jammu and Kashmir Cooperative Union Limited.

Kapoor, D.R. (1992), *"Prospective Planning for the Development of Agricultural Cooperative in India"*, Cooperator's, Bulletin, XXXV (3), March, Jammu, Jammu and Kashmir Cooperative Union Limited.

Kapoor, D.R. (1998), *"Handbook of Cooperative Audit"*, 1st Edition, New Delhi, Anmol Publications Pvt., Ltd.

Kashani, S. (2004), *"State Subject Law in the Eye of the Storm"*, Kashmir Image, Tuesday, March, 09, 8(66), Srinagar.

Kashmir Times (2004), *"Gender Biased State Subject Bill Passed"*, Saturday, March, 06, Jammu.

Kaur, M., Sharma, M.L., and Kour, S. (1988), *"Women and Work in Rural Society"*, in Dak, T.M., (ed.), *'Women and Work in Indian Society'*, Delhi, Discovery Publishing House.

Khan, A.R. (2003), *"Kashmir; Land and People"*, 1st Edition, Srinagar, City Book Centre.

Khan, F.H. (1991), *"The Role of Cooperatives in Water Management"*, The Cooperator, XXIX (7), Oct., New Delhi, National Cooperative Union of India.

Khan, F.N. (1992), *"Women Entrepreneurship Development"*, Co-operator's Bulletin, XXXV (5), May, Jammu, Jammu and Kashmir Cooperative Union Limited.

Khan, I.A. (2001), *"Need of School Cooperatives to Strengthen the Cooperative Movement"*, Cooperator's Bulletin, XXXXIV (8), Aug., Jammu, Jammu and Kashmir Cooperative Union Limited.

Khan, M.A., and Ayesha, N. (1982), *"Status of Rural Women in India: A Study of Karnataka"*, New Delhi, Uppal Publishing House.

Khan, M.I. (1999), *"History of Srinagar; 1846-1947: A Study in Socio-Cultural Change"*, New Delhi, Cosmos Publications.

Khurana, K.M.L. (1981), *"Cooperative Housing in India"*, Cooperative News Digest, XXXII (7), July, Bombay, Reserve Bank of India.

Khurana, K.M.L. (1992), *"Housing Cooperatives and National Integration"*, Cooperator's Bulletin, XXXV (10), Oct., Jammu, Jammu and Kashmir Cooperative Union Limited.

Khurana, K.M.L. (1999), *"Cooperative Banks in Tamil Nadu"*, The Tamil Nadu Journal of Cooperation, 91 (4), July, Tamil Nadu, The Tamil Nadu Cooperative Union.

Khusro, A.M. (1992), *"The Cooperative Sector: Neglecting a Vital Component of Economy"*, Cooperator's Bulletin, XXXV (7), July, Jammu, Jammu and Kashmir Cooperative Union Limited.

Khusro Committee (1989), *"Agricultural Credit Review Committee"*, A Report, Bombay, Reserve Bank of India.

Kodvag, V.B. (2000), *"Indian Grape Export through Cooperatives: A Case Study of Sangli District"*, The Maharashtra Cooperative Quarterly, LXXXIII (4), April-June, Pune, Maharashtra Rajya Sahakari Sangh.

Kodvag, V.B. (2001), *"A Success Story of Shree Varna Vibhag Sahakari Grahak Mandal Limited: Warannagar"*, The Maharashtra

Cooperative Quarterly, LXXXIV (3), Jan-March, Pune, The Maharashtra Rajya Sahakari Sangh.

Kohli, P.P. (2001), *"Kolhapur Women Cooperative Bank for the Dalits"*, Cooperator's Bulletin, XXXXIV (3), March, Jammu, Jammu and Kashmir Cooperative Union Limited.

Kollannavar, G., and Naidu, A.S. (1997), *"Production and Marketing of Footwear"*, Social Welfare, 43(10), Jan., Suchi Query Output, SISN 96899, Shreemati Nathibai Damodar Thackersey Women's University Library, Mumbai, National Information Centre.

Korabik, K. (1992), *"Women Hold Up Half the Sky: The Status of Managerial Women in China"*, in Wedley, W.W., (ed.), *'Advances in Chinese Industrial Studies'*, 3, Greenwich, Conn. J.I. Press.

Korabik, K. (1993), *"Women Managers in the People's Republic of China: Changing Roles in Changing Times"*, Applied Psychology, An International Review.

Korabik, K. (1994), *"Managerial Women in the People's Republic of China: The Long March Continues"*, in Adler, N.J., Izraeli, D.N., (eds.), *'Competitive Frontiers: Women Managers in a Global Economy'*, Cambridge (United States of America)/Oxford (England), Blackwell Publishers.

Kotaiah, P. (1997), *"Banking on Micro Entrepreneurs: Innovative Lending and Credit Programmes"*, National Bank News Review, 13 (2), April-June, Mumbai, National Bank for Agriculture and Rural Development.

Koul, P.A., and Bamzai, P.N.K. (1978), *"Geography of Jammu and Kashmir State"*, New Delhi, Light and Light Publishers.

Krishna, D. (1999), *"Housing Cooperatives to Construct 2 Lakh Houses each Year"*, COOP-Banking, VIII (32), Aug., 8-15, New Delhi, National Federation of Urban Cooperative Banks and Credit Societies.

Krishna, D. (1999), *"Women Cooperative Banking"*, COOP-Banking, VIII (27-33), July-Aug., New Delhi, National Federation of Urban Cooperative Banks and Credit Societies.

Krishnaswamy, K.S., and Rajagopal, S. (1985), *"Women in Employment: A Micro-Study in Karnataka"*, in Jain, D., Banerjee, N., (eds.), *'Women in Poverty: Tyranny of the Household, Investigative Essays on Women's Work'*, New Delhi, Vikas Publishing House.

Krishnaswami, O.R. (1976), *"Cooperative Democracy in Action: An Empirical Study of Democratic Control and Management in Agricultural Cooperative Credit Structure in a State in India"*, Bombay, Somaiya Publications Pvt., Ltd.

Kulkarni, H.S., Patil, H.K., and Bhosale, S.S. (2001), *"Growth of Lead Bank Credit in Ratnagiri District of Maharashtra State"*, The Maharashtra Cooperative Quarterly, LXXXV (1), July-Sept., Pune, Maharashtra Rajya Sahakari Sangh.

Kumar, N. (1982), *"Role of Cooperatives in Economic Development"*, Cooperator's Bulletin, XXV (4), April, Jammu, Jammu and Kashmir Cooperative Union.

Kumar, N. (1983), *"Role of Cooperative Marketing in Agricultural Development"*, Cooperator's Bulletin, XXVI (1), January, Jammu, Jammu and Kashmir Cooperative Union Limited.

Kumar, Rachel (1994), *"Development and Women's Work in Kerala: Interactions and Paradoxes"*, Economic and Political Weekly, 29 (51-52), ICSSR Journal of Abstracts and Reviews, Sociology and Social Anthropology, New Delhi, Indian Council of Social Science and Research.

Kumar, S.R. (2001), *"Working of Urban Cooperative Banks: A Case-Study"*, The Maharashtra Cooperative Quarterly, LXXXIV (4), April-June, Pune, Maharashtra Rajya Sahakari Sangh.

Kurien, V. (1993), *"Cooperative Sector should be Free from Government Interference"*, Cooperator's Bulletin, XXXVI (6), June, Jammu, Jammu and Kashmir Cooperative Union Limited.

Lalitha, N. (1996), *"Women's Empowerment through Cooperatives"*, Social Welfare, 43 (6), Sept., Suchi Query Output, SISN 92904, Shreemati Nathibai Damodar Thackersey Women's University Library, Mumbai, National Information Centre.

Lawrence, S.W. (1985), *"Kashmir and Jammu"*, 1st Edition, Tawi, Jammu, Jay Kay Book House.

Limaya, A. (1988), *"Participation of Women in Industrial Cooperatives"*, Roshni, April-July, Suchi Query Output, SISN 11028, Shreemati Nathibai Damodar Thackersey Women's University Library, Mumbai, National Information Centre.

Maheshwari, A. (1993), *"Cresent Over Kashmir: Politics of Mullaism"*, New Deihi, Rupa and Company.

Majid, A. (1990), *"Philosophy and Methods of Extension Work and Extension Work in Cooperative Movement"*, Cooperator's

Bulletin, XXXIII (1), Jan., Jammu, Jammu and Kashmir Cooperative Union Limited.

Majumdar, U. (1979), *"From Research to Policy: Rural Women in India"*, in Leidenstein, S., (ed.), *'Learning about Rural Women: Studies in Family Planning'*, A Special Issue, 11-12, Nov-Dec., Delhi, Discovery Publishing House.

Malekar, A., and Sakariyapura (2000), *"Land of Milk and Money"*, The Weekly, 18 (12), March-5, ICVF 5894, Suchan Query Output, SISN 14652, Shreemati Nathibai Damodar Thackersey Women's University Library, Mumbai, National Information Centre.

Manchanda, A. (2001), *"Women in Cooperatives: Pivotal Role"*, Cooperator's Bulletin, XXXXIV (5-7), May-July, Jammu, Jammu and Kashmir Cooperative Union Limited.

Manorama Year Book (1999), *'Five Year plans'*, Kottayam, Kerala, Malaya Manorama.

Mansor, N. (1994), *"Women Managers in Malaysia: Their mobility and Challenges"*, in Adler, N.J., Izraeli, D.N., (eds.), *'Competitive Frontiers: Women Managers in a Global Economy'*, Cambridge (United States of America)/Oxford (England), Blackwell Publishers.

Marantz, F. (1992), *"The Flip Side of Fertility"*, Jerusalem Report, Nov., 5, Jerusalem.

Mathew, P.M., and Nair, M.S. (1986), *"Women's Organisations and Women's Interests: Women's Cooperatives"*, New Delhi, Ashish Publishing House.

Mathias, L. (1987), *"Women Storm a Male Bastion"*, The Sunday Observer, Nov., 22, Suchi Query Output, SISN 2125, Shreemati Nathibai Damodar Thackersey Women's University Library, Mumbai, National Information Centre.

Mehta, V.L. (1996), *"Abodana Mahila Kapad Chapkam Utpadak Sahakari Mandali Limited"*, Khadi Gramodyog, 43 (2), Nov., Suchi Query Output, SISN 95747, Shreemati Nathibai Damodar Thackersey Women's University Library, Mumbai, National Information Centre.

Mencher, J. (1982), *"Women's Work and Poverty: Their Contributions to Household Maintenance in South Indian States"*, Paper presented at the Conference on *'Women and Income Control in the Third World'*, N. York, Columbia University.

Menon, M.I. (1981), *"Status of Muslim Women in India"*, New Delhi, Uppal Publishing House.

Miller, J. (1996), *"Statistics for Advanced Level"*, 2nd Edition, N. York, Cambridge University Press.

Ministry of Labour (2001), *"Labour: Part 1"*, 2K-01, Delhi, Government of India.

Misra, R.V. (1999), *"National Policy on Cooperatives"*, Cooperator's Bulletin, XXXXII (4), July-Aug., Jammu, Jammu and Kashmir Cooperative Union Limited.

Mittal, M. (1995), *"Women's Education"*, in Gupta, S., Mittal, M., (eds.), *'Status of Women and Children in India'*, New Delhi, Anmol Publications Pvt., Ltd.

Mohanan, N. (1989), *"The Cooperative Organisations in India"*, Courses on Managing Cooperatives for Rural Development, Hyderabad, National Institute of Rural Development.

Mohanty, T. K. (2000), *"Empowering Women: A Catalyst in Development"*, Employment News, XXV (25), 16-22, Sept.

Moore, D. (1992), *"Labour Market Segmentation and its Implementation: Inequality Deprivation and Entitlement"*, N. York, Garland Publishing.

Mudd, S.M. (1998), *"NDDB Thrust on Women Power in Cooperatives", Land Bank Journal*, XXXVI (III), March, Mumbai, National Cooperative Agriculture and Rural Development Bank's Federation Limited.

Mukerji, A., and Verma, N. (1987), *"Socio-Economic Backwardness in Women"*, New Delhi, Ashish Publishing House.

Mustafa, M. (2002), *"Problems Galore: Emphasis on Solving the Day to Day Problems Facing Women"*, Greater Kashmir, 15 (64), March, Thursday, Srinagar.

Naibitt, J., and Aburdence, P. (1990), *"Magatrend 2000"*, United States of America, Marrow.

Nakabayashi, S. (1976), *"New Trends in the International Cooperative Movement: Economic Growth and Cooperative Principles"*, Anthology of Cooperative Thought, II, New Delhi, National Cooperative Union of India.

Narayanesamy, R., and Roy, A.K. (2000), *"Women Empowerment through Cooperatives: A Case Study of Mahila Vikas in Andhra*

*Pradesh"*, Cooperative Perspective, *Journal of Cooperative Management*, 34 (4), Jan-March, Pune, Vaikunth Mehta National Institute of Cooperative Management.

National Bank of Agricultural and Rural Development (1981), *"Statistical Statements Relating to the Cooperative Movement in India"*, Part-1, Credit Societies, Bombay, NABARD.

National Bank of Agricultural and Rural Development (1985), *"Important Items of Data Credit and Non-Credit Cooperative Societies"*, Bombay, NABARD.

National Bank of Agricultural and Rural Development (1987), *"Important Items of Data: Credit and Non-Credit Cooperative Societies"*, Bombay, NABARD.

National Bank of Agricultural and Rural Development (1993), *"Annual Report"*, Bombay, NABARD.

National Cooperative Agriculture and Rural Development Bank's Federation (1992), *"32nd Annual Report"*, Bombay, NAFCARD.

National Cooperative Agriculture and Rural Development Bank's Federation (1997), *"Statistical Bulletin"*, Mumbai, NAFCARD.

National Cooperative Agriculture and Rural Development Bank's Federation (1998), *"Statistical Bulletin"*, Mumbai, NAFCARD.

National Cooperative Consumer's Federation of India (1997), *"32nd Annual Report"*, New Delhi, NCCF.

National Cooperative Development Corporation (1974), *"Role of Consumer Cooperatives in Rural Areas"*, Annual Report, New Delhi, NCDC.

National Cooperative Union of India (1991), *"Saturating the Consumer Market (Union of Soviet Socialist Republics): Cooperatives Abroad"*, The Cooperator, XXIX (3), Aug., New Delhi, NCUI.

National Cooperative Union of India (1992), *"Agricultural Cooperatives in Thailand: Social Background of Cooperative Movement in Thailand"*, The Cooperator, XXIX (13), March, New Delhi, NCUI.

National Federation of State Cooperative Banks (2000), *"Review of Disbursement of Short Term Agricultural Loans for Rabi and Kharief Crops"*, Mumbai, NAFASCOB.

National Resource Centre (1988), *"Indian Cooperatives: A Profile"*, New Delhi, National Cooperative Union of India.

National Resource Centre (1993), *"Indian Cooperative Movement: A Profile"*, New Delhi, National Cooperative Union of India.

National Resource Centre (1997), *"Indian Cooperative Movement: A Profile"*, New Delhi, National Cooperative Union of India.

National Cooperative Union of India (1998), *"45th All India Cooperative Week"*, 14-20, Nov., New Delhi, NCUI.

National Resource Centre (1998), *"Indian Cooperative Movement: A Profile"*, New Delhi, National Cooperative Union of India.

National Resource Centre (1999), *"Indian Cooperative Movement: A Profile"*, New Delhi, National Cooperative Union of India.

National Resource Centre (2001), *"Indian Cooperative Movement: A Profile"*, New Delhi, National Cooperative Union of India.

Noorpur, I.K. (1999), *"Women in Search of Identity"*, New Delhi, B.R. Publishing Corporation.

Padmini, I.K., and Krishnamoorthy, S. (1994), *"Demographic and Socio-Economic Status of Women in Different Family Structures in Rural Area of South India", International Journal of Sociology of the Family*, 24 (2), ICSSR Journal of Abstracts and Reviews, Sociology and Anthropology, New Delhi, Indian Council of Social Science and Research.

Pai, T.A. (1976), *"Women Should Work Shoulder to Shoulder with Men"*, The Cooperator, XIII (20), April 15, New Delhi, National Cooperative Union of India.

Pandya, D. (1998), *"MPs Call for Reforms in Cooperative Sector"*, The Observer of Business and Politics, New Delhi, Monday, July, 27, Press Clippings on the Meeting of the Members of Parliament with the Cooperative initiative Panel, Anand, Gujarat, Cooperative Initiative Panel.

Parasuraman, S., and Greenhaus, J. (1993), *"Personal Portrait: The Lifestyle of the Women Managers"*, in Fagenson, E.A., (ed.), *'Women in Management: Trends, Issues and Challenges in Managerial Diversity'*, Newbury Park, Calif, Sage Publications.

Parikh, I. J. and Narayana, A.S. (1994), *"Women Managers in Transition: From Homes to Corporate Offices"*, The Indian Journal of Social Work, 45 (2), ICSSR Journal of Abstracts and Review, Sociology and Social Anthropology, New Delhi, Indian Council of Social Science and Research.

Pathania, K., Thakur, Y.S., and Pathania, A. (1998), *"Strengthening Cooperatives in Tribal Areas"*, in Tripathy, S.N., (ed.),

*'Cooperatives for Rural Development'*, New Delhi, Discovery Publishing House.

Patil, D.T. (2001), *"Effectiveness of Short Term [Crop] Loan: A Case Study of PACS in Miraj Taluka"*, The Maharashtra Cooperative Quarterly, LXXXIV (3), Jan-March, Pune, Maharashtra Rajya Sahakari Sangh.

Patil, H.K., Bhosale, S.S., and Patil, N.S. (2000), *"Gokul: A Light House in the Cooperative Milk Marketing in India"*, The Maharashtra Cooperative Quarterly, LXXXIV (1), July-Sept., Pune, Maharashtra Rajya Sahakari Sangh.

Patrick, Martin, and Rajasehan, D. (1994), *"Earnings, Discrimination on and Status: A Study of Sales Women in Ernukulam District"*, The Indian Journal of Labour Economics 37 (1), ICSSR Journal of Abstracts and Review, Sociology and Social Anthropology, New Delhi, Indian Council of Social Science and Research.

Pawan, K. and Kamra (1987), *"Cooperative Management Practices, Problems and Prospects"*, New Delhi, Deep and Deep Publication.

Peres, Y. and Katz, R. (1984), *"The Working Mother and her Family"*, Tel Aviv, Modi, Ezrachi Ltd., Institute of Research.

Pillai, J.K. (1995), *"Women and Empowerment"*, New Delhi, Gyan Publishing House.

Pitchai, C., Narayanasamy, R. and Gopalsamy, R. (2001), *"A Small Candle Beams Light-A Success Story of Mudural Medical College Students Cooperative Stores"*, The Cooperator, XXXIX (6), Dec., New Delhi, National Cooperative Union of India.

Powell, G. N. (1988), *"Women and Men in Management"*, Newbury Park, Calif, Sage Publications.

Prakash, D. (1989), *"Management of Cooperatives: The Concept of Management Extension"*, The Cooperator, XXVI (6), Feb., 15, New Delhi, National Cooperative Union of India.

Prakesh, D. (1992), *"Rural Women Leaders of Agricultural Cooperatives in Asia: A Report"*, New Delhi, International Cooperative Alliance.

Prakash, D. (2000), *"Participation of Women in Decision Making in Agricultural Cooperatives: An Overview"*, The Cooperator, XXXVIII (5), Nov., New Delhi, National Cooperative Union of India.

Prakash, D. (2000), *"Women in Agriculture and Cooperatives"*, NCDC Bulletin, XXXIV (2), June, New Delhi, National Cooperative Development Corporation.

Prakash, D., and Shortriya, G.C. (1999), *"Paradigm Shift in the Management of Agricultural Cooperatives in Asia: An Over View"*, International Cooperative Alliance, New Delhi, Indian Farmers' Fertiliser Cooperative Limited.

Prashar, B. (2002), *"Cooperatives Improve Women's Lot"*, Co-operator's Bulletin, XXXXV (7), July, Jammu, Jammu and Kashmir Cooperative Union Limited.

Press Trust of India (1995), *"Sex Workers of Calcutta Unite to Form Co-op and Marketing Agency"*, Indian Express, July, 31, ICVF 1967, Suchi Query Output, SISN 78343, Shreemati Nathibai Damodar Thackersey Women's University Library, Mumbai, National Information Centre.

Puri, S.S. (1992), *"Cooperative Sector in India: Directions of Changes"*, Cooperator's Bulletin, XXXV (11), Nov., Jammu, Jammu and Kashmir Cooperative Union Limited.

Puspavalli, S. (2000), *"A Study on the Trend in Growth of Cooperatives in Tamil Nadu: With Special Reference to Primary Agricultural Credit Societies"*, in Tripathy, S.N., (ed.), *'Cooperatives—its Growth and New Dimensions'*, New Delhi, Discovery Publishing House.

Raju, K.N.M., and Bhat, T.N. (1994), *"Acceptance of Family Planning Methods in the Cultural Context of Family Structure and Women's Participation in Labour Force"*, Social Action, 44 (3), ICSSR Journal of Abstracts and Review, Sociology and Social Anthropology, 23 (1), Jan-June, New Delhi, Indian Council of Social Science and Research.

Ramanujan, K.N. (1997), *"Women Cooperatives and Economic Development"*, Cooperator's Bulletin, XXXX (1), Jan., Jammu, Jammu and Kashmir Cooperative Union Limited.

Ramanujan, K.N. (1998), *"Global Cooperatives"*, The Tamil Nadu Journal of Cooperation, 90 (5), Aug., Tamil Nadu, The Tamil Nadu Cooperative Union.

Ramesh, R.S. (2001), *"Growth of Dairy Movement in Karnataka: A Case Study of Karnataka Milk Federation"*, The Maharashtra Cooperative Quarterly, LXXXIV (4), April-June, Pune, Maharashtra Rajya Sahakari Sangh.

Rohilla, R.S. (1997), *"Nagpur Mahila Nagri Sahakari Bank Limited: A Case Study"*, Urban Credit, XIX (2), June, New Delhi, National Federation of Urban Cooperative Banks and Credit Societies.

Rao, S.B.N. (1987), *"All Women Cooperatives in Andhra Pradesh"*, Cooperator's Bulletin, XXX (12), Dec., Jammu, Jammu and Kashmir Cooperative Union Limited.

Rao, S., and Hasalkar, S.M. (1997), *"Identification of Entrepreneurship Qualities Among Members of Women Cooperatives: A Study in Dharwad Taluka"*, Research Highlights, 7(4), October, Suchi Query Output, SISN 100615, Shreemati Nathibai Damodar Thackersey Women's University Library, Mumbai, National Information Centre.

Rao, R. (1994), *"Woman Power Fuels: India's Milk Cooperatives"*, Social Welfare, 41 (6), Sept., Suchi Query Output, SISN 72729, Shreemati Nathibai Damodar Thackersey Women's University Library, Mumbai, National Information Centre.

Rao, V.M. (1997), *"Giving Control into Women's Hands"*, Social Welfare, 44 (1), April, Suchi Query Output, SISN 97606, Shreemati Nathibai Damodar Thackersey Women's University Library, Mumbai, National Information Centre.

Rao, Y.V. (2000), *"Incoserva: A Success Story of Cooperative Tea Industry in Tamil Nadu"*, The Maharshtra Cooperative Quarterly, LXXXIII (4), April-June, Pune, Maharashtra Rajya Sahakari Sangh.

Raper, A.F. (1970), *"Rural Development in Action: The Comprehensive Experiment at Comilla—East Pakistan"*, London, Cornell University Press.

Rose, K. (1992), *"Where Women are Leaders: The SEWA Movement in India"*, New Delhi, Sage Publications, ICSSR Journal of Abstracts and Reviews, Sociology and Social anthropology, Jan-June, New Delhi, Indian Council of Social Science and Research.

Rashtra Mahila (2000), *"Task Force on Women and Children"*, A Report, 3 (22), Sept., New Delhi, National Commission for Women.

Rashtra Mahila (2001), *"Eighty-Eight Percent Women Have Gynae Problems"*, A Report, 3 (17), March, New Delhi, National Commission for Women.

Ray, N. (1987), *"One Women's Consumer Cooperative"*, Roshni, July (86)-February (87), Suchi Query Output, SISN 15418, Shreemati Nathibai Damodar Thackersey Women's University Library, Mumbai, National Information Centre.

Reddy, A.V.R.N. (1996), *"Economic Development of Woman: Andhra Pradesh Women's Cooperative Finance Corporation"*, in Shamin,

A., (ed.), *'Women's Development Problems and Prospects'*, New Delhi, APH Publishing Corporation, Suchi Query Output, SISN 96099, Shreemati Nathibai Damodar Thackersey Women's University Library, Mumbai, National Information Centre.

Reddy, G.R. (1989), *"Performance an Prospects of the 7Th Five Year Plan"*, in Reddy, J.M., Reddy, M.Y., Upadhyay, K.S., Reghuran, C., (eds.), *'Seventh Five Year Plan: Performance and Perspective'*, New Delhi, Sterling Publishers Private Ltd.

Rehman, H. (1982), *"Role of Rural Cooperatives in Canalising Savings: Recent Trends"*, Cooperator's Bulletin, XXV (1), Jan., Jammu, Jammu and Kashmir Cooperative Union Limited.

Rekhrao (2001), *"Revision of Licensing Policy of New Urban Cooperative Banks"*, Mumbai, Reserve Bank of India.

Remuneration Economics (1991), *"1990 Salary Survey"*, Corby, U.K., British Institute of Management.

Renzu, F. (1998), *"Discovery of Kashmir"*, Jawahar Nagar, Srinagar, Beenish Publications.

Reserve Bank of India (1979), *"Statisticai Statements Relating to the Cooperative Movement in India"*, Part-1, Credit Societies, Bombay, RBI.

Reshi, M. (1999), *"Unforgettable Kashmir"*, Kashmir, Jammu and Kashmir Tourism and Hindustan Thompson Associates Ltd.

Roy, T.K. (1998), *"Kushmandi Cooperative Marketing Society Proves it's Worth"*, NAFED Market Review, XXVIII (8-10), Aug-Oct., New Delhi, National Agricultural Cooperative Marketing Federation.

Saeed, M., and Ansari, A.A. (1990), *"Cooperative Marketing and Processing"*, New Delhi, Anmol Publications.

Sah, A.K. (1984), *"Professional Management"*, New Delhi, Vikas Publishing House.

Saikia, P.D., Gogoi, K., and Lekharu, A. (1986), *"Indian Rural Women: A Study of Role and Status of Rural Women in Assam"*, Delhi, Mittal Publications.

Saiyed, A.R. (1992), *"Muslim Women in India: An Overview"*, in Anjum, M., (ed.), *'Muslim Women in India'*, New Delhi, Sangam Books.

Selvaraju, R. (1998), *"Supervised Credit System in Land Development Banks", Land Bank Journal*, XXXVI, March, III, Mumbai, National

Cooperative Agriculture and Rural Development Bank's Federation Limited.

Salve, W.N. (2000), *"Development of Consumer's Cooperatives in Kollapur District"*, The Maharashtra Cooperative Quarterly, LXXXIII (4), April-June, Pune, Maharashtra Rajya Sahakari Sangh.

Salve, W.N. (2001), *"Seasonal Schools for Migrant Labour Camps in Cooperative Sugar Factories in Maharashtra"*, The Maharashtra Cooperative Quarterly, LXXXV (1), July-Sept., Pune, Maharashtra Rajya Sahakari Sangh.

Sarojini, T.B., Vijayalakshmi, B., and Himachalam, D. (1997), *"The Growth of Consumer Movement"*, Indian Consumer Cooperator, 24 (4), Oct-Dec., New Delhi, National Cooperative Consumer's Federation Limited.

Sathyanarayna, E. (1984), *"Need to Reactivise Credit Cooperatives"*, Cooperator's Bulletin, XXVII (6), June, Jammu, Jammu and Kashmir Cooperative Union Limited.

Saxena, D. and Tripathi, H. (1998), *"Entrepreneurial Behaviour of Milk Producers According to their Social, Personal, Economic and Psychological Attributes in Women's Dairy Cooperatives"*, IASSI Quarterly, 17 (2), Oct-Dec., Suchan Query Output, SISN 11653, Shreemati Nathibai Damodar Thackersey Women's University Library, Mumbai, National Information Centre.

Sexena, D., and Tripathi, H. (1998), *"Entrepreneurship among Milk Producers in Women Dairy Cooperative Societies"*, Productivity, 38 (4), Jan-March, Suchan Query Output, SISN 2351, Shreemati Nathibai Damodar Thackersey Women's University Library, Mumbai, National Information Centre.

Sehgal, M.N. (1990), *"A Text Book of Cooperative History"*, Jammu, Jammu and Kashmir Cooperative Union Limited.

Sehgal, M.N. (2000), *"Progress Report in Respect of all Projects and Members Education Programmes of Jammu and Kashmir Cooperative Union"*, Annual Report, March, Jammu, Jammu and Kashmir Cooperative Union Limited.

Sehgal, M.N. (2001), *"World Consumer's Day and Cooperatives"*, The State Times, Thursday, March, 15, Jammu.

Sen, G. (2001), *"Centre's Policy for Women's Empowerment"*, Rashtriya Mahila, 3 (20), June, New Delhi, National Commission for Women.

Serd, and Jenian, E. (1994), *"Women Managers in France"*, in Adler, N.J., Izraeli, D.N., (eds.), *'Competitive Frontiers: Women in a Global Economy'*, Cambridge (United States of America)/Oxford (England), Blackwell Publishers.

Sethi, R.M. (1988), *"Status and Power of Working Women Within the Family: A Test of Marxian Perspective"*, in Dak, T.M., (ed.), *'Women and Work in Indian Society'*, Delhi, Discovery Publishing House.

SEWA Academy (2000), *"Labouring Brick by Brick: A Study of Construction Workers"*, Ahmedabad, Self Employed Women's Association Academy.

SEWA Academy (2000), *"Organising Bidi Workers in Gujarat and Madhya Pradesh"*, Ahmedabad, Mahila Self Employed Women's Association Trust.

SEWA Academy (2000), *"Organising for Change: Union and Cooperatives"*, Self Employed Women's Association, Ahmedabad, Mahila Self Employed Women's Association Trust.

SEWA Academy (2000), *"Self Employed Women's Association: Annual Report"*, Ahmedabad, Shri Mahila Self Employed Women's Association Trust.

Shafi, A. (2002), *"Working Women in Kashmir"*, New Delhi, APH Publishing Corporation.

Shah, D. (1985), *"Women Participation and Modern Dairy Industry: A Case of Amul"*, in Jain, S.C., (ed.), *'Women and Technology'*, Jaipur, Rawat Publications.

Shah, M.A. (1992), *"Export Marketing of Kashmir Handicrafts"*, New Delhi, Ashish Publishing House.

Shah, U.M. (1990), *"Cooperative Law and Cooperative Development"*, The Cooperative Law journal, XXVI (1), Jan., New Delhi, National Cooperative Union of India.

Sharan, R. (1988), *"From Tradition to Modernity: A Case of Women Workers and Non-Workers"*, in Dak, T.M., (ed.), *'Women and Work in Indian Society'*, Delhi, Discovery Publishing House.

Sharma, B.D. (1988), *"Role of Cooperatives in the Development of Hill and Tribal Areas"*, Paper Presented on *'National Conference on the Role of Cooperatives in Development of Hill and Tribal Areas'*, Thursday, 29th Sept., New Delhi, National Cooperative Union of India.

Sharma, J.R. (1982), *"Opportunities for the Youth in the Cooperatives"*, Cooperator's Bulletin, XXV (3), March, Jammu, Jammu and Kashmir Cooperative Union Limited.

Sharma, M., and Vanjani, U. (1989), *"Women's Work is Never Done: Dairy Development and Health in the Lives of Rural Women in Rajasthan"*, Economics and Political Weekly, 24(17), April, Suchi Query Output, SISN 11758, Shreemati Nathibai Damodar Thackersey Women's University Library, Mumbai, National Information Centre.

Sharma, N.P. (1987), *"Cooperatives Offer More Opportunity to Women for Self Reliance"*, Cooperative Education News, Education Division, II (2), July, N. Delhi, National Cooperative Union of India.

Sharma, P.S. (1998), *"Role of Cooperatives in the Ninth Plan"*, Cooperator's Bulletin, XXXXI (1), Jan., Jammu, Jammu and Kashmir Cooperative Union Limited.

Sharma, P.S. (2000), *"Cooperatives for Empowerment of the People"*, The Cooperator, XXXVIII (3), Sept., New Delhi, National Cooperative Union of India.

Sharma, S. (1996), *"Indian Renaissance: Concept of Womannood and Dayanand Saraswati"*, in Jain, P., Mahan, R., (eds.), *'Women Images'*, New Delhi, Rawat Publications.

Sharma, S.R. (1990), *"Development of Cooperative Movement in Jammu and Kashmir"*, Cooperator's Bulletin, XXXIII (9), Sept., Jammu, Jammu and Kashmir Cooperative Union Limited.

Sharma, S.R. (1991), *"The Role of Cooperatives in Holding the Price Line"*, Cooperator's Bulletin, XXXV (8), Aug., Jammu, Jammu and Kashmir Cooperative Union Limited.

Sharma, U. (1991), *"Women's Work and Poverty in North-West India"*, in Anita, (ed.), *'Women's Quest for Equality: Land Relations and Women'*, Jaipur, Institute of Public Administration.

Sherlekar, S.A. (1985), *"Marketing and Salesmanship"*, 1st Edition, Bombay, Himalaya Publishing House.

Shobha, V. (1987), *"Rural Women and Development: A Study of Female Agricultural Labourers in Telangana"*, Delhi, Mittal Publications.

Siengthai, S., and Leelakulthanit, O. (1994), *"Women Managers in Thailand"*, in Adler, N.J., Izraeli, D. N., (eds.), *'Competitive Frontiers: Women Managers in a Global Economy'*, Cambridge (United States of America)/Oxford (England), Blackwell Publishers.

Singh, I.P. (1991), *"Indian Women: The Power Trapped"*, 1st Edition, New Delhi, Galaxy Publications.

Singh, J., Chatta, I.S., and Singh, N. (1987), *"A Study into Economic Rationale of the Long Term Cooperative Credit", Indian Cooperative Review*, XXV (2), Oct., ICSSR Journal of Abstracts and Reviews, Economics, XVII (4), Oct-Dec., New Delhi, Indian Council of Social Science and Research.

Singh, K. (2002), *"Development Strategy for Women in Cooperatives", Cooperator's Bulletin*, XXXXV (II), Nov., Jammu, Jammu and Kashmir Cooperative Union Limited.

Singh, K.B. (2001), *"Self-Help Groups: Its Impact on the Women Folk of Manipur", The Cooperator*, XXXIV (6), Dec., New Delhi, National Cooperative Union of India.

Singh, K.S. (1999), *"Women in Cooperative: A Case Study on the Thangjam Leikai Weavers Cooperative Society Limited"*, The Maharashtra Cooperative Quarterly, 83 (1), July- Sept., Suchan Query Output, SISN 11173, Shreemati Nathibai Damodar Thackersey Women's University Library, Mumbai, National Information Centre.

Singh, K. S. (2000), *"Consumer Cooperatives in Manipur: A Case Study of Kongba Bazar Consumer Cooperative Society Limited"*, The Maharashtra Cooperative Quarterly, LXXXIV (1), July-Sept., Pune, Maharashtra Rajya Sahakari Sangh.

Singh, K.S. (2000), *"Nongpok Mustee Cooperative Thrift Society Limited"*, Cooperator's Bullitin, XXXXIII (5-6), May/June, Jammu, Jammu and Kashmir Cooperative Union Limited.

Singh, K.S. (2001), *"Trend in Recovery of Loan in PACS: Its Main Causes and Remedies"*, The Maharashtra Cooperative Quarterly, LXXXIV (4), April-June, Pune, Maharashtra Rajya Sahakari Sangh.

Singh, R. (1987), *"Let More Women Join Cooperative Movement"*, Yojana, 31 (12), July, Suchi Query Output, SISN 762, Shreemati Nathibai Damodar Thackersey Women's University Library, Mumbai, National Information Centre.

Singh, R. (1994), *"Extension Education"*, Ludhiana, Sahitya Kala Prakashan.

Sinha, M.L. (1994), *"Condition of the Women Workers in the Brick Kilns"*, Man in India, 74 (1), *ICSSR Journal of Abstracts and Review, Sociology and Social Anthropology*, New Delhi, Indian Council of Social Science and Research.

Sisodia, S.S. (1999), *"Cooperative Policy Reforms: Urban Credit"*, XXI (1), March, New Delhi, National Federation of Urban Cooperative Banks and Credit Societies.

Sreen, P.S. and Sreen, J.S. (1991), *"Insights from Women Dairy Farms in India: What do they Gain from Participation"*, Social Action, 41 (4), Oct-Dec., Suchi Query Output, SISN 42749, Shreemati Nathibai Damodar Thackersey Women's University Library, Mumbai, National Information Centre.

Srinath, A.R. (2002), *"Leadership Development in Cooperative Sector"*, Cooperator's Bulletin, XXXXV (1), Jan., Jammu, Jammu and Kashmir Cooperative Union Limited.

Srinivasan, T. (1999), *"Ninth Plan: Challenges for Cooperatives"*, Cooperator's Bulletin, XXXXII (4), July-Aug., Jammu, Jammu and Kashmir Cooperative Union Limited.

Srivastava, D. (1995), *"Success of Student Cooperatives"*, NCDC Bulletin, XXVIII (6), Feb., New Delhi, National Cooperative Development Corporation.

Steinhoff, P.G., and Tanaka. K. (1994), *"Women in Japan"*, in Adler N.J., Izraeli, D.N., (eds.), *'Competitive Frontiers: Women Managers in a Global Economy'*, Cambridge (United States of America)/ Oxford (England), Blackwell Publishers.

Subrahmanyam, B. (1994), *"Performance of Primary Agricultural Credit Societies' in 1993-94"*, Bombay, National Federation of State Cooperative Banks Limited.

Subudhi, R.N., and Padhi, S.K. (1991), *"Indian Women in Cooperative Management"*, Khadi Gramodyog, 37 (7), April, Suchi Query Output, SISN 38913, Shreemati Nathibai Damodar Thackersey Women's University Library, Mumbai, National Information Centre.

Sud, S. (2001), *"Cooperatives in 21st Century"*, NCDC Bulletin, XXXV (4, 5), Oct-Dec., New Delhi, National Cooperative Development Corporation.

Sundar, K. (1998), *"Industrial Cooperatives: A Case for Revitalisation"*, The Tamil Nadu Journal of Cooperation, 90 (9), Dec., Tamil Nadu, Tamil Nadu Cooperative Union.

Suresh, K.A., and Joseph, M. (1990), *"Cooperatives and Rural Development in India"*, New Delhi, Ashish Publishing House.

Suri, J.B. (1992), *"Jammu Central Cooperative Bank"*, Cooperator's Bulletin, XXXV (6), June, Jammu, Jammu and Kashmir Cooperative Union Limited.

Swaminathan, M.S. (1991), *"Cooperative Movement in Today's India: Need for Child Development and Conservation Cooperatives"*, Cooperator's Bulletin, XXXIV (1), Jan., Jammu, Jammu and Kashmir Cooperative Union Limited.

Swarajyalaxmi, C. (1992), *"Women at Work: Insights from Indian Organisations"*, New Delhi, Anmol Publications.

Syngal, B.S. (1992), *"Role of Women in Cooperatives"*, The Cooperator, XXIX (12), Feb., New Delhi, National Cooperative Union of India.

Syngal, B.S. (1994), *"Women in Cooperatives"*, Social Welfare, 41 (2), May, Suchi Query Output, SISN 76557, Shreemati Nathibai Damodar Thackersey Women's University Library, Mumbai, National Information Centre.

Taimni, K.K. (1979), *"Training and Development of Human Resources in Cooperatives"*, 1st Edition, New Delhi, Sarin Brothers.

Taimni, K.K. (1981), *"Innovation in Cooperatives: Concept, Need and Scope"*, Cooperative News Digest, XXXII (6), June, Bombay, Reserve Bank of India.

Taimni, K.K. (1995), *"Conference of Principals of National Cooperative Training Institutions in Asia, Anand, India"*, A Report, International Labour Organisation, COOPNET UPDATE for Asia and Pacific, Pune, Human Resource Development for Cooperative Management and Net Working.

Taimni, K.K. (1998), *"Meeting the Capital Needs of Cooperatives"*, International Labour Organisation, Asia-Pacific, COOPNET UPDATE, 5 (2), April, Pune, International Labour Organisation COOPNET Programme.

Tandon, Niti, and Kumar, N. (1994), *"A Study of Employment Status and Income Generating Activities of Socially Underprivileged Slum Women"*, Social Action, 44 (2), ICSSR Journal of Abstract and Review, Sociology and Social Anthropology, New Delhi, Indian Council of Social Science and Research.

Tandon, R.K., (1998), *"Status of Women in Contemporary World"*, New Delhi, Common Wealth Publishers.

Thapar, V. (1998), *"National Convention on Family Life Education: Emerging Challenges,* Background Paper, 18-19, Nov., New Delhi, National Institute of Public Cooperation and Child Development.

Tigges, L.M., and Gary, R.G. (1994), *"Small Business Success among Men and Women: Owned Firms in Rural Areas"*, Rural Sociology,

59 (2), *ICSSR Journal of Abstracts and Review, Sociology and Social Anthropology*, New Delhi, Indian Council of Social Science and Research.

Tiwari, S. (2000), *"Women and Child Development: Encyclopaedia of Indian Government Series"*, 1st Edition, New Delhi, Anmol Publications Pvt., Ltd.

*Two-Days Workshop on Management of Cooperatives* (2001), Workshop Report, Aug., 28-29, Faculty of Rural Development of Jammu and Kashmir, Srinagar, Institute of Management, Public Administration and Rural Development.

Umre, R.S. (1980), *"Consumer Cooperatives for the Rural Poor"*, Cooperative News Digest, XXXI (5), May, Bombay, Reserve Bank of India.

Unni, J. (1994), *"Labour Participation Decisions of Married Women in Rural India"*, Indian Economic Review, 29 (2), ICSSR Journal of Abstracts and Review, Sociology and Social Anthropology, 23 (1), Jan-June, New Delhi, Indian Council of Social Science and Research.

U.S. Department of Labour (1989), *"Women in Management: Facts on Working Women"*, 84 (4), Washington D.C., U.S. Government Printing Office.

U.S., Department of Labour (1990), *"Employment and Earnings"*, Washington D.C., U.S. Government Printing Office.

Vashishtta, N. (1996), *"Images of Women as Reflected in Sculpture"*, in Jain, P., Mahan, R., (eds.), *'Women Images'*, New Delhi, Rawat Publications.

Veerakumaran, G. (2002), *"Need for Higher Education in Cooperative Management"*, Cooperator's Bulletin, XXXXV (5), May, Jammu, Jammu and Kashmir Cooperative Union Limited.

Venkatappiah, B. (1989), *"Cooperation and Rural Development"*, Courses on Managing Cooperatives for Rural Development, Hyderabad, National Institute of Rural Development.

Verkey, V.O. (1994), *"Cooperatives for Poor Women"*, NCDC Bulletin, 28 (1), April, Suchi Query Output, SISN 69287, Shreemati Nathibai Damodar Thackersey Women's University Library, Mumbai, National Information Centre.

Varkey, V.O. (2000), *"Mahila Bank of Mysore"*, The Maharashtra Cooperative Quarterly, LXXXIV (1), July-Sept., Pune, Maharashtra Rajya Sahakari Sangh.

Verma, V.S., and Pathania, K. S. (1988), *"Regional Disparities in the Performance of Cooperatives"*, Indian Cooperative Review, XXV (4), April ICSSR Journal of Abstracts and Review, Economics, XVIII (1-4), Jan-Dec., New Delhi, Indian Council of Social Science and Research.

Verulkar, A.A. (1989), *"Mahila Sahakari Banks: A New Challenge"*, The Banker, 36 (1), June, Suchi Query Output, SISN 13179, Shreemati Nathibai Damodar Thackersey Women's University Library, Mumbai, National Information Centre.

Vinze, and Medha, D. (1987), *"Women Entrepreneurs in India: A Socio-Economic Study of Delhi"*, New Delhi, Mittal Publications.

Weeraman, P.E., (1990), *"Aims and Principles of Cooperatives: Their Application in Developing Countries"*, Jammu, Jammu and Kashmir Cooperative Union Limited.

*Women's Cooperative Mobilization Project* (2000), A Report, Swedish Cooperative Centre, New Delhi, National Cooperative Union of India.

World Conference on Agrarian Reform and Rural Development (1979), *"Proceedings of Conference"*, 12-20th July, Rome, Italy, *Kurukshatra.*

Xi, L. (1985), *"Are Women Intellectually Inferior to Men"?* Women of China, January, Rawat Publications.

Yahya, S.R. (1990), *The Development Process and Women's Labour Force Participation"*, A Macro Level Analysis of Patterns and Trends, 1957-87, Paper Presented at the Colloquium on Women and Development in Malaysia Implications for Planning and Population Dynamics, The Population Studies Unit, FEA, University of Malaysia, Kuala Lumpur.

Yardimci, B. (1995), *"Problems with Credit, Marketing and Cooperatives"*, in Verma, R.K., (ed.), *'Rural Development and Anti-Poverty Programme'*, 5, Jaipur, Rupa Books Pvt., Ltd.